# INNOVATIONS IN EDUCATION
## reformers and their critics

JOHN MARTIN RICH
*The University of Texas at Austin*

*Allyn and Bacon, Inc.*
*Boston, London, Sydney, Toronto*

LIBRARY OF CONGRESS CATALOGING IN PUBLICATION DATA


Rich, John Martin, comp.
  Innovations in education.

  Includes bibliographical references.
  1. Educational innovations—Addresses, essays,
lectures. 2. Education—Philosophy—Addresses, essays,
lectures. I. Title.
LB1027.R513        370        74-19343
ISBN: 0-205-04650-9

Fourth printing . . . July, 1977

# Contents

# Preface

*Perceptive observers are aware that American education is presently in a state of great ferment. Today we hear about "the crisis in the classroom," the dehumanization of schooling, student and teacher militance, and the demands of minority groups. In the face of these significant developments, several reformers have arisen, offering ideas for extricating education from the morass in which it finds itself. These writers are distinguished by their ability to break with tradition and the conventional modes of perceiving educational problems and situations. They have advanced a number of bold and imaginative proposals, and many of the reformers are especially concerned with humanizing education.*

*All too frequently the proposals of these reformers are either accepted uncritically (especially among the young) so that their ideas become dogmas rather than possible ways of liberating thought and action, or else, by others, they are rejected out of hand. To address this situation, selections of reformers are followed by those of their critics (with the exception of two essays included to provide background information). In this way a balance of viewpoints can be gained, the strengths and weaknesses of the reformers can be weighed, and the reader can use this material and his own reasoning ability to develop his own position.*

*There also is considerable interest today in promising alternatives and innovations in education. They exhibit possibilities for new curricula and instructional patterns as well as a break with traditional forms of school organization. Both the pros and cons of these innovations are presented.*

*Thus the book consists of two parts. Part One contains representative selections by today's leading educational reformers. Part Two is composed of selections, both pro and con, on the latest and most prominent educational innovations. The innovations presented may include but are not restricted to those advocated by the specific reformers in Part One. Introductions precede the main parts, laying the background for the ideas which follow. Readers may find it useful to read over the discussion questions and activities following each chapter before reading the selections.*

*I wish to thank Dr. Joyce Ann Rich for useful suggestions, and Mrs. Carol Rhoades for her helpfulness and efficient typing.*

*John Martin Rich*

# Part One

# EDUCATIONAL REFORMERS
# AND THEIR CRITICS

## INTRODUCTION

*Education today is almost everywhere under attack. There are youth cultures and student movements in both economically developed and underdeveloped nations that have drawn up a long list of grievances against both educational and social institutions. While student unrest has been greater in many of the major universities throughout the world, it is spreading to the secondary level and junior high, and even upper elementary schools in some communities.*

*Parents and other citizens also have become increasingly critical of their schools. Many are agreed that most taxes are too high and a rebellion has ensued in some communities over a rise in property taxes to support school bond issues. Communities have delayed opening their schools because of insufficient funding resulting from the defeat of bond issues, while other communities have had to close schools prior to the end of the academic year.*

*How do we correct the widespread dissatisfaction that exists towards public education? Many reformers have spoken out on educational situations that seem to them to need correction. The essays in this anthology provide viewpoints that should inform, stimulate thought, and encourage the reader to reason carefully to clarify his own thinking relating to the topics addressed. If, in fact, the reader can see that neither the reformers nor their critics have adequately surmised a situation, it is his own task to build beyond the essays provided.*

1

## The Tasks of Educational Reform

*Reform can begin either with dissatisfaction or with the perception of a thinker who has conceived of a better way to accomplish certain outcomes. Dissatisfaction, although sometimes a necessary beginning, is not sufficient to bring about reform, for in many cases dissatisfaction leads no further than complaints and grievances expressed to one's peers or to suffering silently through personal feelings of unrest and unease. Dissatisfaction, as the initial stimulus, must lead to a faith that things can be improved and that individuals with new ideas who are willing to act on their convictions do make a difference. While it is reassuring to have the support of a strong organization, access to the media, and generous financial backing, few reformers can initially boast of such advantages. Even though it would be foolish to disregard the politics of educational change, it would be cynical to believe that fresh, cogent ideas do not have force. The reformers whose essays appear in this section have gained a wide hearing through the force of their ideas. Some of them have worked within the established educational system but have since chosen to work outside it in order to gain greater freedom to pursue their ideals.*

*But what does it mean to reform a system? We generally think of an educational reformer as engaged in planned change or innovation so that the system will better fulfill a set of standards based on certain ideals. More specifically, the reformer has in mind his own conception of what education ought to be, and after examining the system and finding that it falls short of his ideals, he proposes new forms of teaching, curricula, or organizational arrangements designed to rectify these deficiencies. There are three aspects to the reform process: normative, factual, and programmatic. The reformer begins with certain normative concerns which influence his inquiry. He brings to the situation a set of values from which he formulates his goals. But he must check his assumptions by gathering data bearing upon his area of inquiry. At this stage he must be certain that he gets facts straight. But even here the normative side intrudes because facts have no meaning apart from the framework used to interpret them and the methodology used in gathering them—and such choices are not based strictly upon factual considerations. Once the factual aspect of the investigation has been completed, the reformer will then be able to evaluate how well those educational conditions under scrutiny fulfill his normative criteria. If they fail to fulfill these criteria, he can make recommendations for new pro-*

*grams (the programmatic aspect) which he believes most likely to correct the deficiency by satisfying the normative criteria. Let us take an example to illustrate this process. During the late 1950's and early 1960's, a number of scholars expressed a concern over existing programs and teaching practices in the sciences and mathematics. They found that some of the material was badly dated, and the teaching methods being used were not effective in getting students to think and to do serious inquiry in the various disciplines. Moreover, students were being taught information that had already been superseded by newer developments. Thus, the scholars developed new curricula and encouraged in-service training programs designed to prepare teachers to handle the new science and the new math.*

*In the above examples the scholars expressed a concern because of their initial conviction that such educational goals as getting students to think and do serious inquiry in the various disciplines were not being fulfilled (normative aspect). Their investigations of existing practices (factual aspect) showed that their concerns were largely warranted. Hence, they proposed new programs and teaching procedures to rectify conditions (programmatic aspect).*

## Response to Reformers

*Societies which provide basic freedoms of speech, press, and assembly are sure to find their institutions under scrutiny and criticism. Since institutional forms which show initial promise may tend to rigidify unless subject to continuous reappraisal and renewal, a need for reexamination by both institutional officials and reformers outside the system is necessary. Thus while intelligent and sensitive reformers are needed, critics are required who will subject the reformers' proposals to searching examination before they are adopted. Social systems must undertake systematic planning that involves determination of priorities, procedures of operation, and the allocation of resources. Periodically, the system's goals must also be reassessed. The ideas of reformers and an appraisal of their ideas by their critics are vital factors in this process.*

*Concerned criticism is always appropriate and legitimate. Recall the preceding discussion of aspects of the reform process: normative, factual, and programmatic. With these aspects in mind, one has a starting point in knowing how to evaluate the essays related to each proposal for reform.  At times, the reader may know that a certain topic has not been properly covered by either reformer or critic.  At this point he might present his own proposal, or refer to a more enlightened view provided by some other thinker.  The reader will, of course, realize that none of the topics presented in this book can be adequately covered in one or two essays; but it is hoped that the essays will stimulate reading in areas of special interest.*

# I. The Saber-Tooth Curriculum

*It is frequently necessary to acquire social distance in order to perceive our problems with greater insight and perspective. This can sometimes be done by attempting to perceive one's world as would peoples from other lands and cultures. So also, by assuming new tasks in dramatically different social contexts, we can gain fresh ways of looking at our world. Through novels, plays, short stories, poetry, and other genres, one can acquire new perspectives. The following selection takes a satirical look at our present educational practices and the rationales offered in their support by its lively portrayal of an imaginary Paleolithic system. There is enough truth in the portrayal to enable the reader to view today's arguments from a new point of view.*

*This satire provides us with an example of the clash of cultural values and the tenacity of tradition. This essay is not followed by one offering constructive criticism of it. It was included for the purpose of illustrating the vital function of educational reformers.*

Harold Benjamin
(J. Abner Peddiwell, pseud.)

# 1. THE SABER-TOOTH CURRICULUM

The first great educational theorist and practitioner of whom my imagination has any record (began Dr. Peddiwell in his best professorial tone) was a man of Chellean times whose full name was *New-Fist-Hammer-Maker* but whom, for convenience, I shall hereafter call *New-Fist*.

New-Fist was a doer, in spite of the fact that there was little in his environment with which to do anything very complex. You have undoubtedly heard of the pear-shaped, chipped-stone tool which archeologists call the *coup-de-poing* or fist hammer. New-Fist gained his name and a considerable local prestige by producing one of these artifacts in a less rough and more useful form than any previously known to his tribe. His hunting clubs were generally superior weapons, moreover, and his fire-using techniques were patterns of simplicity and precision. He knew how to do things his community needed to have done, and he had the energy and will to go ahead and do them. By virtue of these characteristics he was an educated man.

New-Fist was also a thinker. Then, as now, there were few lengths to which men would not go to avoid the labor and pain of thought. More readily than his fellows, New-Fist pushed himself

Under the pseudonym of J. Abner Peddiwell, Harold Benjamin penned *The Saber-Tooth Curriculum*, from which this selection is drawn. Besides *The Saber-Tooth Curriculum*, Harold Raymond Wayne Benjamin was also the author of *The Cultivation of Idiosyncrasy, Democracy in the Administration of Higher Education, La educación superior en las repúblicas americanas*, and *Emergent Conceptions of the School Administrator's Task*.

beyond those lengths to the point where cerebration was inevitable. The same quality of intelligence which led him into the socially approved activity of producing a superior artifact also led him to engage in the socially disapproved practice of thinking. When other men gorged themselves on the proceeds of a successful hunt and vegetated in dull stupor for many hours thereafter, New-Fist ate a little less heartily, slept a little less stupidly, and arose a little earlier than his comrades to sit by the fire and think. He would stare moodily at the flickering flames and wonder about various parts of his environment until he finally got to the point where he became strongly dissatisfied with the accustomed ways of his tribe. He began to catch glimpses of ways in which life might be made better for himself, his family, and his group. By virtue of this development, he became a dangerous man.

This was the background that made this doer and thinker hit upon the concept of a conscious, systematic education. The immediate stimulus which put him directly into the practice of education came from watching his children at play. He saw these children at the cave entrance before the fire engaged in activity with bones and sticks and brightly colored pebbles. He noted that they seemed to have no purpose in their play beyond immediate pleasure in the activity itself. He compared their activity with that of the grown-up members of the tribe. The children played for fun; the adults worked for security and enrichment of their lives. The children dealt with bones, sticks, and pebbles; the adults dealt with food, shelter, and clothing. The children protected themselves from boredom; the adults protected themselves from danger.

"If I could only get these children to do the things that will give more and better food, shelter, clothing, and security," thought New-Fist, "I would be helping this tribe to have a better life. When the children became grown, they would have more meat to eat, more skins to keep them warm, better caves in which to sleep, and less danger from the striped death with the curving teeth that walks these trails by night."

Having set up an educational goal, New-Fist proceeded to con- struct a curriculum for reaching that goal. "What things must we tribesmen know how to do in order to live with full bellies, warm backs, and minds free from fear?" he asked himself.

To answer this question, he ran various activities over in his mind. "We have to catch fish with our bare hands in the pool far up the creek beyond that big bend," he said to himself. "We have to catch fish with our bare hands in the pool right at the bend. We have to catch them in the same way in the pool just this side of the bend. And so we catch them in the next pool and the next and the next. Always we catch them with our bare hands."

Thus New-Fist discovered the first subject of the first curriculum—fish-grabbing-with-the-bare-hands.

"Also we club the little woolly horses," he continued with his analysis. "We club them along the bank of the creek where they come down to drink. We club them in the thickets where they lie down to sleep. We club them in the upland meadow where they graze. Wherever we find them we club them."

So woolly-horse-clubbing was seen to be the second main subject in the curriculum.

"And finally, we drive away the saber-tooth tigers with fire," New-Fist went on in his thinking. "We drive them from the mouth of our caves with fire. We drive them from our trail with burning branches. We wave firebrands to drive them from our drinking hole. Always we have to drive them away, and always we drive them with fire."

Thus was discovered the third subject—saber-tooth-tiger-scaring-with-fire.

Having developed a curriculum, New-Fist took his children with him as he went about his activities. He gave them an opportunity to practice these three subjects. The children liked to learn. It was more fun for them to engage in these purposeful activities than to play with colored stones just for the fun of it. They learned the new activities well, and so the educational system was a success.

As New-Fist's children grew older, it was plain to see that they had an advantage in good and safe living over other children who had never been educated systematically. Some of the more intelligent members of the tribe began to do as New-Fist had done, and the teaching of fish-grabbing, horse-clubbing, and tiger-scaring came more and more to be accepted as the heart of real education.

For a long time, however, there were certain more conservative members of the tribe who resisted the new, formal education system on religious grounds. "The Great Mystery who speaks in thunder and moves in lightning," they announced impressively, "the Great Mystery who gives men life and takes it from them as he wills— if that Great Mystery had wanted children to practice fish-grabbing, horse-clubbing, and tiger-scaring before they were grown up, he would have taught them these activities himself by implanting in their natures instincts for fish-grabbing, horse-clubbing, and tiger-scaring. New-Fist is not only impious to attempt something the Great Mystery never intended to have done; he is also a damned fool for trying to change human nature."

Whereupon approximately half of these critics took up the solemn chant, "If you oppose the will of the Great Mystery, you must die," and the remainder sang derisively in unison, "You can't change human nature."

Being an educational statesman as well as an educational administrator and theorist, New-Fist replied politely to both arguments. To the more theologically minded, he said that, as a matter of fact, the Great Mystery had ordered this new work done, that he even did the work himself by causing children to want to learn, that children could not learn by themselves without divine aid, that they could not learn at all except through the power of the Great Mystery, and that nobody could really understand the will of the Great Mystery concerning fish, horses, and saber-tooth tigers unless he had been well grounded in the three fundamental subjects of the New-Fist school. To the human-nature-cannot-be-changed shouters, New-Fist pointed out the fact that paleolithic culture had attained its high level by changes in human nature and that it seemed almost unpatriotic to deny the very process which had made the community great.

"I know you, my fellow tribesmen," the pioneer educator ended his argument gravely, "I know you as humble and devoted servants of the Great Mystery. I know that you would not for one moment consciously oppose yourselves to his will. I know you as intelligent and loyal citizens of this great cave-realm, and I know that your pure and noble patriotism will not permit you to do anything which will block the development of that most cave-realmish of all our institutions—the paleolithic educational system. Now that you understand the true nature and purpose of this institution, I am serenely confident that there are no reasonable lengths to which you will not go in its defense and its support."

By this appeal the forces of conservatism were won over to the side of the new school, and in due time everybody who was anybody in the community knew that the heart of a good education lay in the three subjects of fish-grabbing, horse-clubbing, and tiger-scaring. New-Fist and his contemporaries grew old and were gathered by the Great Mystery to the Land of the Sunset far down the creek. Other men followed their educational ways more and more, until at last all the children of the tribe were practiced systematically in the three fundamentals. Thus the tribe prospered and was happy in the possession of adequate meat, skins, and security.

It is to be supposed that all would have gone well forever with this good educational system if conditions of life in that community had remained forever the same. But conditions changed, and life which had once been so safe and happy in the cave-realm valley became insecure and disturbing.

A new ice age was approaching in that part of the world. A great glacier came down from the neighboring mountain range to the north. Year after year it crept closer and closer to the headwaters of the creek which ran through the tribe's valley, until at length it reached the stream and began to melt into the water. Dirt and gravel which the glacier had collected on its long journey were dropped into the creek. The water grew muddy. What had once been a crystal-clear stream in which one could see easily to the bottom was now a milky stream into which one could not see at all.

At once the life of the community was changed in one very important respect. It was no longer possible to catch fish with the bare hands. The fish could not be seen in the muddy water. For some years, moreover, the fish in this creek had been getting more timid, agile, and intelligent. The stupid, clumsy, brave fish, of which originally there had been a great many, had been caught with the bare hands for fish generation after fish generation, until only fish of superior intelligence and agility were left. These smart fish, hiding in the muddy water under the newly deposited glacial boulders, eluded the hands of the most expertly trained fish-grabbers. Those tribesmen who had studied advanced fish-grabbing in the secondary school could do no better than their less well-educated fellows who had taken only an elementary course in the subject, and even the university graduates with majors in ichthyology were baffled by the problem. No matter how good a man's fish-grabbing education had been, he could not grab fish when he could not find fish to grab.

The melting waters of the approaching ice sheet also made the country wetter. The ground became marshy far back from the banks of the creek. The stupid woolly horses, standing only five or six hands high and running on four-toed front feet and three-toed hind feet, although admirable objects for clubbing, had one dangerous characteristic. They were ambitious. They all wanted to learn to run on their middle toes. They all had visions of becoming powerful and aggressive animals instead of little and timid ones. They dreamed of a far-distant day when some of their descendants would be sixteen hands high, weigh more than half a ton, and be able to pitch their would-be riders into the dirt. They knew they could never attain these goals in a wet, marshy country, so they all went east to the dry, open plains, far from the paleolithic hunting grounds. Their places were taken by little antelopes who came down with the ice sheet and were so shy and speedy and had so keen a scent for danger that no one could approach them closely enough to club them.

The best trained horse-clubbers of the tribe went out day after day and employed the most efficient techniques taught in the schools, but day after day they returned empty-handed. A horse-clubbing education of the highest type could get no results when there were no horses to club.

Finally, to complete the disruption of paleolithic life and education, the new dampness in the air gave the saber-tooth tigers pneumonia, a disease to which these animals were peculiarly susceptible and to which most of them succumbed. A few moth-eaten specimens crept south to the desert, it is true, but they were pitifully few and weak representatives of a once numerous and powerful race.

So there were no more tigers to scare in the paleolithic community, and the best tiger-scaring techniques became only academic exercises, good in themselves, perhaps, but not necessary for tribal security. Yet this danger to the people was lost only to be replaced by another and even greater danger, for with the advancing ice sheet came ferocious glacial bears which were not afraid of fire, which walked the trails by day as well as by night, and which could not be driven away by the most advanced methods developed in the tiger-scaring courses of the schools.

The community was now in a very difficult situation. There was no fish or meat for food, no hides for clothing, and no security from the hairy death that walked the trails day and night. Adjustment to this difficulty had to be made at once if the tribe was not to become extinct.

Fortunately for the tribe, however, there were men in it of the old New-Fist breed, men who had the ability to do and the daring to think. One of them stood by the muddy stream, his stomach contracting with hunger pains, longing for some way to get a fish to eat. Again and again he had tried the old fish-grabbing technique that day, hoping desperately that at last it might work, but now in black despair he finally rejected all that he had learned in the schools and looked about him for some new way to get fish from that stream. There were stout but slender vines hanging from trees along the bank. He pulled them down and began to fasten them together more or less aimlessly. As he worked, the vision of what he might do to satisfy his hunger and that of his crying children back in the cave grew clearer. His black despair lightened a little. He worked more rapidly and intelligently. At last he had it—a net, a crude seine. He called a companion and explained the device. The two men took the net into the water, into pool after pool, and in one hour they caught more fish—intelligent fish in muddy water— than the whole tribe could have caught in a day under the best fish-grabbing conditions.

Another intelligent member of the tribe wandered hungrily through the woods where once the stupid little horses had abounded but where now only the elusive antelope could be seen. He had tried the horse-clubbing technique on the antelope until he was fully convinced of its futility. He knew that one would starve who relied on school learning to get him meat in those woods. Thus it was that he too, like the fish-net inventor, was finally impelled by hunger to new ways. He bent a strong, springy young tree over an antelope trail, hung a noosed vine therefrom, and fastened the whole device in so ingenious a fashion that the passing animal would release a trigger and be snared neatly when the tree jerked upright. By setting a line of these snares, he was able in one night to secure more meat and skins than a dozen horse-clubbers in the old days had secured in a week.

A third tribesman, determined to meet the problem of the ferocious bears, also forgot what he had been taught in school and began to think in direct and radical fashion. Finally, as a result of this thinking, he dug a deep pit in a bear trail, covered it with branches in such a way that a bear would walk out on it unsuspectingly, fall through to the bottom, and remain trapped until the tribesmen could come up and despatch him with sticks and stones at their leisure. The inventor showed his friends how to dig and camouflage other pits until all the trails around the community were furnished with them. Thus the tribe had even more security than before and in addition had the great additional store of meat and skins which they secured from the captured bears.

As the knowledge of these new inventions spread, all the members of the tribe were engaged in familiarizing themselves with the new ways of living. Men worked hard at making fish nets, setting antelope snares, and digging bear pits. The tribe was busy and prosperous.

There were a few thoughtful men who asked questions as they worked. Some of them even criticized the schools.

"These new activities of net-making and operating, snare-setting, and pit-digging are indispensable to modern existence," they said. "Why can't they be taught in school?"

The safe and sober majority had a quick reply to this naive question. "School!" they snorted derisively. "You aren't in school now. You are out here in the dirt working to preserve the life and happiness of the tribe. What have these practical activities got to do with schools? You're not saying lessons now. You'd better forget your lessons and your academic ideals of fish-grabbing, horse-clubbing, and tiger-scaring if you want to eat, keep warm, and have some measure of security from sudden death."

The radicals persisted a little in their questioning. "Fishnet-making and using, antelope-snare construction and operation, and bear-catching and killing," they pointed out, "require intelligence and skills—things we claim to develop in schools. They are also activities we need to know. Why can't the schools teach them?"

But most of the tribe, and particularly the wise old men who controlled the school, smiled indulgently at this suggestion. "That wouldn't be *education*," they said gently.

"But why wouldn't it be?" asked the radicals.

"Because it would be mere training," explained the old men patiently. "With all the intricate details of fish-grabbing, horse-clubbing, and tiger-scaring—the standard cultural subjects—the school curriculum is too crowded now. We can't add these fads and frills of net-making, antelope-snaring, and—of all things—bear-killing. Why, at the very thought, the body of the great New-Fist, founder of our paleolithic educational system, would turn over in its burial cairn. What we need to do is to give our young people a more thorough grounding in the fundamentals. Even the graduates of the secondary schools don't know the art of fish-grabbing in any complete sense nowadays, they swing their horse clubs awkwardly too, and as for the old science of tiger-scaring—well, even the teachers seem to lack the real flair for the subject which we oldsters got in our teens and never forgot."

"But, damn it," exploded one of the radicals, "how can any person with good sense be interested in such useless activities? What is the point of trying to catch fish with the bare hands when it just can't be done any more. How can a boy learn to club horses when there are no horses left to club? And why in hell should children try to scare tigers with fire when the tigers are dead and gone?"

"Don't be foolish," said the wise old men, smiling most kindly smiles. "We don't teach fish-grabbing to grab fish; we teach it to develop a generalized agility which can never be developed by mere training. We don't teach horse-clubbing to club horses; we teach it to develop a generalized strength in the learner which he can never get from so prosaic and specialized a thing as antelope-snare-setting. We don't teach tiger-scaring to scare tigers; we teach it for the purpose of giving that noble courage which carries over into all the affairs of life and which can never come from so base an activity as bear-killing."

All the radicals were silenced by this statement, all except the one who was most radical of all. He felt abashed, it is true, but he was so radical that he made one last protest.

"But—but anyway," he suggested, "you will have to admit that times have changed. Couldn't you please *try* these other more up-to-date activities? Maybe they have *some* educational value after all?"

Even the man's fellow radicals felt that this was going a little too far.

The wise old men were indignant. Their kindly smiles faded. "If you had any education yourself," they said severely, "you would know that the essence of true education is timelessness. It is something that endures through changing conditions like a solid rock standing squarely and firmly in the middle of a raging torrent. You must know that there are some eternal verities, and the saber-tooth curriculum is one of them!"

# Discussion Questions
## and Activities

1. Every culture has its New-Fists (educational reformers). Even though they may be unappreciated or sometimes scorned by their contemporaries, they are vital in the role of helping to eliminate apathy and subtle forms of tyranny that often exist in education. From your own observations, what educational reforms need to be made?

2. After the ice age came, the elders of the tribe objected to introducing new skills that the bolder members of the tribe had discovered in securing their food. They claimed that to teach these skills would be mere "training," not "education." What is the difference between being "trained" and being "educated"? To what extent are you being trained? Educated?

3. The elders admitted that fish-grabbing was no longer taught for learning to grab fish but for another purpose. What was this purpose? Can you think of a similar argument today?

4. What are you being taught right now that seems to you about as useful as "fish-grabbing"?

5. Certainly it would be difficult to find another satire about education that has been more enthusiastically received or discussed than *The Saber-Tooth Curriculum*. This is not entirely surprising because the author is able to call into question many of our sacred cows in a nimble and delightful manner. List these.

# II.  Requirements for a Valid "New Criticism"

*The reformers, according to Havighurst, are strong on criticism but weak in their proposals for improvement.  While reform and reformers are needed, Havighurst tells us, today's reformers have often failed to consider the positive achievements of the schools and have failed to produce sufficiently researched, viable alternatives to some of our present practices.  In this essay, Havighurst supplies what he believes to be ground rules for evaluating the proposals of the reformers.*

46

Robert J. Havighurst

## 2. REQUIREMENTS FOR A VALID "NEW CRITICISM"

### HOW BAD IS URBAN EDUCATION?

On November 2, 1967, the New York City School Board reported the results of school achievement tests that had been given the preceding April to all pupils in the second and fifth grades. *The New York Times* reported the results in a page of tables and headlined the story on page one with "City Pupils Losing Ground in Reading and Arithmetic." Let us examine some of the test results.

The national average reading scores for these grades in April were 2.7 and 5.7 respectively. New York City school children averaged definitely below these levels, and there was some evidence that the New York City average was lower than it had been the year before.

*The New York Times* did not point out the fact that almost 300 of the 650 elementary schools had reading averages for their second grades of 3.0 or higher—that is, three-tenths of a year above the national average. Nor did *The Times* report that 44 elementary schools had reading scores for their fifth grades averaging 7.0 or more—1.3 of a year above the national average.

Robert J. Havighurst, Professor of Education and Human Development at the University of Chicago, has been a member of the faculty since 1941. He is a prolific writer and, in addition to many articles, is author or co-author of some twenty-five books. He is especially remembered for his influential *Human Development and Education* and such sociological studies with W. Lloyd Warner as *Who Shall Be Educated?* He has conducted a systematic study of the Chicago public schools and is a leading authority on the impact of metropolitan growth on educational systems. He has also served as Fulbright Professor at the University of Canterbury and a consultant on education to the Brazilian government.
Source: Robert J. Havighurst, "Requirements for a Valid 'New Criticism,'" *Phi Delta Kappan* (September 1968), pp. 20–26. Reprinted by permission.

During that same month of November, the New York State Board of Regents called for "a concerted effort to reform urban education." The "Bundy Report" of the Mayor's Advisory Panel on Decentralization of the New York City Schools, which was published November 9, commences with the statement, "The New York City school system, which once ranked at the summit of American public education, is caught in a spiral of decline." *The Times* on that date referred in an editorial to what it called "the deterioration of New York's gigantic school system."

*The Saturday Review* for November 18 carried the following headlines on its front cover—*Requiem for the Urban School* and *Education in Washington: National Monument to Failure.*

The unwary middle-income parent, with several school-age children, is very likely to read these pieces in *responsible* newspapers and journals, and to decide to move to the suburbs, where he is assured by the same press that the schools are good. This person may live in Queens District 27, where 20 out of 27 schools are well above average in reading achievement, or in Queens District 26, where every one of the 24 elementary schools averaged at least .4 of a year above the national average at the second grade and at least one year above the national average at the fifth grade. But if he follows the *responsible* press, unless he explores the fine print, he is misled to suppose that he cannot find "good" public schools in the city.

Although these examples are taken from New York City, they can be duplicated in every large city. In some areas of the city, where the people of average and above-average income live, school achievement is above the national average, and about the same as it is in the "better" suburbs. In the low-income areas, school achievement is low.

How bad is education in our big cities? Does a dispassionate examination of the facts justify such widely publicized statements and slogans as "our children are dying," "requiem for urban education," "the end of the common school," "death at an early age," all applied to the work of the public schools in large cities?

We spend much more on education now than we did in 1955, much more per child, and a great deal more of our gross national product. Yet we are not making much headway with the education of disadvantaged children.

The children who are doing so poorly in our public schools constitute about 15 percent of the total group of children. They come predominantly from the homes of parents who are in the bottom quarter of the population in income, educational level, and occupational status. An equal number of children in such homes do fairly well in school—hence we cannot simply say that the children of the poor do poorly in school. Many of them do very well. But about 15 percent of children come from poor families *and* do poorly in school. We call these children "socially disadvantaged" because there is ample evidence that their home environments give them a very poor preparation for success in school.

Since World War II the families that produce these children have collected in large numbers in the slums of the big cities. Before World War II the majority of these children were living in rural and relatively isolated areas, and consequently their failure in school did not create an obvious social problem.

The other 85 percent of American children are doing quite well in school, according to the ordinary standards of judgment applied by most Americans to the schools.

I find the situation far from desperate. It is encouraging, but rough in spots, and the rough spots are most clearly seen in the big-city slums. We are learning to do the job for disadvantaged children, but making a good many mistakes in the process.

### The Criticisms of Urban Education

What are the criticisms? There are two major themes of criticism of urban education, and they are quite different. The first and most general is that the schools are failing to educate the children of the poor, and it is the fault of the schools rather than the fault of the slum culture and home environment to which the children of the poor are subjected.

The second criticism is that the educational system is doing a poor job for the middle-class child and youth. The argument is that the present middle-class establishment is failing to govern the country effectively and failing to solve the country's international and domestic problems, and at the same time attempting to train the next generation to carry on this pattern of civic failure. One of the leading critics, writing an article entitled "In Praise of Populism," says, "Indeed, the essential idea of this resurgent populism, in my opinion, is that the powers-that-be in the world are incompetent, their authority is irrational, they cannot cope with modern conditions, and they are producing ultimate horrors."[1]

[1] Paul Goodman, "In Praise of Populism," *Commentary* (June 1968), pp. 25–30.

## Who Are the Critics?

There is a group who appear at this time to have easy access to the responsible newspapers and journals. These include Paul Goodman, Edgar Friedenberg, Nat Hentoff, John Holt, Herbert Kohl, and Jonathan Kozol. These are not irresponsible people. On the contrary, they feel a tremendous moral responsibility to report their perceptions of the schools and their hypotheses for the betterment of the schools.

There are certain personal characteristics of these critics which are relevant to their criticisms. I do not propose to psychoanalyze them, and I have shared these qualities at one time or another in my own career. All of these characteristics do not apply equally to all of the critics. For one thing, they tend to be anarchists. That is, they do not like rules and institutions set up by society to regulate the conduct and development of its members. For another, they tend to be hostile to authority and therefore critical of the Establishment. A third characteristic is that some of them are young men agonizing in public over their discovery that the world is a difficult place.

To this group of critics should be added another group who are especially concerned with one or another disadvantaged minority group, and claim that the schools are failing to educate properly the children of these groups either by discriminating against them or by offering them inappropriate forms of schooling. The principal minority group on whose behalf these critics speak is the Negro group, though there are similar arguments on behalf of Puerto Ricans, Spanish-Americans of the Southwest, rural whites of the Appalachian-Ozark mountain area, and American Indians.

## What Is Wrong with the Schools?

The critics tend to attribute the shortcomings of the schools to the fact that they are operated by "the Establishment." The Establishment consists of the bureaucrats who administer the schools and who in turn are supported by the political leadership of the big cities, backed by a middle class satisfied with the school system in its present form. Thus Jason Epstein, writing on the Bundy Report that recommends decentralization of the public schools of New York City, says,

> ... the urgent matter is to wrench the school system away from the bureaucrats who are now running it and whose failure

now threatens the stability of the city itself. As a practical matter the children of the ghetto, who now comprise nearly half the total public school enrollment, are largely without a functioning educational system at all, and the present school administration has shown that it is incapable of supplying them with one.[2]

Related to this criticism is the contention that the size of big-city systems makes them bad. When a single school board and a single superintendent and his staff have to take responsibility for more than about 50 schools or 50,000 pupils, it is argued that the school system becomes rigid, unable to adapt to the various educational needs of various subgroups and sections of the city.

Third, there is the criticism of the common school, or the system of public education. Thus Peter Schrag, editorializing in *The Saturday Review* for April 20, 1968, on the subject, "The End of the Common School," says,

> Although criticism of schools and teachers has always been a great national pastime, there is something fundamentally new in the declining faith in the possibilities of reform, and particularly in the kind of reform that can be accomplished within the existing school structure. The characteristic view, reflected in the pressures for decentralization and for the establishment of competing institutions, is that school systems tend to be self-serving, bureaucratic monsters that need replacement rather than reform. Although these demands have arisen during a time when the schools can attract more resources and more sophisticated staffs than ever before, they also coincide with the moment when the schools have achieved a near-monopoly position as gatekeepers to social and economic advancement. Where the schools were once considered benign, happy institutions for the young, they are now increasingly regarded as instruments of power.

Schrag says that there will have to be a number of alternative forms of education that may replace the single public school.

> A few such competing institutions have already been established. In the large cities there are a few community schools, store-front academies, and programs for dropouts. Most of

[2] Jason Epstein, "The Politics of School Decentralization," *New York Review of Books*, June 6, 1968, p. 26.

these operations are considered in some measure remedial and temporary. Most of them are inadequately financed and do not begin to meet the problems of miseducation, even in the communities where they are located. Yet the problems that led to the establishment of such institutions are going to be with us for a long time, and unless the public schools begin to accommodate far more diversity and to offer far more choice than they now do, the desperate need for alternatives will continue.

## *What Do the Critics Propose?*

As one would expect from critics who tend to be anarchists and who are hostile to the forms of authority, the positive proposals for educational improvement tend to be few and weak. There are three broad approaches.

1. Abolish the present school system and allow new institutions to emerge. This kind of proposal tends to be supported by critics who believe that there is too much bureaucracy with consequent rigidity in the present school system. They are not much concerned with the nature of the new institutions, since they tend to distrust institutions. With John Holt in *How Children Learn*, they follow Rousseau in their belief that children will learn best if allowed to initiate their own education. Paul Goodman writes, "We can, I believe, educate the young entirely in terms of their free choice, with no processing whatsoever."[3]

2. Experiment widely and freely with new procedures, looking for teachers with enthusiasm, creativity, and iconoclasm. New ways of working successfully with disadvantaged children and youth will emerge from such experiments.

3. Require the schools and their teachers to do a much better job of teaching disadvantaged children. This is the proposal especially of some Negro educators, who believe that the school system at present, both North and South, tends to *reject* Negro children, to assume they cannot learn well, and to avoid the effort of teaching them effectively.

There are two principal weaknesses in the positions taken by the

3 Paul Goodman, "Freedom and Learning: The Need for Choice," *Saturday Review*, May 18, 1968, p. 73.

critics. First, many of them, and especially those who speak for minority groups, are ignoring the basic research on the importance of the pre-school years in the preparation of a child for success in school. They ignore the following basic proposition:

The child's cognitive and social development in the years before age five are extremely important in his readiness for school work and his achievement in school. This proposition has been established by the empirical work of Bernstein in London, Martin Deutsch in New York, Robert Hess and his co-workers at the University of Chicago, and Skeels and Skodak at the University of Iowa. This proposition is widely discussed and amplified in the writings of J. McVicker Hunt, Benjamin Bloom, and Jerome Bruner.

Second, they ignore the post-war work on methods and materials of teaching mathematics, science, social studies, and foreign languages which has effectively reformed the curriculum of the intermediate and high school grades, and vastly improved the education of the majority of children and youth who do average and superior work in school.

Nevertheless, the critics serve a valuable purpose in contemporary education. They are sensitive people, aware of the needs for improvement in our society and in our education. They are especially useful as our social conscience.

## WAYS OUT OF THE EDUCATIONAL MESS

Granting the proposition that major changes must be made in big-city education, how shall we decide what changes to make, and how shall we make them? There are three groups of people with something to say on this topic—the establishment, the anarchists, and the activists. All are prepared to talk about changing, though all are not equally prepared to take actual responsibility for changes.

### The Establishment as a Change Agent

It is customary to describe the Establishment as a bureaucratic organization wedded to things as they have been in the past. The national organization of school superintendents and the organization of school principals have been accused of standing athwart the path of progress.

Yet some city school systems have been remarkably ready to

exercise leadership in the making of changes. For instance, the New York City system which has been pilloried in *The New York Times* as a deteriorating system has been one of the most flexible, most experimental, and most responsive of all big-city systems to the social situation and the social needs of the big city. A list of outstanding changes in the New York City schools in the past 30 years would include:

- The establishment of a system of specialized high schools serving the entire city with outstanding programs for the ablest students.

- A long history of special programs for gifted elementary school children, centered at Hunter College.

- Programs in certain high schools to meet the local community needs of a particular ethnic group, such as the program at the Benjamin Franklin High School when Leonard Covello was principal there.

- Science teaching programs in the intermediate grades and the high schools that led the way to the improved science courses which swept the country after 1960.

- The Statement on Integration adopted by the New York City Board of Education in 1954, shortly after the Supreme Court decision on segregation. This was not only the first policy statement on integration to be adopted by a big-city board of education, but one of the strongest; and it was put into effect by a positive open enrollment policy and by a vigorous rezoning program during the first years, when these measures could be fairly effective.

- The Demonstration-Guidance Project in Junior High School 43 and the George Washington Senior High School. This was the first of the attempts by the big-city systems to enrich their programs for socially disadvantaged children.

- The Higher Horizons Project in a large number of elementary schools, which was carefully and critically evaluated by the Research Bureau, and was the first big-city project for the socially disadvantaged to warn us that the job was not going to be easy. While other cities reported rosy but carelessly compiled results of their projects, New York City forced educators to face the facts.

- The More Effective Schools Program, a carefully designed project to improve the education of the socially disadvan-

taged, which has been evaluated carefully and critically
by an independent research agency.

- The study of Puerto Rican children in New York City
schools made by J. Cayce Morrison in the 1950's, which
helped the school system to recognize and go to work on
this special problem.

- A series of experiments in delegating responsibility for the
conduct of schools to local district school boards, stretching over the last 70 years. Notable in this series was
the project in the Bronx headed by Joseph Loretan in the
late 1950's, when he was district superintendent there.

- A set of current experiments in the delegation of responsibility to local community committees for choosing administrators and teaching staff and for adapting the
curriculum to local community conditions. This is a
radical and controversial experiment which no other big-
city school system has been able to try. Whatever becomes of it, it will give us valuable knowledge on the
problem of relations between the school system and local
communities.

It is a curious thing for the critics to proclaim the proposition that
New York City schools are failing, when these schools are leading the
country in working at the problem of educating socially disadvantaged youth, defining the problem, and studying it scientifically and
experimentally.

During this period of the last 30 years, the great majority of
books on the problems of education in the big city have come from
New York City. These have been written by a wide range of people
with a wide range of motives and experience.

Still, many of the great cities have been slow to innovate, and
there certainly is a problem in all big-city systems where a bureaucratic structure stretching from the office of school principal to that
of superintendent tends to perpetuate practices to which the organization has already grown accustomed. An example is the use of federal
funds under Title I of the Elementary and Secondary Education Act
to supplement educational services in schools located in poverty areas.
The tendency has been to use these funds to support "more of the
same" rather than to innovate. That is, the money has been used to
pay teachers for an extra hour of classes after school, for Saturday
morning instruction, for summer instruction, and to reduce the size

of classes.  This has not worked very well, and has given rise to criticism of big city systems for failure to try bold new experiments.

## The Anarchists as Change Agents

The anarchists have been strong on criticism and weak on constructive proposals for change.  They are, of course, opposed to the creation of a new set of organized and institutional practices, since, as anarchists, they mistrust procedures which tend to become rigid and confining.  They proclaim "the end of the common school" and tell us that we are killing off the minds and spirits of children, but they are wary of writing proposals that could be put into an organized educational system.  They favor experimentation of many kinds, but do not argue for careful evaluation of such experiments.  For instance, Peter Schrag, writing in *The Saturday Review* of June 15, 1968, on "Learning in a Storefront" makes the following approving statement:

> The East Harlem Block Schools, which operate nursery and primary classes in four locations, have discovered no new pedagogical secrets, operate according to no rigid theory, and have conducted little validating research.  What they are doing, however, is to demonstrate that educational programs directed by parents and often staffed by parents are not only effective—at least in the judgment of those same parents —but that they represent a community focus and center of interest limited only by the financial resources their sponsors can attract.

He notes in passing, as though it were not an important matter, that there is no validating research on these schools.  He also notes that the project costs $2,000 per child per year for 135 children, but he gives no indication that such a program would have to be supported by a thorough research validation if it would have any chance of gaining the public support that could spread it to cover one hundred times as many children.  It would have to do this to produce a significant impact on the education of disadvantaged children in New York City.  Instead, Schrag points out the importance of getting the schools into the hands of parents.  "It is the parents who are minding the store," he says.  It is this kind of anti-institutional and anti-organizational emphasis which is both the strength and the weakness of the anarchist position.

But the ablest of the anarchists recognize the need for new institutionalized procedures. Thus Paul Goodman, who calls himself an anarchist, also says explicitly that new institutions are necessary. After speaking of the present educational establishment as a hoax on the public and calling for an end to it, he says in the letter which appears in this KAPPAN, "Of course our society would then have to re-open or devise other institutional arrangements for most of the young to grow into the world; and in my books I propose many of these, since this is the problem."

To see the anarchist position most ably stated, and stated in most positive terms, one should read more of Goodman's writing. His article on "Freedom and Learning: The Need for Choice" in *The Saturday Review* for May 18, 1968, expands the ideas expressed in the above-mentioned letter. Here he argues that the educational system which has developed into such a large and expensive set of operations since 1900 is a hoax on American society. It tends to force conformity on the younger generation, and conformity to a set of adult institutions which are bad for everybody. He calls for more free choice in learning and says, "Free choice is not random but responsive to real situations; both youth and adults live in a nature of things, a polity, an ongoing society, and it is these, in fact, that attract interest and channel need. If the young, as they mature, can follow their bent and choose their topics, times, and teachers, and if teachers teach what they themselves consider important—which is all they can skillfully teach anyway—the needs of society will be adequately met; there will be more lively, independent, and inventive people; and in the fairly short run there will be a more sensible and efficient society."

Up to age 12, Goodman says, there is no point to formal subjects or a prearranged curriculum. Teaching should be informal, and should follow the child's interest. If let alone, a normal child of 12 will, Goodman believes, learn most of what is useful in the eight-year elementary curriculum by himself.

However, Goodman recognizes that some families do not provide an adequate setting for their children to learn the elementary school curriculum, and he has a proposal for a kind of school to serve these disadvantaged children. He says, "Since we have communities where people do not attend to the children as a matter of course, and since children must be rescued from their homes, for most of these children there should be some kind of school. In a proposal for mini-schools in New York City, I suggested an elementary group of 28 children with four grownups: a licensed teacher, a housewife who can cook, a college senior, and a teen-age school dropout. Such a group can meet in any storefront, church basement, settlement house, or housing project; more important, it can often go about the city, as is possible when the student-teacher ratio is 7 to 1. Experience at the First Street School in New York has shown that the cost for such a little school is less than for the public school with a student-teacher ratio of 30 to 1. . . . The school should be located near home so the children can escape from it to home, and from home to it. The school should be supported by public money but administered entirely by its own children, teachers, and parents."

Looking at the positive suggestions of the more constructive anarchists, of whom Goodman is a good example, we see that they want education to be institutionalized to a minimal degree, with a wide variety of small school and college units in which pupils and teachers work as far as possible on their own initiative.

### The Activists as Change Agents

A broad group of people are prepared to work within the present educational system but want major changes or additions to it. This group might be called "institutional meliorists," to distinguish them from the anarchists. This group accepts the notion that the educational system must have a complex institutional structure and therefore differs from the anarchists on this major point. The activists want broad and fundamental changes in the educational system.

There is much disagreement among the activists. Many of them have just one program which they emphasize, such as:

- Pre-school programs for disadvantaged children starting as early as age 3.
- Decentralization of the public school system to place responsibility and decision making more in the hands of parents and local community leaders.
- Educational parks.
- Black teachers for black schools.
- Alternative educational systems to the public schools, supported with public funds.

The U.S. Office of Education has been promoting activist programs through its very large funds under Title III of the Elementary and Secondary Education Act. Several of the educational foundations have been supporting activist projects.

To this writer, who is an activist, it appears that there are some serious weaknesses in the activist approach, but that these weaknesses are being corrected.

A major weakness is a general lack of systematic reporting and evaluation of the results of experimental work. Several major big-city programs of compensatory education for disadvantaged children have been given wide publicity as successful on the basis of preliminary and inadequate evaluation, only to withdraw their claims after more systematic study of their outcomes.

But there have been some outstanding examples of careful research evaluation of innovative programs. For instance, the Higher Horizons Program in New York City elementary schools was evaluated by the Bureau of Research, and its successor program, the More Effective Schools, has been carefully studied by the Center for Urban Education. The fact that these evaluations did not support some of the hopes and expectations of the sponsors of the programs is an unfortunate fact which the big city systems must learn to use constructively.

At present there are some serious and sophisticated evaluations of several types of pre-school programs for disadvantaged children supported by the U.S. Office of Education. This should go a long way toward helping the educational systems to make rational judgments about the practical wisdom of expanding pre-school programs at public expense as a regular part of the public school program.

After a period of uncritical spending on innovations designed to improve the education of disadvantaged children and youth, stretching from Head Start through Title I of ESEA to the Job Corps, the federal agencies are now going in for evaluation, under pressure from congressmen and the Bureau of the Budget. The USOE is engaged in cost-benefit studies of the Title I program, and here there is another kind of danger. The educational benefits of pre-school and other innovative programs may not be fully measurable in terms of gains of children on reading-readiness tests and ordinary standardized tests of school achievement, applied immediately after an experimental program lasting a year or so. Yet cost-benefit studies are limited to assessing the costs of benefits that are measured. If the benefits of certain experimental programs cannot be measured simply after a short trial of the program, we should take the time and make the effort to measure the benefits in more complex ways over longer periods of time.

### Working on Motives Rather Than Skills

Recently some of the activists appear to have discovered a principle that may produce much more effective ways of teaching disadvantaged children than the conventional way. The conventional way is to work directly on the mental skills of the child—his vocabulary, reading, writing, arithmetic. *Teach, teach, teach* with all the energy, time, patience, and techniques available. This has not worked very well. Hence some experimental methods have been tried that work on *motives* rather than skills and drills. The aim is to help the pupil *want* to learn, to help him see himself as a learner in school, as he now may see himself as a basketball player, a fighter, an attractive person to the opposite sex, a helper in the home, etc.

The theory underlying this approach might be outlined as follows: When a person *wants* something, he *tries* to get it. For example, when a child wants to read, he tries to read, and will use whatever help he can get from teachers, parents, other pupils, television, street signs, books around the house. He will drill himself, or accept the teacher's drill methods.

The desire to learn may be conscious or unconscious. One may have an explicit desire to be a good basketball player, or a good dancer, or a good reader, or a good singer. In this case, one seeks opportunity to improve oneself. On the other hand, one may have only a generalized and vaguely felt desire to please somebody else, or to be like somebody. In this case one accepts opportunity to move in the desired direction, but does not actively seek it.

Programs aimed directly at improving mental skills have had remarkably little success with children beyond the age of 7 or 8. Only a few people, generally with highly personal methods, appear to have succeeded with classes in slum schools beyond the third grade. For example, Herbert Kohl taught a sixth-grade class in Harlem with a kind of freedom and spontaneity that seems to have motivated many of his pupils to care about their school work. Perhaps it is significant that he did relatively little drilling, and did not bother to correct spelling and grammar. In fact, he drew criticism from his supervisors because he did not emphasize the mental skills in the usual way. And Jonathan Kozol, in Boston, made friends with his pupils, took them on trips with him, visited their homes, but did not seem to stress the conventional training.

A rather common element of motivating situations is the presence of a model—a person who is accepted by the pupil as one he would like to be like. The habit of *modeling* one's behavior after that of others is learned very early in life, and becomes largely unconscious. A person forms the habit of imitating his parents and other persons in authority and persons who are visible to him and attractive to him. Teachers may or may not be effective models, depending on their behavior toward pupils and on the attitudes of pupils toward them.

## Examples of Motivating Situations

There are a growing number of experiments with inner-city youth that seem to be successful and yet do not represent what we think of conventionally as good teaching. The methods are erratic; the teachers are not well-trained. These *experiments have in common a motivating element.*

**Storefront Academies and Mini-schools.** Small, informal schools and classes springing up in the inner city appear to be accomplishing more than the conventional schools with disadvantaged youth. For example, the "street academies" of New York City appear to be working successfully with some dropouts and failing students from the high schools. These are described in an article by Chris Tree in *The Urban Review* for February, 1968, and are now a part of the Urban League's Education and Youth Incentives Program. The mini-school idea has already been presented.

Such projects must have methods, and the methods are being worked out pragmatically. It is too soon to say with any assurance what such a program would accomplish if it were expanded and made a part of the school system. Careful, empirical evaluation will have to be made to find out what kind of children and youth profit from this type of school and what kind do not.

Perhaps the essential factor in whatever success these schools have is that of acceptance by the teachers of the pupils as persons who want to learn, and the acceptance by the pupils of the teachers as people they want to be like.

**Tutoring Projects.** A few years ago there was a wave of tutoring projects which put college students and middle-class adults in the role of tutors to inner-city pupils of the intermediate and high school grades. These seem to have been largely discontinued, even though the tutors often reported that they got great personal satisfaction from their work and that it helped them to understand better the social structure of their society. Several careful evaluations of the effects of tutoring on mental skills of pupils throw some doubt on the value of the project from this point of view.

More recently there has been a development of tutoring by students only a little bit older and more skilled than the pupils being tutored. Some of these projects have shown surprising success. For example, Robert Cloward of Rhode Island University has evaluated a tutoring program in New York City in which teen-agers somewhat retarded in reading tutored middle-grade pupils in slum schools. Both tutees and tutors gained more in reading achievement tests than their controls did in a carefully designed experiment.

I have been told by several teachers of primary grades that they have occasionally asked an older or more advanced child to help a slow first-grader, with good results.

Whatever success these procedures have must be due more to motivation than to method. Getting *involved* with someone in a helping relationship apparently increases the desire to learn on the part of both the helper and the helped.

**Games.** Games have an accepted place in schools, as activities for recess and sometimes physical education and even spelling lessons. Generally they have been used as a change from the serious business of the school. But now games are being used as part of the planned curriculum. The reason is that games are motivating to most players, and they try to learn in order to win the game. There are now a good many mathematical games available, as well as games in geography. James S. Coleman and his colleagues have been working out games for high school students. The Mecklenberg Academy in Charlotte, North Carolina, has a number of games available for high school students.

It is not clear to what extent games can be used in slum schools, though there seems to be no reason to suppose that inner-city children cannot be interested in games aimed at teaching geography and arithmetic.

**Self-Concept Building.**  Middle-class white Americans have difficulty understanding the demand for courses in African culture and history, for African languages such as Swahili, and for units on the Negro in American history in the elementary school.  It is a waste of time if one is only interested in understanding the present world and in learning "useful" foreign languages.

But the need of a disadvantaged minority group to learn about its own cultural history in a positive way is related to the need for a positive self-concept—a self-concept of a person as a member of a social group that has a dignified and competent past.  This need is hardly recognized by the white middle-class American, partly because he does not feel the need consciously and partly because his own competence and success as a person give him a positive self-concept which he can pass on to his children.  Yet many children of Negro and other disadvantaged groups are told by their parents that they come from inferior stock, that they have "bad blood," that they suffer from their social past of slavery or of defeat by the white man.

While the best basis for a positive self-concept as a person who can learn in school and can succeed in American social and economic life is achievement—in school, in play, and in work—it may be that Negro children, in particular, would gain something from a study in school of the contributions of the Negro group to American life and culture, and of African history and culture.

When we find the good and effective ways to teach disadvantaged children and youth, we will still have to solve the problem of social integration of ethnic and poverty-plagued minority groups into the economic and political life of our large metropolitan areas.  The solutions will go hand in hand.  Big city and suburban governments as well as big city and suburban school systems will be remade in this process of social urban renewal.

I see the educational establishment reorganized and revitalized, together with the sociopolitical establishment.  The work will largely be done by activists who learn to innovate creatively and to evaluate their innovations scientifically.

# Discussion Questions and Activities

1. "The anarchists," Havighurst says, "have been strong on criticism and weak on constructive proposals for change." Is this an accurate statement? What would you say makes a proposal for change "constructive"?

2. What are the differences between "anarchists" and "institutional meliorists"? What are the strengths and weaknesses of the latter group's position?

3. Havighurst cites two groups—"anarchists," and critics whose chief concern is the disadvantaged—who have three principal criticisms and three proposals for reform of the schools. Taking cues from these proposals, construct your own proposal, drawing upon what you know about the pre-school child's cognitive and social development.

4. There are a number of conditions that reformers must fully consider, according to Havighurst, before a new criticism will be valid and effective. What are these conditions? Which of these conditions would you eliminate? What conditions would you add?

5. Different types of tests yield different types of information, and the use of a variety of statistical procedures may produce divergent findings. Havighurst cites figures on school achievement from the *New York Times* which he believes have been used in a misleading way. Is Havighurst correct? Check your local newspaper to see how school data are interpreted.

6. From what you know about educational measurement, would you say there is proof that the schools are effectively serving the 85 percent that the author points to as having good records of achievement? (Think in terms of "success" as being equated with scores on achievement tests.)

7. Havighurst cites the many innovations undertaken during the past thirty years by the New York City school system as evidence that it has been one of the most flexible and experimental of all big-city systems. Contrast these findings with David Rogers's study of New York City's schools, *110 Livingston Street.*

8. Evaluate the author's objection to expanding storefront schools.

# III. Joyless Classrooms

*Despite many criticisms of public schools, the schools have registered many tangible achievements which should not be overlooked. The schools have enrolled more youngsters, both absolutely and as a proportion of population, than at any time in history. Expenditures per pupil since the end of World War II (after adjusting for purchasing power) have more than doubled. Three out of four students now finish high school; whereas less than forty years ago less than three out of four went beyond the eighth grade. Improvements have also been made in the education of various ethnic groups.*

*Yet these improvements alone do not tell the full story, for it is possible to have longer and more expensive schooling and still not provide the learning opportunities today's youths need. Schools still may be dehumanizing institutions. Educators disagree over the extent to which this charge is applicable to the majority of schools. However, Charles E. Silberman, after conducting a national survey of today's schools, found them rather "joyless" institutions where emphasis is placed on order and control. Schools, he finds, tend to enforce time-consuming routines, silence rather than interchange of ideas, and to engender a generally repressive atmosphere for learning. Despite this atmosphere, many parents and a majority of students surveyed are essentially in favor of school rules and regulations. Silberman attributes the underlying problems to a prevailing "mindlessness" and lack of attention to meaning and purpose.*

*His study has been enthusiastically received by many educators, and most of the reviewers are quite laudatory. Some educators, however, defend the schools' accomplishments. Others think that Silberman has missed the causes of the schools' malaise and has thereby failed to get at the root of the problem. An example of this is Colin Greer's review which finds numerous shortcomings, oversights, and misdirections in the Silberman study and implies that it is not a panacea because it leaves most of the real problems unresolved.*

Charles E. Silberman

# 3. CRISIS IN THE CLASSROOM

. . . education should prepare people not just to earn a living but to live a life—a creative, humane, and sensitive life. This means that the schools must provide a liberal, humanizing education. And the purpose of liberal education must be, and indeed always has been, to educate educators—to turn out men and women who are capable of educating their families, their friends, their communities, and most importantly, themselves. "Though we cannot promise to produce educated men and women," says the catalogue of the College of the University of Chicago, whose faculty has thought harder about educational purpose than most faculties, "we do endeavour to bring each student . . . to a point beyond which he can educate himself." This must also be the purpose of the public schools. . . .

The most important characteristic schools share in common is a preoccupation with order and control. In part, this preoccupation grows out of the fact that school is a collective experience requiring, in the minds of those who run it, subordination of individual to collective or institutional desires and objectives. . . .

One of the most important controls is the clock; as Jackson puts it, "school is a place where things often happen not because students

Charles E. Silberman, a member of the *Fortune* magazine editorial staff from 1953 to 1971, served as director of the Carnegie Study of the Education of Educators which resulted in his widely heralded report, *Crisis in the Classroom,* a comprehensive survey and critique of public education and the education of teachers. He is also the author of *Crisis in Black and White* and has taught at Columbia University, City University of New York, and the Training Institute of the International Ladies' Garment Workers' Union.
Source: From *Crisis in the Classroom* by Charles E. Silberman. Copyright © 1970 by Charles E. Silberman. Reprinted by permission of Random House, Inc. Reprinted by permission of William Morris Agency, Inc., on behalf of author. Excerpts from pp. 114, 122–123, 130, 138, 145–146, 157.

want them to, but because it is time for them to occur." This in turn means that a major part of the teacher's role is to serve as traffic manager and timekeeper, either deciding on a schedule himself or making sure that a schedule others have made is adhered to.

Several things follow from this. Adherence to a timetable means that a great deal of time is wasted, the experiencing of delay being one of the inevitable outcomes of traffic management. No one who examines classroom life carefully can fail to be astounded by the proportion of the students' time that is taken up just in waiting. The time is rarely used productively. Hence in the elementary grades, an able student can be absent from school for an entire week and, quite literally, catch up with all he has missed in a single morning. . . .

Silence is demanded, moreover, despite the fact that school children work in very close quarters. "Even factory workers are not clustered as close together as students in a standard classroom," Jackson observes. "Once we leave the classroom we seldom again are required to have contact with so many people for so long a time." Yet despite the close contact, students are required to ignore those around them. They "must try to behave as if they were in solitude, when in point of fact they are not. They must keep their eyes on their paper when human faces beckon. Indeed, in the early grades it is not uncommon to find students facing each other around a table while at the same time being required not to communicate with each other." To become successful students, they "must learn how to be alone in a crowd."

Silence is demanded even when students are moving from one class to another. . . .

A major source of the underlying hostility is the preoccupation with grades. . . .

Evaluation per se is not the problem. As we shall argue in greater detail in Chapter 8, evaluation is an important and indeed intrinsic part of education—essential if teachers are to judge the effectiveness of their teaching, and if students are to judge what they know and what they are having trouble learning. The purpose should be diagnostic: to indicate where teachers and students have gone wrong and how they might improve their performance. And since students will have to judge their own performance, they need experience in self-evaluation.

But schools rarely evaluate in this way. They make it clear that the purpose of evaluation is rating: to produce grades that enable administrators to rate and sort children, to categorize them so rigidly that they can rarely escape. . . .

If schools are repressive, then, it is not the teachers' fault, certainly not their fault alone. Nearly two-thirds of the high school students' parents surveyed in early 1969 for *Life* by Louis Harris, for example, believe that "maintaining discipline is more important than student self-inquiry"; the comparable figure among teachers is only 27 percent. The United States, in short, has the kinds of schools its citizens have thus far demanded. The role of taskmaster is thrust upon the teachers, some of whom accept it willingly, some reluctantly; all are affected by it. "The teacher-pupil relationship," Waller writes, "is a special form of dominance and subordination, a very unstable relationship and in quivering equilibrium. . . . It is an unfortunate role, that of Simon Legree, and has corrupted the best of men."

# VI

What schools do to both students and teachers can be understood best if one realizes that in a number of respects, schools resemble "total institutions" like hospitals, armed services, and even prisons. In all of these, as Philip Jackson puts it, "one sub-group of their clientele (the students) are involuntarily committed to the institution, whereas another sub-group (the staff) has greater freedom of movement and, most important, has the ultimate freedom to leave the institution entirely. Under these circumstances it is common for the more privileged group to guard the exits, either figuratively or literally." Even when teachers operate "democratic" classrooms, Jackson insists, "their responsibilities bear some resemblance to those of prison guards. In 'progressive' prisons, as in most classrooms, the inhabitants are allowed certain freedoms, but there are real limits. In both institutions the inmates might be allowed to plan a Christmas party, but in neither place are they allowed to plan a 'break.' "[34]

To survive in school, as in other "total institutions," the students, like the teachers, are forced to develop a variety of adaptive strategies

[34] Cf. Willard Waller, *The Sociology of Teaching*, especially Chapters 2 and 14; and Gertrude H. S. McPherson, "The Role-Set of the Elementary School Teacher: A Case Study," unpublished Ph.D. dissertation, Columbia University Library. [Editor's note: Other footnotes appeared in material not quoted here.]

and attitudes. And survival—getting through and compiling a good record or avoiding a bad record—does become the goal. It is inevitable that this be so, given the obsession with routine and given also the frequency with which students are evaluated, the arbitrariness and mysteriousness (at least to the students) of the criteria by which they are judged, and the importance attached to these evaluations by parents, teachers, colleges, graduate and professional schools, and prospective employers. . . .

To be sure, students are less pliable now than they were even a few years ago. Dissent and protest are becoming widespread high school phenomena, and in his 1969 survey of high school students' attitudes, Louis Harris discovered a large reservoir of discontent with adult authority. Even so, the discontent was rather narrowly focused. Two-thirds of the students Harris surveyed felt that they should have more say in making rules and in deciding on curriculum, but fewer than half felt they should have more say in determining discipline.

More important, while students want some role in making the rules, surprisingly few of them question either the rules themselves or the way they are enforced. A clear majority, for example, think the school regulations are "about right," including rules on dress, haircuts, and use of free time. Three times as many students think the rules are enforced too leniently than feel enforcement is too severe; the great majority (two-thirds) think enforcement is about right. Students are equally satisfied with the curriculum: 50 percent of them think they "learn a lot" in high school, nearly two-thirds think the grading system is fair (they voted over two to one against abolishing grades), and 81 percent rate their teachers as good to excellent.[51] Belief in the beneficence of the paternalism to which they are subject exists, Buford Rhea suggests, "because there is a need for faith of this sort"; without it, students might find school intolerable. It is "the myth of institutional paternalism," in short, that keeps students from being alienated. Whether this is a virtue is something else again.

[51] "What People Think About Their High Schools," *Life* (May 16, 1969). Additional data courtesy of *Life* and Louis Harris and Associates, Inc.

Colin Greer

# 4. MUCH ADO ABOUT JOY

If Charles Silberman's *Crisis in the Classroom* were just an ordinary book, it would not be necessary to review it yet again. It has had plenty of reviews, and all of them favorable. Even the fact that one reviewer considers the innumerable plaudits ill-advised would not be at all noteworthy.

But Silberman's book is not at all ordinary. It is, after all, already making social policy in this country. From Dr. Nyquist's office to Mr. Shanker's office, from grade-school teachers to college presidents, the book has become the contemporary authorized version of education.

Reviewers have generally agreed that the book is a must; an informed analysis, rigorously researched, humanely conceived, if sometimes a little out of touch with the real world in which schools function; a "fine, flawed book." Having noted its deficiency, they dismiss it—its qualities are enough to go on. And yet, while I have found the deficiency—albeit more in terms of mountains than molehills—I have had trouble recognizing its much-praised qualities.

A good deal of space at the beginning of *Crisis in the Classroom* is devoted to the relationship between school and society, school being seen as one of a number of social institutions—an ancient concept discovered anew in the 20th century. But Silberman somehow forgets that schools, despite their humane rhetoric, have never

Colin Greer is a radical critic of the myths about American education, both past and present, and has developed his critiques in such books as *Cobweb Attitudes: Essays on Educational and Cultural Mythology* and *The Great School Legend*. He is senior editor of the journal, *Social Policy*, and a member of the faculty at Hunter College.

Source: Colin Greer, "Much Ado About Joy," *Social Policy*, vol. 1, no. 6 (March–April 1971), pp. 64–65. Reprinted by permission. *Social Policy* is published by Social Policy Corporation, New York, New York 10010.

created an environment in which that rhetoric is honored, that is, an environment in which tension rather than symbiosis is created between school and society. Now that we have such a tension through rapid social and economic change, Silberman provides a dangerous way for the system to cling to its rhetoric without recognizing that the hole is too big for the finger.

His survey of schools and programs in the United States is almost always descriptive rather than analytic. Mrs. Froelich, at P.S. 129 in New York City, does, like the other principals he cites, run an exciting school in which she functions as educator, not executive bureaucrat; Maxine Greene and Lawrence Cremin, at Columbia University, are indeed exciting teachers and seminal thinkers, having given intellectual cohesion to a field long dominated by soft-headed educationese. But Silberman never engages the issues presented by the facts that if Mrs. Froelich is among a handful of unique people, what of the licensing, selection, and tenure patterns that preserve the autonomy of others? Despite Mrs. Froelich's well-run, dedicated school, the children of P.S. 129 seem to do no better or worse in junior high school than other poor children. And whatever the strengths of Silberman's teacher-education heroes, when Teachers College graduates enter into teaching, they fare no better and do no better on behalf of schoolchildren in general than normal-school graduates of more than half a century ago.

Silberman makes no mention of such experiments in public education as, for example, that in the state of Vermont, under Harvey Scribner; Ocean Hill-Brownsville, Brooklyn, under Rhody McCoy; the decentralization movement in general, and the closely related introduction and escalation of the use of paraprofessionals in the classroom; the work in five major cities of The Teachers, Inc.; Caleb Gattegno's work in "Subordinating Teaching to Learning" in the development of reading and math skills; or the hundredfold "learning through teaching" projects across the country, of which Silberman gives neither description nor analysis, though he does pick up the item as one worth trying, as if it were brand new, untried, with no precedent or experience of its own. In a work which pretends to encyclopedic proportions—hailed as a thorough survey of American education now—these omissions are unforgivable.

Thanks to a body of scholarship and criticism which developed in the '60s, the Silberman who was committed to schools' doing old jobs for new kids in his other "crisis" work (*Crisis in Black and White*, which he now retracts with respect to his emphasis on preschool education for poor Black children, but which was no less a policy-setter than this *Crisis*) now recognizes the inability of schools to create mobility, and the joylessness of the classroom; and he concedes that both might be of longer standing than we had ever imagined. Yet he does not seem at all impelled to develop a theoretical framework for understanding the consistency of these facts in relation to the world they serve. As a result, therefore, he does not get into the problem of how much the schools can change while the world in which they function goes unchanged. He is able to conclude that there should be joy in the classroom, that we should simply put joy in the classroom—not mobility, interestingly enough.

In a dangerous way, Silberman is suggesting the very same solution he helped foist on us (wrongly, as he now admits) half a decade ago. Now, instead of putting poor Black kids, in particular, and poor kids, in general, into more of the same preschool classes, he suggests that we meet the same but increased parent complaint and student dissatisfaction with yet another program resolution which ignores both of them. Damning the whole of American education in gross terms for the absence of very vaguely defined kinds of "joy" in the classroom, he is able to forget the extreme seriousness of school failure for poor people in this day and age. He has joined middle-class-student complaint and lower-class aspiration frustration and lost the point of both. They are not the same. They are different.

What, after all, is joy—for whom, when, and how? In this book joy, which is recognized as missing, is somehow to be introduced without initiating any changes in the societal and school structures which have excluded it for so long. Progressivism, Silberman tells us—that is, the 1920s movement toward more open, more informal, less overcrowded classrooms—failed to contribute to real change because it was vulgarized. But the social forces which vulgarized it and muted it are left undiscussed and unengaged except for a rhetorical rallying call for humanism.

In this *Crisis* Silberman wholeheartedly accepts the English infant schools as a radical revolution in public education, forgetting entirely what Brian Jackson repeatedly and rigorously documents for us—that poor and working-class children in British infant schools do no better than their ancestors now in English secondary schools; they infrequently attend the university; and the rigidity of the English class structure remains virtually unaffected, in school and out. Making kids happier in grade school is a fine objective, but it is dangerous unless it clearly means more than a mechanism for the production of smiling, unaspiring, lower classes.

It is worth noting that Silberman ignores entirely the real force behind our current realizations about classroom deadness, which he establishes as conventional wisdom here. We have known for a very long time about the stultifying, formal classroom, from Emerson, from Dewey, from Holt, and now from Silberman. What, however, has caused the dynamic of the *Crisis* to which Mr. Silberman responds now is the voice of dissatisfied students and dissatisfied parents, especially Blacks.

But joylessness is only one small part of their complaint, and not even the crux of it, because joylessness in some schools and for some children is different from that for others. Putting joy in their respective classrooms—that is, encouraging the development of their differences—requires a preparedness for individual choices that neither our schools nor our society seems willing to permit.

The fact that Silberman fails to address the complexity of the school's traditional role in society, or a potentially different one, means inevitably that strategies for change—even at the gross level Silberman discusses it—never appear in *Crisis in the Classroom*. How, for example, do we challenge the entrenched power structure which maintains the institution and therefore the priorities of public education? How do we subvert its tried and tested cooptive apparatus, of which the response to this book is a notable example? How do we institutionalize experimentation while maintaining the integrity of the motives and protections of the experimental situation? How do we go about getting change even assuming the most positive interstices in Silberman's vague, one-word summary of what is missing?

# Discussion Questions
and Activities

1. Does Silberman's statement about the purposes of education
help to clarify your concept of what education should do
for an individual? For a society? What should be the
primary purpose of education? Refer to a dictionary for the
meaning of "education," use your own observations, and
prepare just one clear statement on what education should
do.

2. What are the most important characteristics schools share
in common? Is Silberman's diagnosis of these
characteristics unbiased? Be specific in your analysis.

3. Is evaluation, according to Silberman, the source of the
problem? From your view, is evaluation always
constructive? Explain.

4. Do schools resemble "total institutions"? If so, how?

5. What does it take to "survive" in today's public schools?
Are there basic changes that must be made before schools
can become places where joyous learning experiences
transpire? If changes are needed, what are these changes?

6. How do you explain the fact that a majority of students (in
the study mentioned by Silberman) think school
regulations are "about right"?

7. What is the difference between defying authority and
questioning its legitimacy? Which approach do most of
today's students take, and what significance does it have
for education?

8. Greer calls into question what he alleges to be a belief that
exceptional teachers and programs produce superior
outcomes. Teachers College (Columbia) graduates "do no
better on behalf of school children in general than
normal-school graduates of more than a half a century ago."
Do you consider it pretentious to equate exceptional
teachers with the school from which they obtained a degree?
If you were hiring a teacher to work with children in the
public schools, what qualities would you look for in that
teacher?

9. Greer cites experiments in public education that Silberman
fails to deal with in his book. Because the book has been

hailed as a thorough survey, Greer finds the omissions "unforgivable." Has he overstated his criticism?

10. Silberman, the article claims, provides only a one-word summary—"joyless"— as his explanation of what is wrong in schools. Does Silberman not also stress a "mindlessness" and a lack of meaning and purpose? What is the meaning of the terms "joyless" and "mindlessness"? Are these terms synonymous?

11. Silberman has found schools "joyless" places. Greer claims that putting joy back in schools is not enough: Silberman should not neglect the need of Blacks for social mobility. Actually, both can be achieved—schools can be joyous places of learning and Blacks can give whatever is needed for upward mobility. Achieving this goal involves changing concepts. What are some of the concepts that need to be changed? For example: beliefs and attitudes about skin color, the need to recognize the dignity of each individual, and the responsibility of helping an individual realize his own potential. List concepts that you know need to be changed before much progress can be made in achieving both joy and mobility for students.

12. Visit local school systems and observe the emphasis placed on order and control. What forms of order and control observed do you think are justified and what types are unnecessary? What are your own values and beliefs on which you base your conclusions?

13. How do we challenge the entrenched power structure? Silberman devotes little time to this question. List what you know teachers can do to challenge the power structure.

14. Greer charges Silberman with a failure to deal with the social forces in the larger society which affect the schools. Write a position paper dealing with this charge.

# IV. Progressive Practices and the New Informalism

*In the first four essays in this chapter, the reformer-writers analyze some of the educational problems they have met in their experience and offer proposals for the amelioration of the problems. These essays are followed by Arthur Pearl's critique of some of their proposals.*

*John Holt points out some of the ways that teachers make children seem stupid, create fear in them, and stifle their creativity. He also indicates that some parents expect schools to discipline children to engage in unpleasant tasks as a preparation for adult life. He then presents the type of classroom practices which he believes would overcome these problems.*

*Herbert Kohl is an advocate of the open classroom. Although it has certain fundamental similarities with the types of learning environments created by the early progressives, he claims that the open classroom is not altogether like their "permissive" classrooms. In the permissive classroom the teacher pretends she is not annoyed or angry with pupils when she actually is; whereas in the open classroom the teacher should try to be herself and let the pupils know how she feels. Also in an open classroom the teacher deals with situations as communal problems rather than as in the permissive classroom of permitting pupils to behave only in predetermined ways. In the selection that follows, Kohl relates incidents from open classrooms in operation.*

*We live in a society undergoing rapid change, but many schools are still teaching concepts more*

*appropriate to an earlier age. These outdated con-
cepts, according to Postman and Weingartner, do
not contribute to man's survival. They show what
it would be like for schools to address themselves
to these changes and to teach youth how to deal with
these changes. The authors propose new concepts
that they believe will enable youth to live more effectively in today's world.*

*The plight of youth in today's society is that of
an insecure status replete with strain and pressure
from an adult community that seeks to control and
shape them into desired patterns. The school, by
means of its compulsory nature, its restrictions on
student choices, and its system of authority, is the
primary vehicle to implement society's attitudes
toward youth. Friedenberg thoughtfully explores
these and other problems which youth face.*

*Arthur Pearl takes up the task of providing a
critique of John Holt, Herbert Kohl, Neil Postman
and Charles Weingartner, and Edgar Friedenberg in
a single article. Even more, he makes some telling
points against the ideas of several other educators
while explaining his own position. At the same
time, wherever he finds sound ideas among the
authors under review, he does not hesitate to draw
them to the reader's attention.*

John Holt

# 5. HOW CHILDREN FAIL

Some time ago, in an article on race stereotypes, I read something that stuck in my mind, but that only recently has seemed to have anything to do with children.

The author spent some time in a German concentration camp during the war. He and his fellow prisoners, trying to save both their lives and something of their human dignity, and to resist, despite their impotence, the demands of their jailers, evolved a kind of camp personality as a way of dealing with them. They adopted an air of amiable dull-wittedness, of smiling foolishness, of cooperative and willing incompetence—like the good soldier Schweik. Told to do something, they listened attentively, nodded their heads eagerly, and asked questions that showed they had not understood a word of what had been said. When they could not safely do this any longer, they did as far as possible the opposite of what they had been told to do, or did it, but as badly as they dared. They realized that this did not much impede the German war effort, or even the administration of the camp; but it gave them a way of preserving a small part of their integrity in a hopeless situation.

After the war, the author did a good deal of work, in many parts of the world, with subject peoples; but not for some time did he recognize, in the personality of the "good black boy" of many

John Holt is widely read, especially among youth, for his ideas on the reform of teaching. He is the author of such books as *How Children Fail, How Children Learn, What Do I Do On Monday?* and *The Underachieving School.* He has taught a variety of subjects at all levels and has lectured at Harvard Graduate School of Education and the University of California at Berkeley. Mr. Holt is a consultant with the Fayerweather Street School in Cambridge, Massachusetts.

Source: John Holt, *How Children Fail* (New York: Pitman Publishing Corporation, 1964), pp. 155–159, 160–161, 180–181. Reprinted by permission.

African colonies, or the "good nigger" of the American South, the camp personality adopted during the war by himself and his fellow prisoners. When he first saw the resemblance, he was startled. Did these people, as he had done, put on this personality deliberately? He became convinced that this was true. Subject peoples both appease their rulers and satisfy some part of their desire for human dignity by putting on a mask, by acting much more stupid and incompetent than they really are, by denying their rulers the full use of their intelligence and ability, by declaring their minds and spirits free of their enslaved bodies.

Does not something very close to this happen often in school? Children are subject peoples. School for them is a kind of jail. Do they not, to some extent, escape and frustrate the relentless, insatiable pressure of their elders by withdrawing the most intelligent and creative parts of their minds from the scene? Is this not at least a partial explanation of the extraordinary stupidity that otherwise bright children so often show in school? The stubborn and dogged "I don't get it" with which they meet the instructions and explanations of their teachers—may it not be a statement of resistance as well as one of panic and flight?

I think this is almost certainly so. Whether children do this consciously and deliberately depends on the age and character of the child. Under pressure that they want to resist but don't dare to resist openly, some children may quite deliberately *go stupid*; I have seen it and felt it. Most of them, however, are probably not this aware of what they are doing. They deny their intelligence to their jailers, the teachers, not so much to frustrate them but because they have other and more important uses for it. Freedom to live and to think about life for its own sake is important and even essential to a child. He will only give so much time and thought to what others want him to do; the rest he demands and takes for his own interests, plans, worries, dreams. The result is that he is not all there during most of his hours in school. Whether he is afraid to be there, or just does not want to be there, the result is the same. Fear, boredom, resistance—they all go to make what we call stupid children.

To a very great degree, school is a place where children learn to be stupid. A dismal thought, but hard to escape. Infants are not stupid. Children of one, two, or even three throw the whole of themselves into everything they do. They embrace life, and devour it; it is why they learn so fast, and are such good company. Listlessness, boredom, apathy—these all come later. Children come to school *curious*; within a few years most of that curiosity is dead, or at least silent. Open a first or third grade to questions, and you will be deluged; fifth graders say nothing. They either have no questions or will not ask them. They think, "What's this leading up to? What's the catch?" Last year, thinking that self-consciousness and embarrassment might be silencing the children, I put a question box in the classroom, and said that I would answer any questions they put into it. In four months I got one question—"How long does a bear live?" While I was talking about the life span of bears and other creatures, one child said impatiently, "Come on, get to the point." The expressions on the children's faces seemed to say, "You've got us here in school; now make us do whatever it is that you want us to do." Curiosity, questions, speculation—these are for outside school, not inside.

Boredom and resistance may cause as much stupidity in school as fear. Give a child the kind of task he gets in school, and whether he is afraid of it, or resists it, or is willing to do it but bored by it, he will do the task with only a small part of his attention, energy, and intelligence. In a word, he will do it stupidly—even if correctly. This soon becomes a habit. He gets used to working at low power, he develops strategies to enable him to get by this way. In time he even starts to think of himself as being stupid, which is what most fifth graders think of themselves, and to think that his low-power way of coping with school is the only possible way.

It does no good to tell such students to pay attention and think about what they are doing. I can see myself now, in one of my ninth-grade algebra classes in Colorado, looking at one of my flunking students, a boy who had become frozen in his school stupidity, and saying to him in a loud voice, "Think! Think! Think!" Wasted breath; he had forgotten how. The stupid way—timid, unimaginative, defensive, evasive—in which he met and dealt with the problems of algebra were, by that time, the only way he knew of dealing with them. His strategies and expectations were fixed; he couldn't even imagine any others. He really was doing his dreadful best.

We ask children to do for most of a day what few adults are able to do even for an hour. How many of us, attending, say, a lecture that doesn't interest us, can keep our minds from wandering? Hardly any. Not I, certainly. Yet children have far less awareness of and control of their attention than we do. No use to shout at them to pay attention. If we want to get tough enough about it, as many schools do, we can terrorize a class of children into sitting still with their hands folded and their eyes glued on us, or somebody; but their minds will be far away. The attention of children must be lured, caught, and held, like a shy wild animal that must be coaxed with bait to come close. If the situations, the materials, the problems before a child do not interest him, his attention will slip off to what does interest him, and no amount of exhortation or threats will bring it back.

A child is most intelligent when the reality before him arouses in him a high degree of attention, interest, concentration, involvement—in short, when he cares most about what he is doing. This is why we should make schoolrooms and schoolwork as interesting and exciting as possible, not just so that school will be a pleasant place, but so that children in school will act intelligently and get into *the habit* of acting intelligently. The case against boredom in school is the same as the case against fear; it makes children behave stupidly, some on purpose, most because they cannot help it. If this goes on long enough, as it does in school, they forget what it is like to grasp at something, as they once grasped at everything, with all their minds and senses; they forget how to deal positively and aggressively with life and experience, to think and say, "I see it! I get it! I can do it!" . . .

A mother said to me not long ago, "I think you are making a mistake in trying to make schoolwork so interesting for the children. After all, they are going to have to spend most of their lives doing things they don't like, and they might as well get used to it now."

Every so often the curtain of slogans and platitudes behind which most people live opens up for a second, and you get a glimpse of what they really think. This is not the first time a parent has said this to me, but it horrifies me as much as ever. What an extraordinary view of life, from one of the favored citizens of this most favored of all nations! Is life nothing but drudgery, an endless list of dreary duties? Is education nothing but the process of getting children ready to do them? It was as if she had said, "My boy is going to have to spend his life as a slave, so I want you to get him used to the idea, and see to it that when he gets to be a slave, he will be a dutiful and diligent and well paid one."

It's easy to see how an adult, in a discouraged moment, hemmed in by seemingly pointless and petty duties and responsibilities, might think of life as a kind of slavery. But one would expect that people feeling this way about their own lives would want something better for their children, would say, in effect, "I have somehow missed the chance to put much joy and meaning into my own life; please educate my children so that they will do better."

Well, that's our business, whether parents say it or not.

This woman is attractive, intelligent, fond of her son, and interested in him. Yet she shares with many parents and teachers a belief about her child and children in general which is both profoundly disrespectful and untrue. It is that they never do anything and never will do anything "worthwhile" unless some adult makes them do it. All this woman's stories about herself and her boy have the same plot: at first, he doesn't want to do something; then, she makes him do it; finally, he does it well, and maybe even enjoys it. She never tells me stories about things that her boy does well without being made to, and she seems uninterested and even irritated when I tell her such stories. The only triumphs of his that she savors are those for which she can give herself most of the credit.

Children sense this attitude. They resent it, and they are right to resent it. By what right do we assume that there is nothing good in children except what we put there? This view is condescending and presumptuous. More important, it is untrue, and blinds us to the fact that in our clumsy and ignorant efforts to mold the character of children we probably destroy at least as many good qualities as we develop, do at least as much harm as good. . . .

The alternative—I can see no other—is to have schools and classrooms in which each child in his own way can satisfy his curiosity, develop his abilities and talents, pursue his interests, and from the adults and older children around him get a glimpse of the great variety and richness of life. In short, the school should be a great smorgasbord of intellectual, artistic, creative, and athletic activities, from which each child could take whatever he wanted, and as much as he wanted, or as little. When Anna was in the sixth grade, the year after she was in my class, I mentioned this idea to her. After describing very sketchily how such a school might be run, and what the children might do, I said, "Tell me, what do you think of it? Do you think it would work? Do you think the kids would learn anything?" She said, with utmost conviction, "Oh, yes, it would be wonderful!" She was silent for a minute or two, perhaps remembering her own generally unhappy schooling. Then she said thoughtfully, "You know, kids really like to learn; we just don't like being pushed around."

No, they don't; and we should be grateful for that. So let's stop pushing them around, and give them a chance.

Herbert Kohl

# 6. THE OPEN CLASSROOM

I have been working with another class in that same school [Berkeley Unified School District], a kindergarten class. This room is also a complex place. There are several typewriters in one corner, a music center in another, a doll house and furniture in a third. One door in the room exits to the playground while the other leads to the hall. Throughout the room there are other centers—an open space with low chairs to sit around, tables, a cabinet with a tape recorder, a movable stand with a 16mm projector, bookcases used as dividers creating many small spaces. The teacher and I have tried many things together, but there are two that are particularly interesting.

One day Danny Caracco, one of my colleagues, and I brought a hundred feet of blank film leader to class and showed it to the children. They picked up their magic markers and paints and inks and

Herbert Kohl has received considerable attention for his ideas about working with children and youth. He is the author of *The Age of Complexity*, *36 Children*, *The Open Classroom*, and *Reading, How To*. He studied at Harvard, Teachers College, Columbia University, and Oxford. Kohl has taught for several years in Harlem schools and was formerly on the staff of the Center for Urban Education and director of the Teachers and Writers Collaborative at the Horace-Mann Lincoln Institute of School Experimentation. Recently he has been director of an experimental program in Berkeley schools.
Source: Herbert Kohl, *The Open Classroom*. Reprinted with permission from *The New York Review of Books*. Copyright © 1969 by Herbert Kohl. Excerpt is from pp. 61–65.

made a film of colors and shapes. There was no need for instruction. Before we could say a word about how to make a film, the children were already making one. Before we had a chance to talk about the product of their work we were overwhelmed by their desire to see it —and to make a sound track to it, and to dance to their sound track, and to play the film on their bodies while they were dancing, and to flick the lights in the classroom on and off while all this was happening. In a few hours these kindergarten children had developed their own "mixed media" technology. We had just stepped aside and let them learn and teach us.

The other experience with the kindergarten class is harder to describe. I teach a class at Berkeley High School, which is euphemistically titled Children's Theater. There are twenty young people in the class and we do improvisations, events in supermarkets, buses, anywhere in the community at large. The class meets formally in the costume room of the Berkeley Community Theater, though our classroom is the city we live in. I have found myself increasingly unable to accept the four walls of a schoolroom as the boundaries in which learning is supposed to take place. Our class goes where we feel we can learn and may be able to teach. We have had picnics on weekends, done improvisations on the beach, in parks, on the streets, in the supermarket. We have also talked about the irrelevance of school and the need to work, to become a functioning part of the community while young and full of the energy needed to change institutions. Doing theater in public places is one thing. Another and more important one is infiltrating the institutions that control lives—hospitals, banks, gas stations, supermarkets—and humanizing them. School at its best can be a place where young people can come to know themselves, their strengths and weaknesses, and get themselves ready to change a society which makes so little sense.

The classroom not only segregates young people from society. It segregates them from each other. We have elementary schools, junior high schools, high schools—six-year-olds never meet ten- or fifteen- or seventeen-year-olds in school. It is absurd. Not only do we not let children of the same age teach each other by insisting upon silence in the classroom, we make it impossible in the context of school for older children[2] to teach younger ones. Our "Children's Theater"

---

[2] I feel uneasy about this word. It makes some sense when applied to kindergarten or first grade people but none whatever when applied to high school students. [Editor's note: Footnote 1 appeared in material not quoted here.]

class has moved away from this, and once a week we visit a kindergarten.

The first time ten high school students came to the kindergarten we were all anxious about the visit. No one knew what would happen. A few improvisations were tried and they were fun but something unexpected and perfectly natural happened. The kindergarten children wanted to know who the high school students were, what they did and cared about. They wanted a chance to find people they liked, or whose interests fascinated them. The high school students felt the same way. The teacher and I, adults and the presumed experts in the room, stepped aside and let things happen.

Groups formed and dissolved, a few people went outside to take a walk, one high school student started to explain drawing to the young children and attracted a crowd, another began to use a typewriter, and got another crowd. I don't know everything that happened that morning, because so much was going on at the same time. What was clear was that the rich classroom we had functioned in with the kindergarten class was poor and meager compared to what it became with many young people alive and "unsupervised" in it.

Most of my examples are drawn from English and art classes. That is not because they are the only or easiest subjects in which to develop open environments. The reason I use these examples is that I know them best. Recently I have seen a science class at the Berkeley Community High School that embodies the same principles.

John Rosenbaum is a physicist and an artist. He makes light boxes using polarized lights and filters. It is difficult to walk into his classroom and not be drawn into an exploration of the phenomena of light and sound. There are sounding boards, tuning forks, musical instruments, amplifying equipment, etc., in one part of the room. Another part has strobe lights, polarized lights, filters, colored gels. And there are science books about, too. And art books. It is a magical world where one can start by playing with color and sound, and become involved in studying those phenomena in artistic or scientific ways.

There is another aspect of John's room which I must mention. In a corner is a large closet. It is empty except for rugs on the floor and posters on the walls. It is a meditation room for students (and hopefully for faculty as well), a place to go alone and be alone. It is the only place available for contemplation in Berkeley High School, which has almost 3,000 students, and it is considered strange.

It is legitimate for a kindergarten or first grade classroom to have a clubhouse or private place for young people, but we never think older children need to be alone in classrooms.

Neil Postman
Charles Weingartner

# 7. TEACHING AS A SUBVERSIVE ACTIVITY

The basic function of all education, even in the most traditional sense, is to increase the survival prospects of the group. If this function is fulfilled, the group survives. If not, it doesn't. There have been times when this function was not fulfilled, and groups (some of them we even call "civilizations") disappeared. Generally, this resulted from changes in the kinds of threats the group faced. The threats changed, but the education did not, and so the group, in a way, "disappeared itself" (to use a phrase from *Catch-22*). The tendency

Neil Postman is Professor of English Education at New York University and is currently on the faculty of Harlem Preparatory School. He was recently the director of New York University Linguistics Demonstration Center and is senior author of Holt, Rinehart & Winston's New English Series.
    Charles Weingartner taught for many years at the high school level, and is presently on leave from Queens College. He was formerly consultant to the New Jersey State Department of Education. He is co-author with Neil Postman of *Linguistics: A Revolution in Teaching, The Soft Revolution*, and *Teaching as a Subversive Activity*.
Source: From *Teaching as a Subversive Activity* by Neil Postman and Charles Weingartner. Copyright © 1969 by Neil Postman and Charles Weingartner. Reprinted by permission of the publisher, Delacorte Press, and Sir Isaac Pitman and Sons Limited. Excerpts from pp. 207–208, 211–212, 213, 216–218.

seems to be for most "educational" systems, from patterns of training in "primitive" tribal societies to school systems in technological societies, to fall imperceptibly into a role devoted exclusively to the conservation of old ideas, concepts, attitudes, skills, and perceptions. This happens largely because of the unconsciously held belief that these old ways of thinking and doing are necessary to the survival of the group.   And that is largely true, *IF* the group inhabits an environment in which change occurs very, very slowly, or not at all. Survival in a stable environment depends almost entirely on remembering the strategies for survival that have been developed in the past, and so the conservation and transmission of these becomes the primary mission of education.   But, a paradoxical situation develops when change becomes the primary characteristic of the environment. Then the task turns inside out—survival in a rapidly changing environment depends almost entirely upon being able to identify which of the old concepts are relevant to the demands imposed by the new threats to survival, and which are not.   Then a new educational task becomes critical: getting the group to unlearn (to "forget") the irrelevant concepts as a prior condition to learning. What we are saying is that "selective forgetting" is necessary to survival.

We suggest that this is the stage we have now reached environmentally, and so we must now work to reach this stage educationally. The only thing that is at stake is our survival.

It is not possible to overstate the fact that technologically wrought changes in the environment render virtually all of our traditional concepts (survival strategies)—and the institutions developed to conserve and transmit them—irrelevant, but not merely irrelevant.   If we fail to detect the fact that they are irrelevant, these concepts themselves become threats to our survival.

This idea is not, of course, original with us, even though it is new.   It is new because up until just recently changes in the environment did not require it.   As might be expected, the idea was first articulated by those most familiar with, and concerned about technologically produced change—scientists.   Not all scientists to be sure, since not all scientists themselves have been able to unlearn irrelevant old concepts.   After all, science is itself so new that 95 percent of all the scientists who ever lived are alive right now! . . .

To date, a great deal of human energy has been spent on the search for the "holy grail" of the illusion of certainty.   As a group, we are still in our intellectual infancy, depending much more upon magic and superstition than upon reason to allay our anxieties about the universe in which we are trying to live. After all, we haven't had much practice at figuring things out scientifically. So far, the use of scientific method is still largely confined to producing things normally intended to increase physical comfort. Up until just recently, technological "progress" has been confined almost solely to extending and shifting the function of human physical strength and energy to machines with which we cannot now compete. And while we have yet to figure out solutions to the problems this elementary kind of "progress" has produced, we are just beginning to confront the problems emerging as a consequence of the assumption by electronic machines of human intellectual functions. Electronic machines just happen to perform—already—a range of intellectual tasks better than human beings can. Our space-probing program, for example, would simply not be possible without electronic extensions of human information-handling and decision-making functions. The environmental changes electronic machines will produce in the near future—if not in the immediate present—is the subject of serious concern and discussion right now. One such discussion, accessible to a large public audience via television, occurred on the NBC *Open Mind* program. The participants were Paul Armer, associate head of the Rand Corporation's Computer Science Department, Theodore Kheel, Secretary-Treasurer of the American Foundation on Automation and Employment, Charles De Carlo, Director of Automation Research at I.B.M., and Robert Theobald, consulting economist and author of *The Challenge of Abundance.*

Threaded throughout the expert estimates of actual and imminent changes were references to the educational tasks to be fulfilled if these changes are not to disrupt the society in which they are occurring and will increasingly occur.

Robert Theobald, focusing on education, restated the sense of the discussion by saying that incredible changes are going to take place within 35 years and that no human group has ever before faced the problem of coping with changes of such magnitude. Noting that cultures have failed because they were incapable of changing their old concepts and ways of thinking, he suggested that we have to help the young people in our culture learn a new set of beliefs, a new set of institutions, and a new set of values, which will allow them to live in a totally different world. The issue, he said, lies here: how do you change the thinking of a culture with enormous speed?

Our response is that you do it through the school system—which is the only social institution that exists to fulfill this function—and by explicitly helping students to internalize concepts relevant to new environmental demands. Theobald, emphasizing that this is not a hypothetical problem and synthesizing the sense of the remarks of other participants, made the point that as a culture we have yet to see and understand the changes that have already taken place much less those that are about to. He noted also that the term "future shock" is coming into currency.

Clearly, there is no more important function for education to fulfill than that of helping us to recognize the world we actually live in and, simultaneously, of helping us to master concepts that will increase our ability to cope with it. This is the essential criterion for judging the relevance of all education. . . .

A decade earlier, Lynn White, Jr. (*Frontiers of Knowledge*, New York: Harper and Bros., 1956) summed up the probable meaning of the newest knowledge of that time under the title "Changing Canons of Culture." Possibly illustrating the rate at which change is occurring, White's views now seem much more sanguine than the state of our schools would seem to permit. . . .

If, as he wrote, White had thoughtfully looked at the schools, he would have found that they were deeply devoted to the job of "inculcating" the old canons he said had changed. Anyone who looks at the schools today will find them *still* "inculcating" the old canons. The schools stare fixedly into the past as we hurtle pell-mell into the future.

Not only are the archaic canons—or concepts—White hopefully suggested had changed still being "taught," but so are a series of other equally out-of-joint concepts, some deriving from those he noted. Among the more obvious of these are the following:

1. The concept of absolute, fixed, unchanging "truth," particularly from a polarizing good-bad perspective.
2. The concept of certainty. There is always one and only one "right" answer, and it is absolutely "right."
3. The concept of isolated identity, that "A is A" period, simply, once and for all.
4. The concept of fixed states and "things," with the implicit concept that if you know the name you understand the "thing."
5. The concept of simple, single, mechanical causality; the

idea that every effect is the result of a single, easily identifiable cause.

6. The concept that differences exist *only* in parallel and opposing forms: good-bad, right-wrong, yes-no, short-long, up-down, etc.

7. The concept that knowledge is "given," that it emanates from a higher authority, and that it is to be accepted without question.

This list is not exhaustive, but, alas, it is representative. What difference does it make—now and in the future—whether students internalize these concepts? What kind of people are they as a result? Here we move to what might be called the "nonintellectual" level of attitudes rather than concepts.

Most criticism of the old education, and the old concepts it conserves and transmits, from Paul Goodman to John Gardner, makes the point that the students who endure it come out as passive, acquiescent, dogmatic, intolerant, authoritarian, inflexible, conservative personalities who desperately need to resist change in an effort to keep their illusion of certainty intact.

It would be difficult to imagine any kind of education less liable to help students to be able to meet a drastically changing future than one which fosters the development of concepts and attitudes such as those noted above.

The concepts that we must all learn—that are now the *raison d'être* of education—are those which both shape technological change and derive from it: they are characteristics of the spirit, mood, language, and process of science. They are operative wherever evidence of social change—including theological versions—can be found.

Some of them you may recognize, and perhaps even accept, at least in certain domains. Others may seem odd or obscure, indicating their, to date, "fugitive" status.

Intellectual strategies for nuclear-space-age survival—in all dimensions of human activity—include such concepts as relativity, probability, contingency, uncertainty, function, structure as process, multiple causality (or noncausality), nonsymmetrical relationships, degrees of difference, and incongruity (or simultaneously appropriate difference).

Concepts such as these, as well as others both implicit in and contingent upon them, comprise the ingredients for changing ourselves in ways that complement the environmental demands that we all must face. The learning of such concepts will produce the kinds of people we will need to deal effectively with a future full of drastic change.

The new education has as its purpose the development of a new kind of person, one who—as a result of internalizing a different series of concepts—is an actively inquiring, flexible, creative, innovative, tolerant, liberal personality who can face uncertainty and ambiguity without disorientation, who can formulate viable new meanings to meet changes in the environment which threaten individual and mutual survival.

The new education, in sum, is new because it consists of having students use the concepts most appropriate to the world in which we all must live. All of these concepts constitute the dynamics of the questing-questioning, meaning-making process that can be called "learning how to learn." This comprises a posture of stability from which to deal fruitfully with change. The purpose is to help all students develop built-in, shockproof crap detectors as basic equipment in their survival kits.

## Edgar Z. Friedenberg

## 8. COMING OF AGE IN AMERICA

In my judgment, the kind of tutelage and status that the high school assigns students affects their lives and subsequent development far more crucially than the content and quality of formal instruction. What is learned most thoroughly by attendance at Milgrim or Harts-

Edgar Z. Friedenberg was educated at Centenary College, Stanford University, and the University of Chicago. He has taught at a number of universities in this country and is presently Professor of Education at Dalhousie University, burgh is certain core assumptions that govern the conditions of life of most adolescents in this country and train them to operate as adult, if not as mature, Americans. The first of these is the assumption that the state has the right to compel adolescents to spend six or seven hours a day, five days a week, thirty-six or so weeks a year, in a specific place, under the charge of a particular group of persons in whose selection they have no voice, performing tasks about which they have no choice, without remuneration and subject to specialized regulations and sanctions that are applicable to no one else in the community nor to them except in this place. So accustomed are we to assuming that education is a *service* to the young that this statement must seem flagrantly biased. But it is a simple statement of what the law provides. Whether this provision is a service or a burden to the young—and, indeed, it is both, in varying degrees— is another issue altogether. Compulsory school attendance functions as a bill of attainder against a particular age group, so the first thing the young learn in school is that there are certain sanctions and restrictions that apply only to them, that they do not participate fully in the freedoms guaranteed by the state, and that, *therefore, these freedoms do not really partake of the character of inalienable rights.*

When services are to be provided to an individual whom the law respects as it does the agency providing the services, the normal legal instrument is, of course, a contract, which defines the rights and obligations of both parties and provides each with legal remedies against the contract's breach.

Compulsory school attendance, however, is provided by a law which recognizes no obligation of the school that the students can enforce. He cannot petition to withdraw if the school is inferior, does not maintain standards, or treats him brutally. There are other laws, certainly, that set standards for school construction and maintenance, the licensing of teachers, technics of discipline, and so forth; and proceedings under these may be invoked if the school does not abide by them. But they do not abate the student's obligation to attend the school and accept its services. His position is purely that

Nova Scotia. One of the most perceptive observers of youth, he has offered his observations in leading journals and in such books as *The Vanishing Adolescent, Coming of Age in America, The Anti-American Generation,* and *Society's Children: A Study of Ressentiment in the Secondary School* (co-author). Source: From *Coming of Age in America* by Edgar Z. Friedenberg. Copyright © 1965 by Edgar Z. Friedenberg. Reprinted by permission of Random House, Inc. Excerpt from pp. 41–49.

of a conscript who is protected by certain regulations but in no case permitted to use their breach as a cause for terminating his obligation.

Of course not. The school, as schools continually stress, acts *in loco parentis*; and children may not leave home because their parents are unsatisfactory. What I have pointed out is no more than a special consequence of the fact that students are minors, and minors do not, indeed, share all the rights and privileges—and responsibilities—of citizenship. Very well. However one puts it, we are still discussing the same issue. The high school, then, is where you really learn what it means to be a minor.

For a high school is not a parent. Parents may love their children, hate them, or, like most parents, do both in a complex mixture. But they must, nevertheless, permit a certain intimacy and respond to their children as persons. Homes are not run by regulations, though the parents may think they are, but by a process of continuous and almost entirely unconscious emotional homeostasis, in which each member affects and accommodates to the needs, feelings, fantasy life, and character structure of the others. This may be, and often is, a terribly destructive process; I intend no defense of the family as a social institution. Salmon, actually, are much nicer than people: more dedicated, more energetic, less easily daunted by the long upstream struggle and less prudish and reticent about their reproductive functions, though inclined to be rather cold-blooded. But children grow up in homes or the remnants of homes, are in physical fact dependent on parents, and are too intimately related to them to permit their area of freedom to be precisely defined. This is not because they have no rights or are entitled to less respect than adults, but because intimacy conditions freedom and growth in ways too subtle and continuous to be defined as overt acts.

Free societies depend on their members to learn early and thoroughly that public authority is *not* like that of the family; that it cannot be expected—or trusted—to respond with sensitivity and intimate perception to the needs of individuals but must rely basically, though as humanely as possible, on the impartial application of general formulae. This means that it must be kept functional, specialized, and limited to matters of public policy; the meshes of the law are too coarse to be worn close to the skin. Especially in an open society, where people of very different backgrounds and value systems must function together, it would seem obvious that each must understand that he may not push others further than their common undertaking demands or impose upon them a manner of life that they feel to be alien.

After the family, the school is the first social institution an individual must deal with—the place in which he learns to handle himself with strangers. The school establishes the pattern of his subsequent assumptions as to which relations between the individual and society are appropriate and which constitute invasions of privacy and constraints on his spirit—what the British, with exquisite precision, call "taking a liberty." But the American public school evolved as a melting pot, under the assumption that it had not merely the right but the duty to impose a common standard of genteel decency on a polyglot body of immigrants' children and thus insure their assimilation into the better life of the American dream. It accepted, also, the tacit assumption that genteel decency was as far as it could go. If America has generally been governed by the practical man's impatience with other individuals' rights, it has also accepted the practical man's respect for property and determination to protect it from the assaults of public servants. With its contempt for personal privacy and individual autonomy, the school combines a considerable measure of Galbraith's "public squalor." The plant may be expensive —for this is capital goods; but nothing is provided graciously, liberally, simply as an amenity, either to teachers or students, though administrative offices have begun to assume an executive look. In the schools I know, the teachers' lounges are invariably filled with shabby furniture and vending machines. Teachers do not have offices with assigned clerical assistance and business equipment that would be considered satisfactory for, say, a small-town, small-time insurance agency. They have desks in staffrooms, without telephones.

To justify this shabbiness as essential economy and established custom begs the question; the level of support and working conditions customarily provided simply defines the status of the occupation and the value the community in fact places on it. An important consequence, I believe, is to help keep teachers timid and passive by reminding them, against the contrasting patterns of commercial affluence, of their relative ineffectiveness; and to divert against students their hostilities and their demands for status. Both teachers and students, each at their respective levels, learn to regard the ordinary amenities and freedoms of middle-class life as privileges. But the teacher has a few more of them. He hasn't a telephone, but he may make calls from a phone in the general office, while, in some schools, the public pay phone in the hallway has a lock on it and the student must get a key from the office before he can dial his call. Where a hotel or motel, for example, provides in its budget for normal wear and tear and a reasonable level of theft of linens and equipment and quietly covers itself with liability insurance, the school—though it may actually do the same thing—pompously indoctrinates its students with "respect for public property," "good health habits," and so forth before it lets them near the swimming pool. In a large city, the pool may have been struck out of the architect's plans before construction began, on the grounds that it would be unfair to provide students in a newer school with a costly facility that students in older schools do not have.

If the first thing the student learns, then, is that he, as a minor, is subject to peculiar restraints, the second is that these restraints are general, and are not limited to the manifest and specific functions of education. High school administrators are not professional educators in the sense that a physician, an attorney, or a tax accountant are professionals. They are not practitioners of a specialized *instructional* craft, who derive their authority from its requirements. They are specialists in keeping an essentially political enterprise from being strangled by conflicting community attitudes and pressures. They are problem-oriented, and the feelings and needs for growth of their captive and disfranchized clientele are the least of their problems; for the status of the "teen-ager" in the community is so low that even if he rebels the school is not blamed for the conditions against which he is rebelling. He is simply a truant or juvenile delinquent; at worst the school has "failed to reach him." What high school personnel become specialists in, ultimately, is the *control* of large groups of students even at catastrophic expense to their opportunity to learn. These controls are not exercised primarily to facilitate instruction, and, particularly, they are in no way limited to matters bearing on instruction. At several schools in our sample boys had, for example, been ordered by the assistant principal—sometimes on the complaint of teachers—to shave off beards. One of these boys, who had played football for the school all season, was told that, while the school had no legal authority to require this, he would be barred from the banquet honoring the team unless he complied. Dress regulations are another case in point.

Of course these are petty restrictions, enforced by petty penalties. American high schools are not concentration camps; and I am not complaining about their severity but about what they teach their students concerning the proper relationship of the individual to society. The fact that the restrictions and penalties are petty and unimportant in themselves in one way makes matters worse. Gross invasions are more easily recognized for what they are; petty restrictions are only resisted by "troublemakers." What matters in the end, however, is that the school does not take its own business of education seriously enough to mind it.

The effects on the students of the school's diffuse willingness to mind everybody's business but its own are manifold. The concepts of dignity and privacy, notably deficient in American adult folkways, are not permitted to develop here. The high school, certainly, is not the material cause of this deficiency, which is deeply rooted in our social institutions and values. But the high school does more than transmit these values—it exploits them to keep students in line and develop them into the kinds of people who fit the community that supports it.

A corollary of the school's assumption of custodial control of students is that power and authority become indistinguishable. If the school's authority is not limited to matters pertaining to education, it cannot be derived from educational responsibilities. It is a naked, empirical fact, to be accepted or controverted according to the possibilities of the moment. In this world power counts more than legitimacy; if you don't have power it is naive to think you have rights that must be respected; wise up. High school students experience regulation only as control, not as protection; they know, for example, that the principal will generally uphold the teacher in any conflict with a student, regardless of the merits of the case. Translated into the high school idiom, *suaviter in modo, fortiter in re* becomes "If you get caught, it's just your ass."

Students, I find, do not resent this; that is the tragedy. All weakness tends to corrupt, and impotence corrupts absolutely. Identifying, as the weak must, with the more powerful and frustrating of the forces that impinge upon them, they accept the school as the way life is and close their minds against the anxiety of perceiving alternatives. Many students like high school; others loathe and fear it. But even these do not object to it on principle; the school effectively obstructs their learning of the principles on which objection might be based; though these are among the principles that, we boast, distinguish us from totalitarian societies.

Yet, finally, the consequence of submitting throughout adolescence to diffuse authority that is not derived from the task at hand—

as a doctor's orders, or the training regulations of an athletic coach, for example, usually are—is more serious than political incompetence or weakness of character. There is a general arrest of development. An essential part of growing up is learning that, though differences of power among men lead to brutal consequences, all men are peers; none is omnipotent, none derives his potency from magic but only from his specific competence and function. The policeman represents the majesty of the State, but this does not mean that he can put you in jail; it means, precisely, that he cannot—at least not for long. Any person or agency responsible for handling throngs of young people—especially if it does not like them or is afraid of them—is tempted to claim diffuse authority and snare the youngster in the trailing remnants of childhood emotion, which always remain to trip him. Schools are permitted to infantilize adolescence and control pupils by reinvoking the sensations of childhood punishment, effective because it was designed, with great unconscious guile, to dramatize the child's weakness in the face of authority. In fact, they are strongly encouraged to do so by the hostility to "teen-agers" and the anxiety about their conduct that abound in our society.

In the process, the school affects society in two complementary ways. It alters individuals: their values, their sense of personal worth, their patterns of anxiety and sense of mastery and ease in the world on which so much of what we think of as our fate depends. But it also performs a Darwinian function. The school endorses and supports the values and patterns of behavior of certain segments of the population, providing their members with the credentials and shibboleths needed for the next stages of their journey, while instilling in others a sense of inferiority and warning the rest of society against them as troublesome and untrustworthy. In this way, the school contributes simultaneously to social mobility and social stratification. It helps to see to it that the kinds of people who get ahead are those who will support the social system it represents; while those who might, through intent or merely by their being, subvert it are left behind as a salutary moral lesson.

Arthur Pearl

# 9. WHAT'S WRONG WITH THE NEW INFORMALISM IN EDUCATION?

There are two major trends in education today, each of which is equally misleading. The first is that of the programmers of the mind, the educational engineers. Its guru is B. F. Skinner, the architect of the mindless man who has only a central nervous system to be programmed. Admiral Rickover was one of this trend's earliest proponents. Current spin-offs include Siegfried Engelmann and Carl Bereiter. The most recent disciple is Max Rafferty. The present fashion of performance contracting is a part of this vogue.

This approach is mindless, authoritarian, and anti-intellectual. For example, Engelmann recommends, in his approach to reading instruction, that his young charges jump up and down 40 times before they begin their reading lesson. There is no logic or evidence that reading is facilitated by jumping up and down.

## THE BEHAVIORIST BILL OF GOODS

The behaviorist psychologists have effectively sold the bill of goods that specific skills can be learned through consistent reinforcement

Arthur Pearl is Professor of Education at the University of Oregon. He has contributed to many journals and presented a full treatment of his own position in *The Atrocity of Education.* He has engaged in public health work and has directed youth and community studies projects. His professional interests are in the area of disadvantaged youth.

Source: Arthur Pearl, "What's Wrong with the New Informalism in Education" *Social Policy* 1, no. 6 (March–April 1971), pp. 15–23. Reprinted by permission. *Social Policy* is published by Social Policy Corporation, New York, New York 10010.

of desired behaviors. The reinforcement is immediate, so at superficial glance it would appear that the behaviorist is giving utility to the learning process. Not so! The reinforcement is usually extraneous to the intellectual activity; the student is forced into a *token economy!* If he learns what the instructor desires in the form and in the style and tempo that the instructor desires, he may receive from the instructor praise, a blue star, or even a piece of candy guaranteed to melt only in the mouth.

A token economy distorts the education process; the reward becomes the end in itself. Both the immediate utility of the *knowledge* and its connection to a system of thought are lacking.

## TEST-TAKING SKILLS ARE NOT EDUCATION

Operant conditioning psychologists are wont to sneer, "But we get results." However, this claim doesn't hold up under much examination. The crucial factor in evaluating the effectiveness of a program is selection of the criteria. It is true that, in some instances, operant conditioning techniques have improved student scores on standardized achievement tests; the problem is that the test performance has little bearing on culture-carrying competence. It is also true that almost any teacher committed to students produces changes in achievement on standardized tests. Herbert Kohl (*36 Children*), whose lack of system defies all of the behaviorists' principles, reports one to two years of gain on standardized tests in six months. *The mere mastering of test-taking skills does not ensure that the test-taker is literate, articulate, knowledgeable, or analytical. Because we rarely reflect upon this truth, persons without any of these attributes succeed to advanced degrees.*

Of course, the computer, the talking typewriter, and the programmed text are important to a good education, but the roles they will play are definitely subordinate. They will only make it possible for *good teachers* to be *better.* They will also, as is the case now, make it possible for *bad teachers* to be *worse.* Technology has contributed to bureaucratic intransigence and has fortified authoritarianism. More of it will not automatically reverse these tendencies. On the contrary, there must be *well-enunciated strategies if technological advancement is to be restricted to advancing humanity.*

## OVERSELLING ECSTASY

Unfortunately, it is not just the engineers who fail to see the necessity of such precaution. George Leonard, recognized as an advocate of humane education since publication of his book *Education and Ecstasy*, presents a cure for education's ills concocted of equal parts of electronic devices, biochemistries, and staged confrontations. His book is at best a journalistic tour de force in which lack of profundity is camouflaged by innumerable references. However, the references only mislead; and in every instance Leonard oversells the product.

The use of group encounters he favors so much, in which people go at each other with no holds barred and break down inhibitions through contrived physical contact, isn't where-it-is-at either. These activities may train persons to become sensitive; but it is quite clear, from years of evaluation, that most of this new-found sensitivity wears off quickly when the participants are returned to the "real world."

Leonard's fascination with psychoactive drugs is not very well balanced. He considers only the possible good things that can happen. He discounts completely the possible horror. He ignores how drugs may isolate man from his social environment and may further involute an already too involuted psychological existence. The quest for an elixir to produce inter- and intra-personal tranquility and intellectual potency is as old as man. There is nothing, Leonard's rhetoric notwithstanding, in its dismal history to lend much encouragement for the future.


## CITIZENSHIP FOR HEAVEN OR HELL?

Leonard is vague about educational goals. He is particularly sloppy when he discusses democratic citizenship—for example, "To learn heightened awareness and control of emotional, sensory, and bodily states and through this, increased empathy for other people (a new kind of citizenship education). . . ."

Leonard's new kind of citizenship education picks up all of the worst elements of the old kind. One of the things wrong today is the unwillingness of the school to open up for honest examination the flaws and failures of governmental workings. Leonard closes his eyes to brutal exploitation of man by man, to the domination of political processes by the very wealthy, and to abuse of power by those elected to office. He never deals with institutionalized racism. He is oblivious to the imminent threat of totalitarianism. His goal of citizenship education could have been surrounded by a bubble emanating from the mouth of the cartoon strip character Mary Worth.

Nowhere in Leonard's book is there a recognition that dynamic leadership is required if democratic processes are to be kept alive for the limited number who now enjoy them and that even more intense effort must be made if the fruits of democracy are to be extended to the large numbers who have been denied the pleasure. Depersonalization of man through bureaucratic organization and segregation is not going to wither away—nor is the oppressiveness of school going to magically disappear. Leonard does us a disservice in arguing that they will.

Leonard's work, like so much in "education," takes on the dimensions of a fairy tale because real problems are blissfully ignored. Nowhere does he deal with the problem of political control and the possible misuse of electronics, drugs, or psychological manipulations. He assumes that as man progresses technically, he also progresses socially. History does not bear him out. He has composed a modern siren's song, one that many find as hard to resist as did the shipmates of Odysseus. He calls his approach to education "ecstasy." He has made a common mistake; he has confused heaven with hell.

## THE OPEN MIND

If the first approach can be symbolized by the closed mind, the second can be represented by the open mind, the open school, in which there are no goals and no ideology, and the student is turned loose, unleashed to discover himself and the world. This is reflected in the new fetish with informalization, as though informalizing the over-regimented educational process will of itself produce significant learning and development. There is a basic Rousseauian assumption here that what is in man is basically good and intent on acquiring knowledge to promote that goodness, and that it simply needs to be let out; it does not require direction, guidance, or accountability. Education—that is, learning, personal development, and intellectual growth—is not to be painful, but rather a pleasant, open, entirely student-determined process. As the first approach has its roots in simplistic traditional education, so the new trend is rooted in Dewey and Neill and the progressive educators.   Its modern advocates include such spokesmen as Paul Goodman, John Holt, Neil Postman, Herbert Kohl, and Edgar Friedenberg.

All of these new educational leaders surrender leadership to the children.   John Holt ("Education for the Future," in Robert Theobald, *Social Policy for America in the '70s,* Doubleday, 1968) would not have teachers play a vital leadership role in changing and developing children; he would have each child determine his own educational goals—"School should be a place where children learn what they want to know, instead of what we think they ought to know."

Let me add here that I am in complete agreement with Holt when he accuses most schools—public schools, especially—of rigidity, irrelevance, unnecessary restrictions, lack of spontaneity, adult domination, and coerciveness.   But then he throws up his hands.   Just shake it all up, remove the teachers, abolish the teacher's leadership role in the classroom altogether, and thereby deny his responsibility in changing the current condition.   He keeps stating: take it all off— and just that haphazardly.   Regarding all learning as essentially the same, he ridicules the concept of curriculum as well as the teacher's leadership role.   Because what is now taught in school is often irrelevant, Holt concludes that it is impossible to identify relevance.   And so he insists:

> The most we can do is try to help, by letting him know roughly what is available and where he can look for it. Choosing what he wants to learn and what he does not is something he must do for himself. . . . In short, the school should be a great smorgasbord of intellectual, artistic, creative, and athletic activities from which each child could take whatever he wanted, and as much as he wanted or as little.

I disagree.   I believe that there is a body of knowledge to be taught and a position to be taken through it, and supported by it, against racism, against parochialism, against poverty and misery. It is important to remember once again that John Holt is a good man —at least by the criteria we all measure the goodness of a man.   He agrees with me about most things.   He is for peace and freedom, and against poverty.   The problem is that his dissatisfactions have diverted his concentration so that he can only identify alternatives to what is.   As a result, this relieves the teacher of responsibility for a better society once a student makes his choice to be a racist, a jingoist, a waster of resources, or a selfish accumulator of wealth.

Holt thinks that persons can be educated to be above these frailties "by creating in the school an atmosphere of freedom, respect, and trust within which true kindness and generosity can be expected to grow. It has little or nothing to do with content, curricula, or learning, and a great deal to do with the human heart and spirit." I have less faith in the undisciplined heart and less despair over what is really possible for us to achieve through schools. John Holt exhibits an anti-intellectual distortion of equalitarianism. Because he could not eliminate fear of failure in the classroom, he assumes it cannot be done. Because what is now taught in school is irrelevant, he believes that it is impossible to identify relevance and teach it. I disagree! I believe, as I said before, that there is a body of knowledge to be taught to prevent racism and provincialism.

## THE TEACHER'S LEADERSHIP ROLE

There is no place for bullies or sadists in the teaching profession! Any activity whose purpose is to inflict pain or embarrassment or to cause guilt must be eliminated from schools. But it is irresponsible to believe that the protection of the enterprise and the assurance of other students' rights will not require that some children's behavior will have to be restricted and that, in very rare instances, some children will have to be removed from the classroom. The incidence of restriction should be much less than it is now; and when it is required, the children affected must be ensured due process.

Neil Postman and Charles Weingartner oppose teacher leadership, too; they oppose what they see as its inevitable corollary—teacher domination of education. They have written a book—*Teaching as a Subversive Activity.* They see all of the structure of education as insulting to the student and good only for training students for playing the trivia game. They want a "revolution," which will become visible when "young revolutionary teachers" take the following steps:

1. Eliminate all conventional "tests" and "testing."
2. Eliminate all "courses."
3. Eliminate all "requirements."

4. Eliminate all full-time administrators and administrations.

5. Eliminate all restrictions that confine learners to sitting still in boxes made of boxes.

And specifically (in a list of 16 proposals), Postman and Weingartner recommended that teachers

> Declare a moratorium on all tests and grades. That would remove from the hands of teachers their major weapons of coercion and would eliminate two of the major obstacles to their students learning anything significant.

Postman and Weingartner would scrub grades entirely. *They are all wrong!* They fail to develop accountability. They don't establish a basis for evaluating student performance that has validity. Because they have not developed educational goals that make sense in a rapidly changing world, they have no legitimate basis for evaluating students.

I believe in the evaluation of both students and faculty. I believe that both not only need evaluation—both want it. But meaningful evaluation depends upon accountability and negotiability. *A test has to be defended to students. Each question must be defended as educationally relevant.* Each question must be upheld as a necessary link in the chain that leads ultimately to the goals of occupational, political, cultural, and personal competence. The student must be encouraged to exercise his right to challenge the teacher's arguments. If his "answer" doesn't correspond with that of the teacher, he, too, should be asked to be accountable. He, too, should be asked to defend his answer in the context of the goals of education. The classroom must become the market where, as Oliver Wendell Holmes Jr. expressed it, "truth [can] be determined through open competition of thought." Assessment, which is fundamental to this competence, requires negotiation. A social contract must be established. There is no possibility of a contract if there is no commonality of goals. But even agreement on goals does not assure meaningful negotiation. There is also the elemental issue of power. Again Holmes offers legal advice that has relevance to the classroom and grading procedure: if open competition of ideas from which grades are to be given is to become a reality, then there must be the understanding that "freedom of contract begins where equality of bargaining power begins."

## BINDING ARBITRATION FOR STUDENTS

The student must have access to binding arbitration and conciliation. In my classes, students can always ask for a sample of ten students to be drawn at random to determine the legitimacy of their grievances—either about tasks to be performed or evaluation of the worth of those tasks. I believe that standards should be negotiable and that the grades should be either "pass" or "haven't passed yet." *It makes little sense to me that a person who almost passes a course has to take it over, or that everyone should have to pass a course in exactly the same period of time.* Why can't a student complete this work two weeks later than the others in the class and receive full credit for his efforts? Suppose an agreed-upon standard for a class is to determine the ingredients in an unknown chemical substance. A student may not have deciphered the problem by the semester's end; but if ten days later he has finished the job, is there any earthly reason why the student shouldn't be given a "pass" for his accomplishment? Of course not.

Clearly, though more by implication than explication, Postman and Weingartner argue that one of the essentials for deflecting the world from its charted course to doom is a markedly changed school. I heartily concur with all the things they find wrong with school—dreariness, irrelevance, sterility, brutalization, etc.—but they present a solution that would in no way move the school toward widely effecting the changes we would all like to see.

## SUBSTITUTING QUESTIONS FOR ANSWERS

We really do not improve education if we merely substitute questions for answers. But Postman and Weingartner identify themselves with those who recommend "inquiry training" as a reformation of current educational emphasis. They believe that they have hit upon something new and vital. They think that what they have is of the electronic age.

Inquiry training can be identified by the following characteristic teacher behaviors:

> "The teacher rarely tells the students what he thinks they ought to know."

"His basic mode of discourse with students is questioning."

"He encourages student-student interaction as opposed to student-teacher interaction."

"And generally he avoids acting as a mediator or judge of the quality of ideas expressed."

"He rarely summarizes the positions taken by students on the learning that occurs."

"His lessons develop from the responses of students and not from a previously determined 'logical' structure."

"Generally, each of his lessons poses a problem for students."

"He measures his success in behavioral changes in students."

What's wrong with this behavior? Nothing, really; and everything, really! Nothing is wrong because the teacher behaviors are all desirable attributes, and everything is wrong because what is depicted is insufficient. The behaviors are not connected to educational goals. They represent processes without reference to outcomes. It is not possible even to guess what a student can *do* about saving the world from its impending disaster as a result of the described teacher behaviors. The teacher is postulated to be a part of a process designed to produce enormous change, yet he is without even a map specifying where he is and where he is trying to go.

What Postman and Weingartner will not recognize is that they have generated a system that is every bit as anti-intellectual as the "fact training" they oppose. In both instances the teacher is not projected as an intellectual leader. I sympathize completely with the criticism of "right-answer"-oriented education. It *is* sterile and ritualistic. Teaching students how to pass examinations has limited utility. The information gained is not useful in the solution of real problems. Even in that rare instance in which the information can be put to use, it is almost always learned in such a way that it is minimally transferable. All of this is true, and Postman and Weingartner dispatch the advocates of performance goals neatly. They are brilliant, devastating, and witty in their denunciation of the "tough-minded," fact-dominated dolts who are gaining ascendancy in schools. But in their desperate effort to avoid Scylla, Postman and Weingartner *become* Charybdis.

There is a romantic, recurring notion that powerful and valid criticism of existing conditions automatically leads to relief from those conditions. Persons who hold such a belief stubbornly refuse to learn the lessons of history. The most reasonable and probable result of criticism without a defensible alternative is a change that really is no change. I'm afraid that that is all we have to look forward to from Postman and Weingartner. The only thing subversive about their book, alas, is the title.

Asking questions can be just as sterile and ritualistic as answering questions. In fact, Postman and Weingartner warn us against this eventuality. But warning against sterility is no big thing. Everyone who favors a question-answering approach to education also opposes sterility—in fact, it can be safely said of *everyone* in education (particularly the most sterile) that he is against sterility. In practice, the warning against *stupidity* in education by educators is the *ritual* that exonerates the practice of stupidity and allows education to exercise it with total impunity. Teachers need to define goals, goals with which students can disagree; and the students must be helped to develop processes and techniques and atmospheres for disagreeing. But the teacher must be able to say "That's a stupid question" when the discovery-method-trained child raises one.

## TEACHER ACCOUNTABILITY

For good education, the student or the teacher (an arbitrary distinction) can neither a questioner nor an answerer be, all the time. What-he-is-when is determined by the goals of the enterprise. To solve man's heretofore unsolved problems, the student must have an enormous amount of facts at his command. He must continually apply those facts to the high-priority ecological puzzles. The problems must be analyzed so that manpower concerns (from the vantage points of both the individual and the greater society) are treated. The political issues (and *all* important problems will require a complex political solution) must be considered. The substantive knowledge of man must be applied to solve man's struggle for survival in such a way that the dignity of each individual is kept within the learner's consciousness. And although it is true that no important question has but one right answer, it is also true that some answers are more right than others. It is disputable whether the answer to "Who discovered America and when?" is Columbus in 1492, but that answer is quite superior to "George Wallace in 1968." The answer regarded right (or extremely right) affects greatly how a student attacks man's major challenges to survival.

In contrast to Postman and Weingartner, I believe that a good teacher *does* start off by telling students what he thinks they ought to know—but he then has to defend to students why he believes what he believes. Not only must he be accountable to them but he must also be willing to negotiate with them. The negotiation can have meaning and be something more than a senseless tug-of-war for power only if there are agreed-upon goals that keep discussion within bounds. In the context of his functioning as an accountable authority, the teacher questions, answers, debates, disputes facts, and summarizes. He always has a logical structure in the form of a plan that can be amended or even abrogated, but only when a better plan more consistent with educational goals is forthcoming. Without continual reference to goals, without "factual" support for arguments, without new concepts introduced by the teacher, the student will wallow in his prejudices and his ignorance. It is inconceivable that an accountable educational system can, or should, avoid an evaluative system. The student has a right to know where he stands. Postman and Weingartner actually concede such a point relatively early in their book, but then vehemently deny it at the end.

Postman and Weingartner are confusing in this respect because they are obviously confused. The call for measurable indices of success isn't made with much conviction because the authors do not believe that man can really communicate very much, let alone measure anything. The main thrust of the book is a plea for recognition that men's isolation from one another is inevitable and essential. "Each man is an island," they argue. "We now know that each man creates his own unique world, that he, and he alone, generates whatever reality he can ever know."

## THE MEDIUM IS NOT THE MESSAGE

Postman and Weingartner are all entangled in the silliness of Marshall McLuhan. Because they are unable to divorce process from purpose, they assert as unassailable truth the palpable falsehood that the medium is the message. *The medium is not the message.* The medium is subordinate to the message. A message must have content. Not only must something be said in a message but that something, if it has educational value, must relate to important problems. And here is where the "inquiry" boys fall apart. They cannot make a commitment. They are unable to take sides because they cannot tell right from wrong. Weingartner and Postman, in their approach to language and perception, stress only subjectivity, imprecision, and privacy. In the end they defy all that they claim to believe. In a book that demands that teachers be limited to "three declarative sentences per class, and fifteen interrogatives," they string together hundreds of declarations and offer no interrogatives. They are shallow where they should be deep, ambiguous where they should be forthright, and cynically humorous where they should be serious.

Postman and Weingartner have written a book that opens with a bang and ends with a whimper. They start off with a powerful first chapter. That chapter, entitled "Crap Detecting," suggests that students must learn in school to separate importance from trivia and truth from misconception. It is unfortunate that they did not heed the advice they offered in that first chapter. If they had, they would have written no more.

Certainly teachers should declare less and inquire more; certainly teachers should stimulate students to question more and answer less; but "inquiry," like any other tactic, remains just that. To elevate it to what it is not, to call it the essence of education, to label it the *new* education, is to do education a disservice. The ends of education should influence the means. Any educational process that fails to tie itself specifically to a long-range outcome (cultural, political, personal, and occupational) is not only inadequate but probably worthless.

Herbert Kohl's experience with his *36 Children* is an important case in point. He managed to "make it" with his students. But it was more happenstance than design. He capitalized on his sensitivity, insight, wit, and dedication. He had no plan; he endured day by day. He had no evaluation scheme. He used informal feedback from his students and kept his antennae out for signals that indicated approaching danger or safe passage. And yet, for all that he accomplished, if he intended to keep his children in the school until they had attained the goals of education, he failed abysmally. One by one the students were overcome by the system.

> Robert is not the only one of the thirty-six children who is now close to being a dropout—John, Margie, Carol, Sam— I stopped searching, don't want to know the full extent of the

misery and tragedy of the children's present lives. Recently one of the kids told me: "Mr. Kohl, one good year isn't enough." (p. 205)

Herbert Kohl could not have known when the students had become educated because he had no terminal goals. He had no theory, and he needed one. He had no strategy or tactics to win allies within the system over to his side. He needed tactics and strategy. He lacked overtures to other instructors. He was in the best tradition of the American Western folk hero. He was there all by himself when both hands of the clock were at twelve—but life isn't like the movies (although Californians obviously don't understand that); and he, not the bad guys, died in the dust.

Education must threaten ignorance and the tendency to put forth the least effort. Discipline and powerful input and stimulation from teachers are necessary. The teaching staff must challenge youngsters, interest them, lead them to confront and disagree. Only a fraction of students are self-starters. And in this sense the new trend is elitist, because it is really directed toward only this fraction.

Paul Goodman believes every mature adult can be a teacher. I disagree strongly. When my students in college played the teaching role, they came to learn very rapidly that there was more to it than simply maturity and openness; and the students whom they were teaching also wanted more than group process.

The problem with the new informalists is that they have no goals to offer, no rules to suggest. Either they produce anarchy or appeal to a tiny group of youngsters who are self-starters; or they fall back on some strong rules of their own and, like George Dennison (*The Lives of Children*), a disciple of Holt in his imposition of freedom, pick out or exclude youngsters who do not fit this pattern; or, like Edgar Friedenberg, who opposes democracy, they move toward appealing to elite, middle-class youngsters. School cannot be simply a place of questions with no answers; this is as bad as answers with no questions, the error of the educational engineers who have no appreciation of the open-ended aspect of learning.

If most "open mind" advocates are softheaded about the implicit elitism in the way they gloss over problems of preparing students for democracy, no such criticism can be leveled at Edgar Friedenberg. His explicit anti-democracy stands, in fact, as a revealing testament to the inevitable logic of democratic "open-minders" who look to him for leadership, confusing his criticism of current formal schooling with broadly based democratic goals.  Edgar Friedenberg advances a most disturbing proposition.  He questions the feasibility of democracy itself.  He concludes that it is more accurate to reject the notion that democracy has become corrupted and perverted and recognize that "What is wrong with America may be characteristic of mass democracy itself" (*Change in Higher Education*, May–June 1969, p. 16).

Friedenberg generates a cogent argument.  He points to a record of nonresponsiveness to social issues:

> In a society as open, invidious and competitive as ours, the kinds of people who succeed are usually incapable of responding to human demands; and the political power of the masses is used merely to express the hatreds and the envy, and to destroy anything that looks like genuine human satisfaction.

According to Friedenberg, we are presently on a collision course with disaster:

> Tyranny has taken many forms in history, but the graceless vulgarity and egregious clumsy brutality of fascism are its most hideous forms; and these grow best out of the democratic process itself.

Friedenberg is dubious of reform—

> The present political structure of America is precisely what is wrong, and there is no a priori reason to assume that it bears within itself the seeds of its own reform.

The hope of the future, according to Friedenberg, cannot now be accurately described, but whatever it is, it will fall outside the pale of established procedures.

> But I am sure that if radical improvement in the quality of our national life can be made—and our survival depends on this—the devices by which it can be done will seem outrageous and will, indeed, cause widespread outrage.

I concur with Friedenberg on the portentous nature of our times.  I differ with him on interpretation.  If one perceives that education merely reflects the dominant society, then Friedenberg's assessment is correct, and we are doomed.  But if one attributes some vitality to education and democracy and potential political power in a coalition of teachers and students, then there is hope.

Friedenberg's contempt for the common man's ability to perform the citizenship role concerns me.  He alludes to a lack of capability. It is my view that mass democracy fails only because so little effort has been made to educate "the masses" for democracy.  I believe that such education is possible.  I don't believe that the masses are any less receptive to such education than the privileged who have always benefited from it, and I believe that they have the most to gain from it.

Friedenberg's pessimism may be based on an accurate assessment of where we are going.  I remain an optimist, because pessimism is a luxury I don't believe we can afford.  The forces that oppose democracy are strong; and if those who support democracy are discouraged or halfhearted in their efforts, then certainly all is lost.  Too often, unfortunately, these latter are just that halfhearted—and softheaded, too.  They constitute the raw materials of bandwagons and the fabric of fads.  They divert us from the realities of the problems of school responsibility and yet, even more important, it is the direction they point to that our best hopes must be channeled.

In essence, education must have accountability.  There must be goals that are more than those set by the youngsters, even though the youngsters must play a powerful participatory role in evaluating and contributing to the goals.  No one teacher can have all the attributes or make all the inputs that are necessary.  The aim is to generate all that is necessary through a wide range of teaching staff for whom the major criteria of classroom interaction are:

1. Acceptance of pluralism in dress, manners, behavior. The staff must itself be diverse enough to make advocacy of all the different groups within a school a reality.
2. Accountability.  No one questions the fact that rules and regulations are essential, but the authority must explain the necessity for the restrictions, and the explanation must be based on logic and evidence.
3. Negotiation.  Differences between students and staff must be reconciled on a basis of mutual concern.  The staff must be willing to accept student suggestions for alternative ways of doing things.
4. Awareness of the inevitability of conflict.  Teachers must not crush all who differ: they must learn to live with people who differ in values and goals.
5. Rules as means, not as goals.  The educator will be in far

less difficulty if he keeps rules in a proper perspective. If
rules are seen only as a means to attain a legitimate goal
of education, then violation of the rules can be handled
rationally.

There must be a strategy for changing the schools; otherwise,
teachers may simply reflect the more pernicious aspects of our society
related to war, racism, and poverty. The new teachers must be able
to win the youngsters, the parents, and their colleagues to a recognition that the old values are inadequate and that a new society is
necessary. This must be done carefully through the whole teaching
process, not by postulating advanced radical goals and posturing
about them. We don't need a lot of rhetoric about change; rather, we
need lots more education and politics—persuasion of people through
everyday processes.

Finally, the educator has still another responsibility: he has to be
an effective citizen himself. The lame-leading-the-halt approach to
teaching of citizenship must be altered. If enlightened citizenship
is to be obtained in the mass, it must begin with a politically enlightened teaching force.

# Discussion Questions and Activities

1. Explain the analogy between "subject peoples" and students. Is Holt's analogy sound?

2. Has Holt overstated his case when he says "school is a place where children learn to be stupid"? Explain.

3. Is it a fact that schools have a tendency to kill the child's curiosity? If so, how is this accomplished? Draw on your own school experiences.

4. "We ask children to do for most of a day what few adults are able to do even for an hour." Do you agree or disagree with this statement? If you agree, how would you teach in order to overcome the problem?

5. Explain your reaction to the statement: Life is hard, so it is best that children learn to do things that are unpleasant and uninteresting.

6. Kohl illustrates the open classroom. Discuss its distinctive features as compared to some of the more traditional classrooms with which you are familiar. Of the two types, which would you prefer to teach in? Give reasons for your choice.

7. Critics of the open classroom claim that it is too unstructured and permissive; students do not learn discipline and thereby develop poor work habits. Does this mean that all students from the traditional classrooms do develop self-discipline and good work habits? How would you say these traits are developed?

8. If you were hiring a teacher to work in an open classroom, what character traits would you expect this teacher to have? Would you look for different character traits if you were hiring a teacher for a more traditional classroom?

9. What do Postman and Weingartner mean by "survival"? Is survival only a means to a higher form of education and life rather than an end in itself? Are the authors clear on this point?

10. Is "selective forgetting" necessary in a culture that is changing rapidly? Support your answer.

11. Is it dangerous for the schools to be devoted to "inculcating the old canons"? If the schools no longer do so, will they

then fail to transmit the cultural heritage?   What is your
position on this matter?

12. Review Postman and Weingartner's list of "archaic canons."
Are all of them archaic?   Can you think of others that they
omitted?

13. Consider your own teachers.   Have they oriented their
courses to help you to cope more effectively with rapid
change?

14. Imagine that a younger sister or brother of a close friend
were to enter the institution you are now attending.   Make
a list of "survival skills" that would equip this person to
earn a degree.

15. Can you refute Friedenberg's assertion that "the kind of
tutelage and status" that high school assigns youth is more
important than the program of formal instruction?   Is
Friedenberg basically making a claim for the student's
dignity?

16. Why would Friedenberg disagree in part with the statement
that education is a "service to the young"?   Do you share
his position on this matter?

17. Has compulsory schooling actually been used to deny
students' rights?   Can you think of any evidence in your
own experience where this has been the case?

18. What general differences are found between the school and
the family, according to Friedenberg, in their mode of
treating youth?

19. In what sense do schools show "contempt for personal privacy
and individual autonomy"?   State specific examples from
your reading and your own experiences.

20. Is the status of teenagers so low in the community that even
if they rebel against the school, the school will usually not
be blamed for the conditions against which they are
rebelling?   Is this true in your own community?   If your
answer is positive, what can be done to improve the
situation?

21. Clarify what you think Friedenberg means by the following
statement: "High school students experience regulation
only as control, not as protection. . ."

22. What difference does Pearl find between those he calls
"programmers of the mind" and proponents of the
"open mind" and the "open school"?

23. Summarize Pearl's criticisms of John Holt's position.   Have

weaknesses of Holt's proposals been effectively exposed, or is the critique misguided?

24. Explain Pearl's disagreement with Postman and Weingartner over grades and evaluation. What does Pearl mean by "accountability" and "negotiability" within the classroom? Do you believe that the undesirable effects that the author claims will result from Postman and Weingartner would actually materialize? What is your position on grades and evaluation?

25. What is wrong with the type of inquiry training advocated by Postman and Weingartner? Are Pearl's criticisms well taken?

26. Pearl tells us that Herbert Kohl was able to "make it" with his students; yet, he later asserts that in another way Kohl "failed abysmally." Explain this discrepancy.

27. We are told that Kohl "could not have known when the students had become educated . . ." Is this a sound criticism? True but overstated? Unsupportable? Support your decision.

28. Edgar Friedenberg is charged with an anti-democratic stance. Evaluate this claim.

29. Has mass democracy failed because "so little effort has been made to educate 'the masses' for democracy"?

30. Give your evaluation of the overall incisiveness and effectiveness of Pearl's criticisms.

# V. Nondirective Learning

*Resting at the heart of educational reform are the concepts we hold of teaching and learning, as well as our convictions about the learner. The teaching process has been studied recently in considerable depth by a number of investigators. We now have not only the findings on learning and motivation but a body of new knowledge on the teaching process and recommendations for its improvement. Knowledge is available about the teacher's verbal behavior and logical reasoning and his nonverbal and affective behavior as well.*

*Traditional models of teaching have long been under attack, and numerous educators have proposed alternative models for the teaching-learning process. Although Rogers would be an educator of this type, he has gone much further than his colleagues by seriously calling into question the efficacy of teaching itself. He believes that much that goes under the name of "teaching" does not help the student to live meaningfully in a continually changing world. He finds that teaching itself is a relatively over-valued activity and proposes instead that we think in terms of the "facilitation of learning." Rogers presents what he means by this concept in terms of the teacher's relations with students, and ends his essay by citing research evidence to support his position.*

*While it would be natural to expect some persons to object to a position that marks a considerable departure from established thought—and many have objected to Rogers's views on these grounds—few, however, have penetrated the underlying conceptual structure of Rogers's position and offered a significant critique of it.   R. S. Peters has penetrated this structure, attempted to show where it is weak and strong, and offered some of his own ideas as a substitute.*

Carl R. Rogers

# 10. THE INTERPERSONAL RELATIONSHIP IN THE FACILITATION OF LEARNING

I wish to begin this paper with a statement which may seem surprising to some and perhaps offensive to others. It is simply this: Teaching, in my estimation, is a vastly overrated function.

Having made such a statement, I scurry to the dictionary to see if I really mean what I say. Teaching means "to instruct." Personally I am not much interested in instructing another. "To impart knowledge or skill." My reaction is, why not be more efficient, using a book or programmed learning? "To make to know." Here my hackles rise. I have no wish to *make* anyone know something. "To show, guide, direct." As I see it, too many people have been shown, guided, directed. So I come to the conclusion that I *do* mean what I said. Teaching is, for me, a relatively unimportant and vastly overvalued activity.

Carl R. Rogers is both an educator and a psychologist, known for his nondirective approach to counseling. He received his formal education at the University of Wisconsin and Columbia University and has taught and served in counseling centers at many universities, both public and private. He has been the recipient of numerous awards for his contributions to psychology and counseling. Among his many writings are such well-known books as *Counseling and Psychotherapy*, *Client-Centered Therapy*, *On Becoming a Person*, *Freedom to Learn*, and he is co-author of *Psychotherapy and Personality Change*. He is presently a staff member at the Center for Studies of the Person, La Jolla, California.
Source: Carl R. Rogers, "The Interpersonal Relationship in the Facilitation of Learning," *Humanizing Education: The Persons in the Process*, Robert R. Leeper, ed. (Washington, D.C.: Association for Supervision and Curriculum Development, 1967), pp. 1–12. Reprinted with permission of the Association for Supervision and Curriculum Development and Carl R. Rogers. Copyright © 1967 by the Association for Supervision and Curriculum Development.

But there is more in my attitude than this. I have a negative reaction to teaching. Why? I think it is because it raises all the wrong questions. As soon as we focus on teaching, the question arises, what shall we teach? What, from our superior vantage point, does the other person need to know? This raises the ridiculous question of coverage. What shall the course cover? (Here I am acutely aware of the fact that "to cover" means both "to take in" and "to conceal from view," and I believe that most courses admirably achieve both these aims.) This notion of coverage is based on the assumption that what is taught is what is learned; what is presented is what is assimilated. I know of no assumption so obviously untrue. One does not need research to provide evidence that this is false. One needs only to talk with a few students.

But I ask myself, "Am I so prejudiced against teaching that I find no situation in which it is worthwhile?" I immediately think of my experience in Australia only a few months ago. I became much interested in the Australian aborigine. Here is a group which for more than 20,000 years has managed to live and exist in a desolate environment in which a modern man would perish within a few days. The secret of his survival has been teaching. He has passed on to the young every shred of knowledge about how to find water, about how to track game, about how to kill the kangaroo, about how to find his way through the trackless desert. Such knowledge is conveyed to the young as being *the* way to behave, and any innovation is frowned upon. It is clear that teaching has provided him the way to survive in a hostile and relatively unchanging environment.

Now I am closer to the nub of the question which excites me. Teaching and the imparting of knowledge make sense in an unchanging environment. This is why it has been an unquestioned function for centuries. But if there is one truth about modern man, it is that he lives in an environment which is *continually changing*. The one thing I can be sure of is that the physics which is taught to the present day student will be outdated in a decade. The teaching in psychology will certainly be out of date in 20 years. The so-called "facts of history" depend very largely upon the current mood and temper of the culture. Chemistry, biology, genetics, sociology, are in such flux that a firm statement made today will almost certainly be modified by the time the student gets around to using the knowledge.

We are, in my view, faced with an entirely new situation in education where the goal of education, if we are to survive, is the *facilitation of change and learning*. The only man who is educated is the man who has learned how to learn; the man who has learned how to adapt and change; the man who has realized that no knowledge is secure, that only the process of *seeking* knowledge gives a basis for security. Changingness, a reliance on *process* rather than upon static knowledge, is the only thing that makes any sense as a goal for education in the modern world.

So now with some relief I turn to an activity, a purpose, which really warms me—the *facilitation of learning*. When I have been able to transform a group—and here I mean all the members of a group, myself included—into a community of *learners*, then the excitement has been almost beyond belief. To free curiosity; to permit individuals to go charging off in new directions dictated by their own interests; to unleash curiosity; to open everything to questioning and exploration; to recognize that everything is in process of change—here is an experience I can never forget. I cannot always achieve it in groups with which I am associated but when it is partially or largely achieved then it becomes a never-to-be-forgotten group experience. Out of such a context arise true students, real learners, creative scientists and scholars and practitioners, the kind of individuals who can live in a delicate but ever-changing balance between what is presently known and the flowing, moving, altering, problems and facts of the future.

Here then is a goal to which I can give myself wholeheartedly. I see the facilitation of learning as the aim of education, the way in which we might develop the learning man, the way in which we can learn to live as individuals in process. I see the facilitation of learning as the function which may hold constructive, tentative, changing, process answers to some of the deepest perplexities which beset man today.

But do we know how to achieve this new goal in education, or is it a will-of-the-wisp which sometimes occurs, sometimes fails to occur, and thus offers little real hope? My answer is that we possess a very considerable knowledge of the conditions which encourage self-initiated, significant, experiential, "gut-level" learning by the whole person. We do not frequently see these conditions put into effect because they mean a real revolution in our approach to education and revolutions are not for the timid. But we do find examples of this revolution in action.

We know—and I will briefly describe some of the evidence—that the initiation of such learning rests not upon the teaching skills of the leader, not upon his scholarly knowledge of the field, not upon his curricular planning, not upon his use of audio-visual aids, not upon the programmed learning he utilizes, not upon his lectures and presentations, not upon an abundance of books, though each of these might at one time or another be utilized as an important resource. No, the facilitation of significant learning rests upon certain attitudinal qualities which exist in the personal *relationship* between the facilitator and the learner.

We came upon such findings first in the field of psychotherapy, but increasingly there is evidence which shows that these findings apply in the classroom as well. We find it easier to think that the intensive relationship between therapist and client might possess these qualities, but we are also finding that they may exist in the countless interpersonal interactions (as many as 1,000 per day, as Jackson [1966] has shown) between the teacher and his pupils.

What are these qualities, these attitudes, which facilitate learning? Let me describe them very briefly, drawing illustrations from the teaching field.

## REALNESS IN THE FACILITATOR OF LEARNING

Perhaps the most basic of these essential attitudes is realness or genuineness. When the facilitator is a real person, being what he is, entering into a relationship with the learner without presenting a front or a facade, he is much more likely to be effective. This means that the feelings which he is experiencing are available to him, available to his awareness, that he is able to live these feelings, be them, and able to communicate them if appropriate. It means that he comes into a direct personal encounter with the learner, meeting him on a person-to-person basis. It means that he is *being* himself, not denying himself.

Seen from this point of view it is suggested that the teacher can be a real person in his relationship with his students. He can be enthusiastic, he can be bored, he can be interested in students, he can be angry, he can be sensitive and sympathetic. Because he accepts these feelings as his own he has no need to impose them on his students. He can like or dislike a student product without implying that it is objectively good or bad or that the student is good or bad. He is simply expressing a feeling for the product, a feeling which exists within himself. Thus, he is a person to his students, not a faceless embodiment of a curricular requirement nor a sterile tube through which knowledge is passed from one generation to the next.

It is obvious that this attitudinal set, found to be effective in psychotherapy, is sharply in contrast with the tendency of most teachers to show themselves to their pupils simply as roles. It is quite customary for teachers rather consciously to put on the mask, the role, the facade, of being a teacher, and to wear this facade all day removing it only when they have left the school at night.

But not all teachers are like this. Take Sylvia Ashton-Warner, who took resistant, supposedly slow-learning primary school Maori children in New Zealand, and let them develop their own reading vocabulary. Each child could request one word—whatever word he wished—each day, and she would print it on a card and give it to him. "Kiss," "ghost," "bomb," "tiger," "fight," "love," "daddy"— these are samples. Soon they were building sentences, which they could also keep. "He'll get a licking." "Pussy's frightened." The children simply never forgot these self-initiated learnings. Yet it is not my purpose to tell you of her methods. I want instead to give you a glimpse of her attitude, of the passionate realness which must have been as evident to her tiny pupils as to her readers. An editor asked her some questions and she responded: " 'A few cool facts' you asked me for. . . . I don't know that there's a cool fact in me, or anything else cool for that matter, on this particular subject. I've got only hot long facts on the matter of Creative Teaching, scorching both the page and me" (Ashton-Warner, 163, p. 26).

Here is no sterile facade. Here is a vital *person,* with convictions, with feelings. It is her transparent realness which was, I am sure, one of the elements that made her an exciting facilitator of learning. She does not fit into some neat educational formula. She *is,* and students grow by being in contact with someone who really *is.*

Take another very different person, Barbara Shiel, also doing exciting work facilitating learning in sixth graders.[1] She gave them a great deal of responsible freedom, and I will mention some of the reactions of her students later. But here is an example of the way she shared herself with her pupils—not just sharing feelings of sweetness and light, but anger and frustration. She had made art materials freely available, and students often used these in creative ways, but the room frequently looked like a picture of chaos. Here is her report of her feelings and what she did with them.

> I find it (still) maddening to live with the mess—with a capital M! No one seems to care except me. Finally, one

[1] For a more extended account of Miss Shiel's initial attempts, see Rogers, 1966a. Her later experience is described in Shiel, 1966.

day I told the children . . . that I am a neat, orderly person by nature and that the mess was driving me to distraction. Did they have a solution? It was suggested they could have volunteers to clean up. . . . I said it didn't seem fair to me to have the same people clean up all the time for others— but it *would* solve it for me. "Well, some people *like* to clean," they replied. So that's the way it is (Shiel, 1966).

I hope this example puts some lively meaning into the phrases I used earlier, that the facilitator "is able to live these feelings, be them, and able to communicate them if appropriate." I have chosen an example of negative feelings, because I think it is more difficult for most of us to visualize what this would mean. In this instance, Miss Shiel is taking the risk of being transparent in her angry frustrations about the mess. And what happens? The same thing which, in my experience, nearly always happens. These young people accept and respect her feelings, take them into account, and work out a novel solution which none of us, I believe, would have suggested in advance. Miss Shiel wisely comments, "I used to get upset and feel guilty when I became angry—I finally realized the children could accept *my* feelings, too. And it is important for them to know when they've 'pushed me.' I have limits, too" (Shiel, 1966).

Just to show that positive feelings, when they are real, are equally effective, let me quote briefly a college student's reaction, in a different course. ". . . Your sense of humor in the class was cheering; we all felt relaxed because you showed us your human self, not a mechanical teacher image. I feel as if I have more understanding and faith in my teachers now. . . . I feel closer to the students too." Another says, ". . . You conducted the class on a personal level and therefore in my mind I was able to formulate a picture of you as a person and not as merely a walking textbook." Or another student in the same course,

> . . . It wasn't as if there was a teacher in the class, but rather someone whom we could trust and identify as a "sharer." You were so perceptive and sensitive to our thoughts, and this made it all the more "authentic" for me. It was an "authentic" *experience*, not just a class (Bull, 1966).

I trust I am making it clear that to be real is not always easy, nor is it achieved all at once, but it is basic to the person who wants to become that revolutionary individual, a facilitator of learning.

## PRIZING, ACCEPTANCE, TRUST

There is another attitude which stands out in those who are successful in facilitating learning. I have observed this attitude. I have experienced it. Yet, it is hard to know what term to put to it so I shall use several. I think of it as prizing the learner, prizing his feelings, his opinions, his person. It is a caring for the learner, but a non-possessive caring. It is an acceptance of this other individual as a separate person, having worth in his own right. It is a basic trust—a belief that this other person is somehow fundamentally trustworthy.

Whether we call it prizing, acceptance, trust, or by some other term, it shows up in a variety of observable ways. The facilitator who has a considerable degree of this attitude can be fully acceptant of the fear and hesitation of the student as he approaches a new problem as well as acceptant of the pupil's satisfaction in achievement. Such a teacher can accept the student's occasional apathy, his erratic desires to explore byroads of knowledge, as well as his disciplined efforts to achieve major goals. He can accept personal feelings which both disturb and promote learning—rivalry with a sibling, hatred of authority, concern about personal adequacy. What we are describing is a prizing of the learner as an imperfect human being with many feelings, many potentialities. The facilitator's prizing or acceptance of the learner is an operational expression of his essential confidence and trust in the capacity of the human organism.

I would like to give some examples of this attitude from the classroom situation. Here any teacher statements would be properly suspect, since many of us would like to feel we hold such attitudes, and might have a biased perception of our qualities. But let me indicate how this attitude of prizing, of accepting, of trusting, appears to the student who is fortunate enough to experience it.

Here is a statement from a college student in a class with Morey Appell.

> Your way of being with us is a revelation to me. In your class I feel important, mature, and capable of doing things on my own. I want to think for myself and this need cannot be accomplished through textbooks and lectures alone, but through living. I think you see me as a person with real feelings and needs, an individual. What I say and do are significant expressions from me, and you recognize this (Appell, 1959).

One of Miss Shiel's sixth graders expresses much more briefly her misspelled appreciation of this attitude, "You are a wounderful teacher period!!!"

College students in a class with Dr. Patricia Bull describe not only these prizing, trusting attitudes, but the effect these have had on their other interactions.

> ... I feel that I can say things to you that I can't say to other professors. . . . Never before have I been so aware of the other students or their personalities. I have never had so much interaction in a college classroom with my classmates. The climate of the classroom has had a very profound effect on me . . . the free atmosphere for discussion affected me . . . the general atmosphere of a particular session affected me. There have been many times when I have carried the discussion out of the class with me and thought about it for a long time.

> ... I still feel close to you, as though there were some tacit understanding between us, almost a conspiracy. This adds to the in-class participation on my part because I feel that at least one person in the group will react, even when I am not sure of the others. It does not matter really whether your reaction is positive or negative, it just *is*. Thank you.

> ... I appreciate the respect and concern you have for others, including myself. . . . As a result of my experience in class, plus the influence of my readings, I sincerely believe that the student-centered teaching method does provide an ideal framework for learning; not just for the accumulation of facts, but more important, for learning about ourselves in relation to others. . . . When I think back to my shallow awareness in September compared to the depth of my insights now, I know that this course has offered me a learning experience of great value which I couldn't have acquired in any other way.

> ... Very few teachers would attempt this method because they would feel that they would lose the students' respect. On the contrary. You gained our respect, through your ability to speak to us on our level, instead of ten miles above us. With the complete lack of communication we see in this school, it was a wonderful experience to see people listening to each other and really communicating on an adult, intelligent level. More classes should afford us this experience (Bull, 1966).

As you might expect, college students are often suspicious that these seeming attitudes are phony. One of Dr. Bull's students writes:

> . . . Rather than observe my classmates for the first few weeks, I concentrated my observations on you, Dr. Bull. I tried to figure out your motivations and purposes. I was convinced that you were a hypocrite. . . . I did change my opinion, however. You are not a hypocrite, by any means. . . . I do wish the course could continue. "Let each become all he is capable of being." . . . Perhaps my most disturbing question, which relates to this course is: When will we stop hiding things from ourselves and our contemporaries? (Bull, 1966).

I am sure these examples are more than enough to show that the facilitator who cares, who prizes, who trusts the learner, creates a climate for learning so different from the ordinary classroom that any resemblance is, as they say, "purely coincidental."


## EMPATHIC UNDERSTANDING

A further element which establishes a climate for self-initiated, experiential learning is empathic understanding. When the teacher has the ability to understand the student's reactions from the inside, has a sensitive awareness of the way the process of education and learning seems *to the student,* then again the likelihood of significant learning is increased.

This kind of understanding is sharply different from the usual evaluative understanding, which follows the pattern of, "I understand what is wrong with you." When there is a sensitive empathy, however, the reaction in the learner follows something of this pattern, "At least someone understands how it feels and seems to be *me* without wanting to analyze me or judge me. Now I can blossom and grow and learn."

This attitude of standing in the other's shoes, of viewing the world through the student's eyes, is almost unheard of in the classroom. One could listen to thousands of ordinary classroom interactions without coming across one instance of clearly communicated, sensitively accurate, empathic understanding. But it has a tremendously releasing effect when it occurs.

Let me take an illustration from Virginia Axline, dealing with a second grade boy. Jay, age 7, has been aggressive, a trouble maker, slow of speech and learning. Because of his "cussing" he was taken to the principal, who paddled him, unknown to Miss Axline. During a free work period, he fashioned a man of clay, very carefully, down to a hat and a handkerchief in his pocket. "Who is that?" asked Miss Axline. "Dunno," replied Jay. "Maybe it is the principal. He has a handkerchief in his pocket like that." Jay glared at the clay figure. "Yes," he said. Then he began to tear the head off and looked up and smiled. Miss Axline said, "You sometimes feel like twisting his head off, don't you? You get so mad at him." Jay tore off one arm, another, then beat the figure to a pulp with his fists. Another boy, with the perception of the young, explained, "Jay is mad at Mr. X because he licked him this noon." "Then you must feel lots better now," Miss Axline commented. Jay grinned and began to rebuild Mr. X. (Adapted from Axline, 1944.)

The other examples I have cited also indicate how deeply appreciative students feel when they are simply *understood*—not evaluated, not judged, simply understood from their *own* point of view, not the teacher's. If any teacher set herself the task of endeavoring to make one non-evaluative, acceptant, empathic response per day to a pupil's demonstrated or verbalized feeling, I believe he would discover the potency of this currently almost nonexistent kind of understanding.

Let me wind up this portion of my remarks by saying that when a facilitator creates, even to a modest degree, a classroom climate characterized by such realness, prizing, and empathy, he discovers that he has inaugurated an educational revolution. Learning of a different quality, proceeding at a different pace, with a greater degree of pervasiveness, occurs. Feelings—positive and negative, confused —become a part of the classroom experience. Learning becomes life, and a very vital life at that. The student is on his way, sometimes excitedly, sometimes reluctantly, to becoming a learning, changing being.

## THE EVIDENCE

Already I can hear the mutterings of some of my so-called "hard-headed" colleagues. "A very pretty picture—very touching. But these are all self reports." (As if there were any other type of expression! But that's another issue.) They ask, "Where is the evidence? How do you know?" I would like to turn to this evidence.

It is not overwhelming, but it is consistent. It is not perfect, but it is suggestive.

First of all, in the field of psychotherapy, Barrett-Lennard (1962) developed an instrument whereby he could measure these attitudinal qualities: genuineness or congruence, prizing or positive regard, empathy or understanding. This instrument was given to both client and therapist, so that we have the perception of the relationship both by the therapist and by the client whom he is trying to help. To state some of the findings very briefly it may be said that those clients who eventually showed more therapeutic change as measured by various instruments, perceived *more* of these qualities in their relationship with the therapist than did those who eventually showed less change. It is also significant that this difference in perceived relationships was evident as early as the fifth interview, and predicted later change or lack of change in therapy. Furthermore, it was found that the *client's* perception of the relationship, his experience of it, was a better predictor of ultimate outcome than was the perception of the relationship by the therapist. Barrett-Lennard's original study has been amplified and generally confirmed by other studies.

Se we may say, cautiously, and with qualifications which would be too cumbersome for the present paper, that if, in therapy, the client perceives his therapist as real and genuine, as one who likes, prizes, and empathically understands him, self-learning and therapeutic change are facilitated.

Now another thread of evidence, this time related more closely to education. Emmerling (1961) found that when high school teachers were asked to identify the problems they regarded as most urgent, they could be divided into two groups. Those who regarded their most serious problems, for example, as "Helping children think for themselves and be independent"; "Getting students to participate"; "Learning new ways of helping students develop their maximum potential"; "Helping students express individual needs and interests"; fell into what he called the "open" or "positively oriented" group. When Barrett-Lennard's Relationship Inventory was administered to the students of these teachers, it was found that they were perceived as significantly more real, more acceptant, more empathic than the other group of teachers whom I shall now describe.

The second category of teachers were those who tended to see their most urgent problems in negative terms, and in terms of student deficiencies and inabilities. For them the urgent problems were such as these: "Trying to teach children who don't even have the ability to follow directions"; "Teaching children who lack a desire to learn"; "Students who are not able to do the work required for their grade"; "Getting the children to listen." It probably will be no surprise that when the students of these teachers filled out the Relationship Inventory they saw their teachers as exhibiting relatively little of genuineness, of acceptance and trust, or of empathic understanding.

Hence we may say that the teacher whose orientation is toward releasing the student's potential exhibits a high degree of these attitudinal qualities which facilitate learning. The teacher whose orientation is toward the shortcomings of his students exhibits much less of these qualities.

A small pilot study by Bills (1961, 1966) extends the significance of these findings. A group of eight teachers was selected, four of them rated as adequate and effective by their superiors, and also showing this more positive orientation to their problems. The other four were rated as inadequate teachers and also had a more negative orientation to their problems, as described above. The students of these teachers were then asked to fill out the Barrett-Lennard Relationship Inventory, giving their perception of their teacher's relationship to them. This made the students very happy. Those who saw their relationship with the teacher as good were happy to describe this relationship. Those who had an unfavorable relationship were pleased to have, for the first time, an opportunity to specify the ways in which the relationship was unsatisfactory.

The more effective teachers were rated higher in every attitude measured by the Inventory: they were seen as more real, as having a higher level of regard for their students, were less conditional or judgmental in their attitudes, showed more empathic understanding. Without going into the details of the study it may be illuminating to mention that the total scores summing these attitudes vary sharply. For example, the relationships of a group of clients with their therapists, as perceived by the clients, received an average score of 108. The four most adequate high school teachers as seen by their students, received a score of 60. The four less adequate teachers received a score of 34. The lowest rated teacher received an average score of 2 from her students on the Relationship Inventory.

This small study certainly suggests that the teacher regarded as effective displays in her attitudes those qualities I have described as facilitative of learning, while the inadequate teacher shows little of these qualities.

Approaching the problem from a different angle, Schmuck (1963) has shown that in classrooms where pupils perceive their teachers as understanding them, there is likely to be a more diffuse liking structure among the pupils. This means that where the teacher is empathic, there are not a few students strongly liked and a few strongly disliked, but liking and affection are more evenly diffused throughout the group. In a later study he has shown that among students who are highly involved in their classroom peer group, "significant relationships exist between actual liking status on the one hand and utilization of abilities, attitude toward self, and attitude toward school on the other hand" (1966, pp. 357–58). This seems to lend confirmation to the other evidence by indicating that in an understanding classroom climate every student tends to feel liked by all the others, to have a more positive attitude toward himself and toward school. If he is highly involved with his peer group (and this appears probable in such a classroom climate), he also tends to utilize his abilities more fully in his school achievement.

But you may still ask, does the student actually *learn* more where these attitudes are present? Here an interesting study of third graders by Aspy (1965) helps to round out the suggestive evidence. He worked in six third-grade classes. The teachers tape-recorded two full weeks of their interaction with their students in the periods devoted to the teaching of reading. These recordings were done two months apart so as to obtain an adequate sampling of the teacher's interactions with her pupils. Four-minute segments of these recordings were randomly selected for rating. Three raters, working independently and "blind," rated each segment for the degree of congruence or genuineness shown by the teacher, the degree of her prizing or unconditional positive regard, and the degree of her empathic understanding.

The Reading Achievement Tests (Stanford Achievement) were used as the criterion. Again, omitting some of the details of a carefully and rigorously controlled study, it may be said that the children in the three classes with the highest degree of the attitudes described above showed a significantly greater gain in reading achievement than those students in the three classes with a lesser degree of these qualities.

So we may say, with a certain degree of assurance, that the attitudes I have endeavored to describe are not only effective in facilitating a deeper learning and understanding of self in a relationship such as psychotherapy, but that these attitudes characterize teachers who are regarded as effective teachers, and that the students of these teachers learn more, even of a conventional curriculum, than do students of teachers who are lacking in these attitudes.

## REFERENCES

**M. L. Appell.** "Selected Student Reactions to Student-centered Courses." Mimeographed manuscript, 1959.

**S. Ashton-Warner.** *Teacher.* New York: Simon and Schuster, 1963.

**D. N. Aspy.** "A Study of Three Facilitative Conditions and Their Relationship to the Achievement of Third Grade Students." Unpublished Ed.D. dissertation, University of Kentucky, 1965.

**Virginia M. Axline.** "Morale on the School Front." *Journal of Educational Research* 38: 521–33; 1944.

**G. T. Barrett-Lennard.** "Dimensions of Therapist Response as Causal Factors in Therapeutic Change." *Psychological Monographs,* 76, 1962. (Whole No. 562.)

**R. E. Bills.** Personal correspondence, 1961, 1966.

**Patricia Bull.** Student reactions, Fall 1965. State University College, Cortland, New York. Mimeographed manuscripts, 1966.

**F. C. Emmerling.** "A Study of the Relationships Between Personality Characteristics of Classroom Teachers and Pupil Perceptions." Unpublished Ph.D. dissertation, Auburn University, Auburn, Alabama, 1961.

**P. W. Jackson.** "The Student's World." University of Chicago. Mimeographed, 1966.

**C. R. Rogers.** "To Facilitate Learning." In Malcolm Provus, editor, NEA Handbook for Teachers, *Innovations for Time To Teach.* Washington, D.C.: Department of Classroom Teachers, NEA, 1966a.

**R. Schmuck.** "Some Aspects of Classroom Social Climate." *Psychology Schools* 3: 59–65; 1966.

**R. Schmuck.** "Some Relationships of Peer Liking Patterns in the Class-Pupil Attitudes and Achievement." *The School Review* 71: 337–59; 1963.

**Barbara J. Shiel.** "Evaluation: A Self-directed Curriculum, 1965." Mimeographed, 1966.

# R. S. Peters

# 11. ON *FREEDOM TO LEARN*

It is, to a certain extent, inevitable that a person's thinking about education will be an extrapolation from a situation with which he is most familiar. Perry (1965) has developed this point with regard to what he calls the "traditional" and the "child-centred" models of education. It is not surprising, therefore, that Carl Rogers' views about education should reflect, in the main, his experiences as a therapist. What is surprising, however, is that an author who strongly advocates openness to the experiences of others should put together a collection of papers that are meant to be of general relevance to educational problems in such a seeming state of ignorance and innocence about educational theory and practice. Freedom is fine; and so is self-directed exploration. But there are other values, both in life and in education—truth, for instance, humility, and breadth of understanding.

Carl Rogers' book about education exemplifies both the strengths and weaknesses of his own emphasis. He builds on what he learns and values and much of what he says is perceptive, if rather repetitive; but his passionate assurance is not clouded by any hint of what

R. S. Peters is a professor at University of London's Institute of Education and is one of today's leading educational philosophers. A member of the National Academy of Education in the United States, he has served as a visiting professor at Harvard University and a visiting fellow at Australian National University. Peters studied at Clifton College, Bristol University, Queens College, Oxford University, and Birbeck College, University of London. He has written in the areas of psychology, political thought, philosophy, and philosophy of education. Among his books are *The Concepts of Motivation*, *Brett's History of Psychology*, rev. ed., *Hobbes*, *Social Principles and the Democratic State* (co-author), *Authority, Responsibility, and Education*, *Ethics and Education*, *The Concept of Education* (editor), *The Logic of Education* (co-author), and *Education and the Development of Reason* (co-editor).
Source: R. S. Peters, "On *Freedom to Learn*," Interchange, vol. 1, no. 4 (1970), pp. 111–114. Review of the Carl Rogers book, reprinted by permission.

he does not know and he even seems unaware of the light that others have already shed on some of the positions that he has made his own. Surely, one reflects, as one reads about self-directed learning, work contracts, and the problem-solving approach, Carl Rogers must have heard of the Dalton plan. Surely he has battled his way through Dewey and Kilpatrick as have most American educators; surely he is not so uneducated as to have missed out on Cremin's *The Transformation of the School*. But then, as one reads on, one begins to understand the free-floating character of the book, its lack of any proper historical, social, or philosophical dimensions. It is not really an attempt to think systematically about the actual problems of teaching and learning in a concrete historical context. It is Carl Rogers "doing his thing" in the context of education. Much of the book was actually given as distinct papers and addresses on specific occasions. These various addresses are strung together with other chapters in which Rogers restates his now familiar themes about the organism, interpersonal relationships, self-enhancement, etc., and tries to demonstrate their general relevance for education. This exposition is prefaced by three case studies in which a sixth grade teacher, a college professor of psychology, and himself try experiments in facilitating learning.

So much by way of general comment on *Freedom to Learn* as a serious sortie into educational theory. But what is to be made of Rogers' specific themes, when due allowance has been made for the limitations of their launching pad? Most of them are to be found in Chapters 4 to 7, after Rogers has presented his case studies in Part I. He gets off to a very shaky start in contrasting teaching, which he thinks unimportant, with the facilitation of learning, which is the proper concern of the educator. He is led to make this rather stark contrast because the dictionary tells him that teaching means "to instruct" and "to impart knowledge and skill"—some, e.g., Oakeshott (1967), actually wish to *contrast* "instruct" with "impart"—and because he thinks that it is concerned only with the passing on of a static body of knowledge and skill. The Australian aborigines managed all right with teaching because of their unchanging environment; it is, however, useless for modern man because his environment is constantly changing. The goal of education for us must therefore be the facilitation of change and learning.

Every aspect of this thesis is dubious. If Rogers had thought more about the concept of "teaching," or if he had taken the trouble to examine what modern philosophers of education had written about it, instead of just looking it up in the dictionary, he would have grasped that "teaching" is a much more polymorphous concept than this. Was not Socrates teaching the slave in *The Meno*, even though he was not telling him anything? He would have grasped, too, that it is not only knowledge that can be imparted but also modes of thought and experience by means of which knowledge has been acquired and by means of which it can be criticized and revised. Also what is the point, on his own showing, of equipping people to *seek* knowledge, if no value is to be accorded to its acquisition? It may be salutary, at a time of change, to stress the importance of learning how to learn. But this goal is not inconsistent with acquiring information. My guess, too, is that, in spite of change, modern man needs to acquire much more of it to survive than ever was required by the Australian aborigine.

Having got teaching out of the way, Rogers is then able to give voice to his excitement about a real community of learners, which is worth quoting because, apart from its style, it could have come straight out of Dewey. "To free curiosity; to permit individuals to go charging off in new directions dictated by their own interests; to unleash the sense of inquiry; to open everything to questioning and exploration; to recognize that everything is in process of change— here is an experience I can never forget" (p. 105). How then, is this process of real "self-initiated, significant, experiential, 'gut-level' learning" to be facilitated? And, at this point, Rogers makes his distinctive contribution. It is through "certain attitudinal qualities which exist in the personal relationship between the facilitator and the learner" (p. 106). Findings in the field of psychotherapy apply in the classroom as well. Rogers then outlines the qualities that a facilitator of learning should exhibit to learners, qualities that parallel those of a client-centred therapist to his patients—genuineness, being a real person with his pupils, prizing the learner and caring for him, empathic understanding, and trust. Rogers claims that "individuals who hold such attitudes, and are bold enough to act on them, do not simply modify classroom methods—they revolutionize them. They perform almost none of the functions of teachers. It is no longer accurate to call them teachers. They are catalyzers, facilitators, giving freedom and life and the opportunity to learn, to students" (p. 126).

This is surely an extremely important point to make about teaching. If we avert our eyes from the naive contrast between "teaching" and "the facilitation of learning" there remains a strong case for saying that personal relationships between teacher and pupil, of the type advocated by Rogers, do seem to facilitate learning. This needs to be said loudly at a time when educational institutions are becoming larger and more impersonal and when students are increasingly being treated as subject-fodder and as operatives to be slotted into the occupational structure. Teachers can function as human beings as well as teachers; and if they do so, learning is probably facilitated.

Rogers, however, does not seem altogether clear about what makes a relationship a personal one as distinct from a role relationship. What seems to me distinctive of a personal relationship is that a response is made to another individual just as a human being— not as an occupant of a role, not as a sharer in a common quest, including that of learning, not even as another moral being who is regarded with respect as the subject of rights (Peters, 1966). Yet Rogers constantly speaks of such relationships as if he views them, in an educational situation, mainly as facilitators of learning. But if they are entered into by the teacher *because he sees them* as facilitating learning they surely cease to be proper personal relationships; for the aspect under which the other is viewed, as a learner, now makes them a species of role relationship. Their spontaneity can thus be spoilt and endless possibilities for *mauvaise foi* are opened up. There is thus inherent in the teacher-pupil relationship a paradox akin to the paradox of hedonism. Learning is facilitated by the teacher entering into personal relationships with his pupils; but such relationships must not be viewed by the teacher as facilitating learning. Indeed a pupil would surely resent being at the receiver end of a "personal relationship" with a "facilitator" that is viewed as aiding his learning, much more than being subject to a straightforward attempt to instruct him. Rogers seems unaware of these difficulties because he does not appreciate that being a facilitator of learning is just as much a role relationship as instructing and that what makes an action a performance of a role is the aspect under which it is viewed by the agent. In other words, Rogers' ideal teacher must, to a certain extent, be capable of forgetting, in his dealing with pupils, that he is a facilitator of learning. He must, from time to time, just respond to his pupils as fellow human beings. This response is something that is valuable in its own right.

Rogers' preoccupations with personal relationships between teacher and pupil are very salutary because progressives, who stress freedom and self-initiated learning, sometimes stress too much "do it yourself" methods. Rogers, of course, advocates these, but he is more than mindful of the bond between teacher and taught that is one of the most potent influences in the development of knowledge, sensitivity, and skill. He does not, however, bring the teacher's role fully out into the open because he is squeamish about direction, and superficial about knowledge. He believes in the growth and self-actualization of the individual. He finds that his clients and pupils move towards genuineness, acceptance of self, openness to others, and self-direction. In other words the self that is realized is not any old self, but one that exemplifies moral values as old as Socrates. Rogers seems to see this as some sort of spontaneous unfolding of dormant potentialities. But he surely must appreciate that there are dormant potentialities for all sorts of other selves and that the emergence of this type of self is very intimately connected with the study influence of persons such as Rogers. Rogers is, of course, an inveterate moralist who passes on his values more by exemplifying them than by trying to instruct others in them—except, of course, when he writes books. This kind of influence is a form of "direction"— perhaps a much more effective form than explicit instruction. I myself share Rogers' moral convictions. But I do think that their ethical status should be made explicit and that some sort of justification of them should be attempted. I also think that persons who believe in them should stop being so squeamish about the manifest "directiveness" involved in passing them on to others—especially if they are teachers.

Rogers' squeamishness about the role of the teacher is connected with his tendency to regard teaching as just instruction in a body of knowledge or code of behaviour. He does not appreciate that a more important aspect of teaching is the initiation of others into modes of thinking and experience that lie behind such bodies of knowledge and codes of behaviour. In teaching science, for instance, one does not just pass on facts and laws; nor does one seek simply to encourage the nebulous sort of adaptability, or learning how to learn, that Rogers advocates. One attempts to get others on the inside of a public form of thinking in which assumptions are challenged and techniques mastered for deciding who is right. Specific types of concepts and truth criteria have to be understood. Above all the passion for truth must be conveyed that gives point to the search for evidence, the abhorrence of irrelevance, incoherence, and arbitrariness, and the love of clarity and precision. Similarly moral education is not just a matter of imposing rules such as those prohibiting stealing and the breaking of promises; it is also a matter of sensitizing persons to principles such as respect for others, truthfulness, fairness, freedom, and the consideration of interests, which are presuppositions of moral experience. Rogers' valuations are intimately connected with this form of experience. It is one that has taken the human race thousands of years to develop and that is constantly threatened by powerful and more primitive tendencies within human nature. It is institutionalized in democratic institutions at their best, and will be perpetuated only if it also is fostered in the consciousness of countless individuals.

Rogers does no service to the tradition that he had inherited by suggesting that his values are private possessions that develop miraculously within the individual soul. And he does a positive disservice by minimizing the role of the teacher as one of the main transmitters of these public forms of life. Rogers contrasts the teacher, who imposes his values, with the facilitator of learning, who sets people free to discover their own. Both pictures are inadequate; for both ignore the public forms of experience underlying, e.g., scientific, moral, and aesthetic achievements and discoveries. The teacher, ideally speaking, is a person whose experience and special training has given him some mastery of one or other of these modes of experience. Rogers himself manifestly has achieved this in the particular mode of interpersonal understanding. His function, in the same way as that of any other teacher, is to initiate others into this form of experience so they can manage on their own. But, as with "creative" artists or scientists, they cannot do so without being introduced in a whole variety of ways, with which good teachers are familiar, into the mode of experience in question. It is against this general background of the role of the teacher that Rogers' important insights about personal relationships are to be seen in proper perspective.

In Part III Rogers outlines some assumptions about learning and its facilitation and discusses graduate education in the light of them. Generalizations are put forward about the importance of relevance to the learner's purposes, about learning through doing and participation, and about the relationship of threats to the self to learning. Much of this discussion is very apposite; but there is nothing very novel in it. What is missing, however, is any sense of the great differences between the sorts of things that have to be learnt—skills, attitudes, principles, facts, etc., within different modes of experience. Some generalizations such as those of Rogers can be made about general conditions of learning. But equally crucial for education are the specific features of different types of learning that derive from differences in what is being learnt—these differences affect very much the role of the "facilitator."

Part IV includes a personal confession of what is most significant to Rogers in "being in relationship," some thoughts about the "valuing process," a chapter on Freedom and Commitment in which he outlines his views on free will in contrast to those of Skinner, and an account of the goal of the "fully functioning person." There is no mention of any of the recent work done on moral development and Rogers' handling of the issues in ethics that he raises is so superficial, limited, and confined to his own frame of reference that it would be difficult to know quite where to begin in discussing them. The book ends with a model for revolution in which Rogers recommends T groups, etc., for educational administrators, teachers, and faculty members. This is mildly reminiscent of Plato's suggestion that society can be saved only if philosophers become kings or kings become philosophers. But Plato did know something about politics and institutional change.

## REFERENCES

**Oakeshott, M.**   Learning and teaching. In R. S. Peters (Ed.), *The concept of education*. London: Routledge & Kegan Paul, 1967.

**Perry, L. R.**   What is an educational situation? In R. D. Archambault (Ed.), *Philosophical analysis and education*. London: Routledge & Kegan Paul, 1965.

**Peters, R. S.**   Teaching and personal relationships. In E. L. French (Ed.), *Melbourne studies in education*. Melbourne: Melbourne University Press, 1966.

## Discussion Questions and Activities

1. How does Rogers define teaching? Do you accept his definition? Construct your own definition.

2. What specific reasons does he give for his assertion that teaching is "a vastly overrated function"? Are his reasons valid in terms of what you know about teaching? Give specific reasons for your answer.

3. By assuming that teaching is only applicable in a certain type of culture, does Rogers thereby lead you to believe that his definition of teaching is overly restrictive?

4. What, according to Rogers, is the goal of education? Evaluate his proposed goal. Develop your own goal.

5. What does it mean to be "a facilitator of learning"? How is being a facilitator different from being a teacher?

6. Evaluate the evidence that Rogers presents as corroborating his position. Do you think that his evidence is adequate?

7. Peters charges that Rogers's book does not attempt to think about teaching and learning in a concrete historical context. In other words, the works of his predecessors are ignored. Is it Rogers's responsibility to show the contributions of earlier educators to his ideas?

8. Peters attacks Rogers's concept of teaching. Explain and evaluate Peters's critique of the concept.

9. Peters argues that Rogers's relationship as a facilitator of learning is a role relationship as distinct from a personal relationship. Evaluate the validity of this charge.

10. What problems, if any, are involved in the concept of spontaneous unfoldment of dormant potentialities?

11. Peters says that Rogers is a moralist but is squeamish about taking a directive role in such matters with students. Peters thinks that Rogers should be less squeamish about doing so. Add ideas of your own if you do not accept the ideas of either author.

12. Peters finds that the teacher who imposes values and the person who is a facilitator of learning are both inadequate because they ignore the public forms of experience underlying codes of behavior and bodies of knowledge. What are the strengths and weaknesses of Peters's counter-argument?

13. Peters briefly states his own position. Does it have any weaknesses? If so, what are they? Is it clearly superior to what Rogers has proposed? If so, in what ways?

14. Make observations of one of your teachers for at least one hour. Was your teacher's behavior more in accordance with the ideas of Rogers or Peters?

# VI.  The Process of Discovery

*New approaches to teaching mathematics, the sciences, and, to a lesser extent, the humanities and social studies were developed by a number of leading scholars in the disciplines in collaboration with curriculum specialists. The approach generally taken is a structure of the disciplines approach, which involves introducing to a child in language he can understand the basic concepts, principles, theories, axioms, and postulates of the discipline. The child also learns, on a miniature scale, how to think about a discipline the way a scholar would do in uncovering the structure and gaining new knowledge. This process involves the method of discovery in which the pupil puts forward guesses and hunches, develops hypotheses, and uses intuitive as well as logical reasoning to arrive at generalizations that lie behind particular operations. The use of the discovery method enables the student to perceive previously unrecognized relations and similarities between ideas. Understanding the fundamental structure and intellectual operations makes a discipline more comprehensible.*

*Jerome Bruner attempts to show that we have underestimated the ability of the child to grasp concepts which traditionally have been reserved for the upper grades. He explains why he thinks it is possible to introduce concepts earlier and speculates as to how it can be accomplished. Underlying his rationale is the structure of the disciplines approach and the use of the discovery method.*

*Robert M. W. Travers reports the research on the discovery method and compares the results to*

*the more traditional expository form of teaching.*
*The results are not as promising as Bruner's enthu-*
*siastic advocacy would lead us to believe.*

Jerome S. Bruner

# 12. READINESS FOR LEARNING

Mastery of the fundamental ideas of a field involves not only the grasping of general principles, but also the development of an attitude toward learning and inquiry, toward guessing and hunches, toward the possibility of solving problems on one's own. Just as a physicist has certain attitudes about the ultimate orderliness of nature and a conviction that order can be discovered, so a young physics student needs some working version of these attitudes if he is to organize his learning in such a way as to make what he learns usable and meaningful in his thinking. To instill such attitudes by teaching requires something more than the mere presentation of fundamental ideas. Just what it takes to bring off such teaching is something on which a great deal of research is needed, but it would seem that an important ingredient is a sense of excitement about discovery—discovery of regularities of previously unrecognized relations and similarities between ideas, with a resulting sense of self-confidence in one's abilities. Various people who have worked on curricula in science and mathematics have urged that it is possible to present the funda-

Jerome S. Bruner studied at Duke University and took his doctorate at Harvard University where, except for short stints at institutions in the United States and Europe, he has taught since 1945. Presently he is Professor of Psychology and directs the Center for Cognitive Studies. Recognized for his contributions to the curriculum reform movement of the 1960's and his studies of cognitive development, his book *The Process of Education* has had as much impact as any single title on curriculum reform during the 1960's. Bruner is also the author of *Toward A Theory of Instruction, Process of Cognitive Growth in Infancy, On Knowing: Essays for the Left Hand, The Relevance of Education,* and is co-author of *A Study of Thinking* and *Studies in Cognitive Growth.*

Source: Jerome S. Bruner, *The Process of Education* (Cambridge, Mass.: Harvard University Press, Copyright, 1960, by the President and Fellows of Harvard College), pp. 20–22, 33–40. Reprinted by permission.

mental structure of a discipline in such a way as to preserve some of the exciting sequences that lead a student to discover for himself.

It is particularly the Committee on School Mathematics and the Arithmetic Project of the University of Illinois that have emphasized the importance of discovery as an aid to teaching. They have been active in devising methods that permit a student to discover for himself the generalization that lies behind a particular mathematical operation, and they contrast this approach with the "method of assertion and proof" in which the generalization is first stated by the teacher and the class asked to proceed through the proof. It has also been pointed out by the Illinois group that the method of discovery would be too time-consuming for presenting all of what a student must cover in mathematics. The proper balance between the two is anything but plain, and research is in progress to elucidate the matter, though more is needed. Is the inductive approach a better technique for teaching principles? Does it have a desirable effect on attitudes?

That the method of discovery need not be limited to such highly formalized subjects as mathematics and physics is illustrated by some experimentation on social studies carried out by the Harvard Cognition Project. A sixth-grade class, having been through a conventional unit on the social and economic geography of the Southeastern states, was introduced to the North Central region by being asked to locate the major cities of the area on a map containing physical features and natural resources, but no place names. The resulting class discussion very rapidly produced a variety of plausible theories concerning the requirements of a city—a water transportation theory that placed Chicago at the junction of the three lakes, a mineral resources theory that placed it near the Mesabi range, a food-supply theory that put a great city on the rich soil of Iowa, and so on. The level of interest as well as the level of conceptual sophistication was far above that of control classes. Most striking, however, was the attitude of children to whom, for the first time, the location of a city appeared as a problem, and one to which an answer could be discovered by taking thought. Not only was there pleasure and excitement in the pursuit of a question, but in the end the discovery was worth making, at least for urban children for whom the phenomenon of the city was something that had before been taken for granted. . . .

We begin with the hypothesis that any subject can be taught effectively in some intellectually honest form to any child at any stage of development. It is a bold hypothesis and an essential one in thinking about the nature of a curriculum. No evidence exists to contradict it; considerable evidence is being amassed that supports it.

To make clear what is implied, let us examine three general ideas. The first has to do with the process of intellectual development in children, the second with the act of learning, and the third with the notion of the "spiral curriculum" introduced earlier.

*Intellectual development.* Research on the intellectual development of the child highlights the fact that at each stage of development the child has a characteristic way of viewing the world and explaining it to himself. The task of teaching a subject to a child at any particular age is one of representing the structure of that subject in terms of the child's way of viewing things. The task can be thought of as one of translation. The general hypothesis that has just been stated is premised on the considered judgment that any idea can be represented honestly and usefully in the thought forms of children of school age, and that these first representations can later be made more powerful and precise the more easily by virtue of this early learning. To illustrate and support this view, we present here a somewhat detailed picture of the course of intellectual development, along with some suggestions about teaching at different stages of it.

The work of Piaget and others suggests that, roughly speaking, one may distinguish three stages in the intellectual development of the child. The first stage need not concern us in detail, for it is characteristic principally of the pre-school child. In this stage, which ends (at least for Swiss school children) around the fifth or sixth year, the child's mental work consists principally in establishing relationships between experience and action; his concern is with manipulating the world through action. This stage corresponds roughly to the period from the first development of language to the point at which the child learns to manipulate symbols. In this so-called preoperational stage, the principal symbolic achievement is that the child learns how to represent the external world through symbols established by simple generalization; things are represented as equivalent in terms of sharing some common property. But the child's symbolic world does not make a clear separation between internal motives and feelings on the one hand and external reality on the other. The sun moves because God pushes it, and the stars, like himself, have to go to bed. The child is little able to separate his own goals from the means for achieving them, and when he has to make corrections in his activity after unsuccessful attempts at manipulating reality, he does so by what are called intuitive regulations rather than by symbolic operations, the former being of a crude trial-and-error nature rather than the result of taking thought.

What is principally lacking at this stage of development is what the Geneva school has called the concept of reversibility. When the shape of an object is changed, as when one changes the shape of a ball of plasticene, the preoperational child cannot grasp the idea that it can be brought back readily to its original state. Because of this fundamental lack the child cannot understand certain fundamental ideas that lie at the basis of mathematics and physics—the mathematical idea that one conserves quantity even when one partitions a set of things into subgroups, or the physical idea that one conserves mass and weight even though one transforms the shape of an object. It goes without saying that teachers are severely limited in transmitting concepts to a child at this stage, even in a highly intuitive manner.

The second stage of development—and now the child is in school —is called the stage of concrete operations. This stage is operational in contrast to the preceding stage, which is merely active. An operation is a type of action: it can be carried out rather directly by the manipulation of objects, or internally, as when one manipulates the symbols that represent things and relations in one's mind. Roughly, an operation is a means of getting data about the real world into the mind and there transforming them so that they can be organized and used selectively in the solution of problems. Assume a child is presented with a pinball machine which bounces a ball off a wall at an angle. Let us find out what he appreciates about the relation between the angle of incidence and the angle of reflection. The young child sees no problem: for him, the ball travels in an arc, touching the wall on the way. The somewhat older child, say age ten, sees the two angles as roughly related—as one changes so does the other. The still older child begins to grasp that there is a fixed relation between the two, and usually says it is a right angle. Finally, the thirteen- or fourteen-year-old, often by pointing the ejector directly at the wall and seeing the ball come back at the ejector, gets the idea that the two angles are equal. Each way of looking at the phenomenon represents the result of an operation in this sense, and the child's thinking is constrained by his way of pulling his observations together.

An operation differs from simple action or goal-directed behavior in that it is internalized and reversible. "Internalized" means that the child does not have to go about his problem-solving any longer by overt trial and error, but can actually carry out trial and error in his head. Reversibility is present because operations are seen as characterized where appropriate by what is called "complete compensation"; that is to say, an operation can be compensated for by an inverse operation. If marbles, for example, are divided into subgroups, the child can grasp intuitively that the original collection of marbles can be restored by being added back together again. The child tips a balance scale too far with a weight and then searches systematically for a lighter weight or for something with which to get the scale rebalanced. He may carry reversibility too far by assuming that a piece of paper, once burned, can also be restored.

With the advent of concrete operations, the child develops an internalized structure with which to operate. In the example of the balance scale, the structure is a serial order of weights that the child has in his mind. Such internal structures are of the essence. They are the internalized symbolic systems by which the child represents the world, as in the example of the pinball machine and the angles of incidence and reflection. It is into the language of these internal structures that one must translate ideas if the child is to grasp them.

But concrete operations, though they are guided by the logic of classes and the logic of relations, are means for structuring only immediately present reality. The child is able to give structure to the things he encounters, but he is not yet readily able to deal with possibilities not directly before him or not already experienced. This is not to say that children operating concretely are not able to anticipate things that are not present. Rather, it is that they do not command the operations for conjuring up systematically the full range of alternative possibilities that could exist at any given time. They cannot go systematically beyond the information given them to a description of what else might occur. Somewhere between ten and fourteen years of age the child passes into a third stage, which is called the stage of "formal operations" by the Geneva school.

Now the child's intellectual activity seems to be based upon an ability to operate on hypothetical propositions rather than being constrained to what he has experienced or what is before him. The child can now think of possible variables and even deduce potential relationships that can later be verified by experiment or observation. Intellectual operations now appear to be predicated upon the same kinds of logical operations that are the stock in trade of the logician, the scientist, or the abstract thinker. It is at this point that the child is able to give formal or axiomatic expression to the concrete ideas that before guided his problem-solving but could not be described or formally understood.

Earlier, while the child is in the stage of concrete operations, he is capable of grasping intuitively and concretely a great many of the basic ideas of mathematics, the sciences, the humanities, and the social sciences. But he can do so only in terms of concrete operations. It can be demonstrated that fifth-grade children can play mathematical games with rules modeled on highly advanced mathematics; indeed, they can arrive at these rules inductively and learn how to work with them. They will flounder, however, if one attempts to force upon them a formal mathematical description of what they have been doing, though they are perfectly capable of guiding their behavior by these rules. At the Woods Hole Conference we were privileged to see a demonstration of teaching in which fifth-grade children very rapidly grasped central ideas from the theory of functions, although had the teacher attempted to explain to them what the theory of functions was, he would have drawn a blank. Later, at the appropriate stage of development and given a certain amount of practice in concrete operations, the time would be ripe for introducing them to the necessary formalism.

What is most important for teaching basic concepts is that the child be helped to pass progressively from concrete thinking to the utilization of more conceptually adequate modes of thought. But it is futile to attempt this by presenting formal explanations based on a logic that is distant from the child's manner of thinking and sterile in its implications for him. Much teaching in mathematics is of this sort. The child learns not to understand mathematical order but rather to apply certain devices or recipes without understanding their significance and connectedness. They are not translated into his way of thinking. Given this inappropriate start, he is easily led to believe that the important thing is for him to be "accurate"—though accuracy has less to do with mathematics than with computation. Perhaps the most striking example of this type of thing is to be found in the manner in which the high school student meets Euclidian geometry for the first time, as a set of axioms and theorems, without having had some experience with simple geometric configurations and the intuitive means whereby one deals with them. If the child were earlier given the concepts and strategies in the form of intuitive geometry at a level that he could easily follow, he might be far better able to grasp deeply the meaning of the theorems and axioms to which he is exposed later.

But the intellectual development of the child is no clockwork sequence of events; it also responds to influences from the environment, notably the school environment. Thus instruction in scientific ideas, even at the elementary level, need not follow slavishly the natural course of cognitive development in the child. It can also lead intellectual development by providing challenging but usable opportunities for the child to forge ahead in his development. Experience has shown that it is worth the effort to provide the growing child with problems that tempt him into next stages of development. As David Page, one of the most experienced teachers of elementary mathematics, has commented: "In teaching from kindergarten to graduate school, I have been amazed at the intellectual similarity of human beings at all ages, although children are perhaps more spontaneous, creative, and energetic than adults. As far as I am concerned young children learn almost anything faster than adults do if it can be given to them in terms they understand. Giving the material to them in terms they understand, interestingly enough, turns out to involve knowing the mathematics oneself, and the better one knows it, the better it can be taught. It is appropriate that we warn ourselves to be careful of assigning an absolute level of difficulty to any particular topic. When I tell mathematicians that fourth-grade students can go a long way into 'set theory' a few of them reply: 'Of course.' Most of them are startled. The latter ones are completely wrong in assuming that 'set theory' is intrinsically difficult. Of course it may be that nothing is intrinsically difficult. We just have to wait until the proper point of view and corresponding language for presenting it are revealed. Given particular subject matter or a particular concept, it is easy to ask trivial questions or to lead the child to ask trivial questions. It is also easy to ask impossibly difficult questions. The trick is to find the medium questions that can be answered and that take you somewhere. This is the big job of teachers and textbooks." One leads the child by the well-wrought "medium questions" to move more rapidly through the stages of intellectual development, to a deeper understanding of mathematical, physical, and historical principles. We must know far more about the ways in which this can be done.

Robert M. W. Travers

# 13. PROBLEM SOLVING AND TEACHING

Those concerned with the practical business of teaching have long
been intrigued with the idea that the most careful education may
well be provided by problem-solving situations in which the student
derives from his own experience the truths that constitute the major
outcomes of his studies. This conception of education has generally
been stated in the form that the student should *discover* the truths
that are to be learned or that he should engage in *discovery learning*.
The assumption is that he will benefit more from knowledge acquired
through problem solving and discovery than from the same knowledge
presented to him on the page of a textbook or presented to him by the
teacher through a lecture. This has long been an attractive proposition that has intrigued generations of teachers. The fascination for
this concept has not waned, as is evident from the support it has
received in recent years from such persons as Jerome Bruner and
J. R. Suchman. The latter prefers to use the term *inquiry training*
rather than the more conventional terms of *discovery learning* or
*discovery teaching*. Teaching by the discovery method is contrasted
with what is called *expository teaching*, which amounts to a teaching
technique of presenting to the student the information he is to acquire.

Robert M. W. Travers studied at the University of London and Columbia
University. He has held offices in the American Educational Research Asso-
ciation and served as a consultant to the U.S. Office of Education. His many
publications include numerous articles in his field and such works as *Introduc-
tion to Educational Research, Essentials of Learning*, and *Man's Information
System*. He is presently serving as Distinguished Professor of Education at
Western Michigan University.
Reprinted with permission of The Macmillan Company from *Essentials of
Learning*, 3rd ed., by Robert M. W. Travers, pp. 289–293. Copyright © 1972
by Robert M. W. Travers.

The issue is of particular interest in connection with the topic under discussion, in that a major claim for discovery teaching has been that it leads to greater transfer of training than teaching involving the direct memorization of subject matter.

It was not until after World War II that the problem was studied experimentally. Worthen (1968), who has reviewed many of the studies made of this problem, points out that the main outcome has been a set of conflicting results. Some studies purportedly gave results that supported discovery teaching, while others, often supposedly attacking the same problem, led to completely opposite results. Worthen concludes that the apparent conflict among the findings is due to the fact that no clear meaning has been assigned to such terms as discovery learning, guided discovery learning, and expository teaching. Indeed, the confusion is so great that what one person refers to as guided discovery learning another may label as expository teaching. Another excellent review of the problem by Wittrock (1966) emphasizes the point that one of the basic weaknesses of research in the area is that most research workers have not specified just what is to be discovered by the student.

The difficulties of deriving generalizations from research on discovery learning that can be applied to teaching can be most readily explored by considering an example. Let us suppose that the pupil is concerned with understanding the conditions under which a beam can be balanced by placing weights on it on opposite sides of the fulcrum. The student might be started on this exploration by being given two weights and a beam marked off in inches from the center. He might be given the beam balanced on a knife edge and be left to place the weights on the beam in such a way that they balanced. This would represent a very unstructured situation in which he would have few cues provided that would help him to arrive at a solution. Given the two weights, the beam, and the balancing edge, few pupils in the elementary school would be likely to discover the principle involved. Most teachers would want to provide more cues so that the pupil would have a greater chance of discovering the principle involved. One way of doing this would be to present the pupil with the balanced beam, as shown in Figure 15, and to ask him to state the rule of how the weights are to be placed on the beam if they are to balance. At this point he could be left to manipulate the two weights, or he could be shown other examples, such as are shown in Figure 15B and Figure 15C. He may be given unlimited time to solve this problem or he may be given additional cues. One helpful

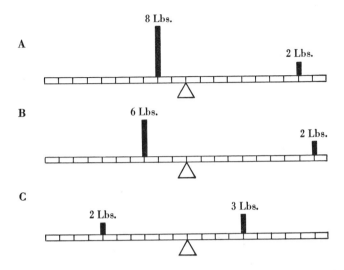

**Figure 15.** Example of task used in discovery learning procedures.

cue that might be given might involve the statement, "Now look at A. The beam is balanced when an 8-pound weight is placed 2 inches from the balance point and when the 2-pound weight is placed 8 inches from the balance point. Write down these numbers: 8 at 2 and 2 at 8. What do you notice about them?" If the pupil still does not see the relationship, tell him to write down the corresponding numbers from B which would read 6 at 3 and 2 at 9. If, by that time, he has not multiplied $6 \times 3$ and $2 \times 9$, then he can be given the additional prompt of being told to multiply each weight by its distance from the point of balance. As the number of cues increases, the procedure becomes more and more closely similar to expository teaching.

In few discovery learning situations is the pupil left with almost no cues to discover a simple principle. Indeed, he would have to have the intellect of a Newton to find a principle under such circumstances. The pupil generally has to be provided with extensive cues in order to arrive at the principle he is to discover. Under such circumstances, there is likely to be very little discovery involved in the student's work. Studies of discovery learning rarely state the degree to which cues are provided. Some of the apparent inconsistency of findings can be attributed to differences in this respect.

Another source of inconsistency across studies of discovery learning is that in some, the effect of learning is appraised through a measure of the pupil's ability to recall what has been learned, while others have used a measure of the ability to transfer what has been learned to the solution of new problems. The previously cited study by Worthen shows that conditions that favor the recall of what is learned may not be the most favorable for transfer. One can easily see how this might happen. If the goal is to parrot back information, then rote learning may be efficient, but the acquisition of understanding may lead to effective transfer even though it may interfere with giving quick answers to short questions.

Mention must also be made of a very important condition, not discussed in most studies of discovery learning. This is the matter of the amount of time spent on learning. Discovery learning procedures are generally much more time-consuming than those involving expository teaching. When more time is spent in learning, more learning is likely to take place. Indeed, learning is generally limited by the time factor rather than by any other. One suspects that in many studies that compare discovery learning with learning by expository methods, much more time is spent with the discovery methods and there should be small surprise that the additional time results in additional learning.

For reasons given here, little research support can be found at this time for using discovery methods of teaching. Although direct evidence to support the procedure is lacking, there is some indirect evidence for using discovery methods so long as they do not use much more time than expository methods. One argument is that methods of learning requiring learner activity are generally superior to learning conditions that require only relatively passive reception of information. However, discovery is only one of many activities that can be introduced. The application of the knowledge that has been acquired also represents an activity that has long been used to promote learning and is probably a successful technique.

The Worthen study provides some of the better data in the area of discovery learning. Unlike most other studies, the characteristics of expository and discovery teaching were quite well defined and the pupils were exposed to sufficiently large doses of these two kinds of pedagogy that any notable difference should have shown up. Worthen was also able to collect data on what the teachers did in the classroom and was able to provide some evidence that teachers assigned to the different methods actually did behave differently. In addition, instruction by each method involved the same amount of time. The children were tested for the knowledge and skill acquired from instruction in mathematics by expository and discovery methods at the end of the six-week period of instruction, and also five weeks and eleven weeks later. The tests involved both measures of the ability to use the knowledge directly and the ability to transfer the knowledge to the solution of novel problems. The results showed very small differences in the learning of the pupils exposed to the different teaching procedures. On the immediate measure of retention there seemed to be a very slight superiority among the pupils exposed to the expository teaching. On the delayed measures of retention there was a very slight superiority for the pupils exposed to the discovery methods. In the case of the tests of transfer of training to new situations, differences were of negligible magnitude. The chief weakness of the study is that the account of it does not specify precisely just what the students discovered nor what was presented to them in the expository teaching, perhaps because scientific accounts have to be brief and often cannot give all the details that the reader would like to know.

The results of the Worthen study follow closely a much earlier study of Wittrock (1963), in which pupils worked problems involving the deciphering of a code. In the Wittrock study the pupils could learn, either by discovery or by expository teaching, the rule needed to solve each problem and the answer to each problem. The only really clear results of this study were that on the test of immediate retention the expository method, which involved the giving of both the rule and the answer, produced superior results. However, when the test was delayed or when a test for transfer of training was involved, then a mixture of the expository and discovery methods showed slight superiority. The mixture involved giving the rule but not giving the answer to the problem.

An interesting hypothesis has been injected into the controversy concerning the relative virtues of expository and discovery methods of learning through a study by Roughead and Scandura (1968). These research workers have taken the position that whatever is learned by a discovery method can be learned by an expository method. They argue, for example, that if the use of a discovery method teaches children how to discover principles, then there must surely be rules that guide behavior in the discovery of principles and these rules can surely be learned by expository methods. The difficulty in teaching such rules by expository methods is that they have not yet been adequately identified, but there is also another difficulty involved, even when the rules are known. In expository teaching, because the children do not have to derive the rules and understand the rationale for them, there is little incentive for acquiring insight into the derivation of the rule. For this reason, they may never discover why a rule is sound. For example, the child taught the rule for multiplying simple fractions may not be interested in knowing the reason why, for a knowledge of the rule alone enables him to get the right answers. On the other hand, the discovery method forces him to go through the procedure of inventing the rule and this he cannot do without understanding how the rule is derived.

1. Is the task of introducing material formerly considered too advanced for the lower grades resolved by finding ways to translate the structure of the subject in terms of the child's way of viewing the world? Are there some concepts which must be withheld until the child grows in intellectual development? Examine some of the latest studies to determine whether they corroborate Bruner's position.

2. Do the stages of intellectual development contradict Bruner's thesis about the early introduction of concepts formerly reserved for the upper grades?

3. Is Bruner correct when he states that no evidence exists to contradict his view? Can you find studies that refute his statement? If so, what is the quality of these studies?

4. Explain how the following statement supports Bruner's thesis: "Of course it may be that nothing is intrinsically difficult. We just have to wait until the proper point of view and corresponding language for presenting it are revealed."

5. Distinguish the discovery method of teaching from expository teaching.

6. Can we conclude that the discovery method, the expository method, or a combination of the two is most likely to facilitate learning? Think of variables that possibly contribute as much as or more than the particular approach used in teaching—for example, the personality of the teacher, the alertness of the student, and so on.

7. In light of the findings provided in the Travers essay, is Bruner's enthusiasm for the discovery method warranted? Give reasons for your answer.

8. Visit a number of classrooms and look for examples of both the discovery method and expository teaching. To what extent do they deviate in practice from the descriptions given in the essay?

9. In what respects do Bruner's ideas about introducing subjects and basic concepts to children far earlier than was formerly the case run counter to the prevailing views about grade level of materials, maturity, and "readiness"?

10. Make a survey of local schools to determine to what extent material is being introduced earlier than it was ten years ago. Concentrate your work in the areas of math and science.

# VII.   Summerhill

*There are few educators who question the entire ritual of established schooling and its attendant successes and failures. One of the most prominent of these is A. S. Neill, who for many years has been an exemplification of his own ideals through Summerhill, the school that he founded. Neill was an early progressive, one who addressed himself many decades earlier to some of the problems with which present-day reformers are struggling.*

*Summerhill is one of the most famous progressive schools in the world, yet prior to 1960 the school was little known in the United States. What accounts for this incredible growth of interest in the Summerhill idea? Since 1960, A. S. Neill's books have been widely read and have been translated into many languages. A new generation of questioning youth have discovered Neill's ideas and have discussed them with interest and enthusiasm. And some educators, finding certain educational practices have not succeeded, are more receptive to new and even radical proposals. All of these changes contribute to a lively debate over the importance of the Summerhill approach and the impact of Neill's imagination and leadership.*

*The usual fare of basic subjects, homework, testing, and grading are dispensed with. Utilizing play, the child's own interest and creativity, his capacity to work and live with his peers in a cooperative arrangement by means of developing his own rules and regulations and seeing that they are enforced, form the basis of Summerhill. The impact of Neill's own personality and the ability to convey his ideas to a growing audience is in large part responsible for Summerhill's renown.*

# A. S. Neill

# 14. WHY HAVE EXAMS?

An H.M.I. said to me: "What would you teach if there were no G.C.E. exams?" I could not think of an answer, possibly because when one has been conditioned from infancy to accept school subjects as education, no one is free enough to answer.

That the products of schools are much more interested in things outside the school system—football pools, cheap press, television, sex, games—than they are in all the subjects we teach suggests that our schools are never adapted to the life outside. This is primarily due to the fact that emotion is of infinitely more moment than is intellect; the above mentioned post-school interests are emotional ones, whereas G.C.E. subjects are all head subjects. We see the same result of this unbalance in books like *Blackboard Jungle* in the U.S.A. and *The Young Devils* at home. This raising of the leaving has too often meant adolescents having to continue sitting at desks saying what has no appeal to their minds or senses. It is just nonsense to say that our schools give children culture—the sales of our most sensational newspapers prove this point—education precedes a national interest in the inferior and unessential.

A. S. Neill studied at his father's village school and later at Edinburgh and Newcastle Universities. In 1921, he was joint founder of the International School, Hellerau, Dresden, and three years later he established Summerhill. He began writing in 1916 and produced such books as *The Problem Child, The Problem Parent, That Dreadful Parent*, and numerous other works. Surprisingly, it was not until *Summerhill* (a compilation) was published in the United States that his ideas became widely known in this country. Summerhill is located in Leiston, Suffolk, England. Neill died in 1973.
Source: A. S. Neill, "Why Have Exams?" *The Times Educational Supplement* (London), May 8, 1959.

## LA PLUME DE . . .

Cultures! Thousands of our pupils learn French up to G.C.E. standard. Few ever will go to France, few will ever read French books; in two years most of what they learnt has gone. So with other subjects. Math! What passer of the O level exams could do a quadratic equation five years later? English! What proportion of G.C.E. passers read whodunnits instead of the cultural reading their grammar schools taught them—Lamb's Essays, Shakespeare, Milton, Coleridge? Geography! How do we apply what we learn after we leave school? Whenever I go to Scotland I cannot get rid of the notion that I am going uphill: the wall map had Scotland at the top. The only geography we use is of the place-on-the-map variety and that vaguely to be sure. How many of us know exactly where these places are—Thursday Island, Vermont, Salzburg? Post-school life does not concern itself with the exports of Brazil or the climate of Timbuctu.

## WHAT TO TEACH

I feel like replying to the H.M.I. by saying: "I'd scrap the lot," but then would have the painful task of saying what my school would teach. Painful because it is so difficult to assess change of values. In my youth a university education was the criterion of an educated man; the scholar with his Latin and Greek and philosophy was the man to respect and emulate. Today that is not so. The standard has altered, mainly because of the great and rapid advance in mechanical theory and practice. In terms of utility today the expert who can make or even repair a television set is of more importance than an M.A. who has specialized in—say—English, for the M.A. can only teach in a small circle while the other man can do in a large one. We see the same in music. Whatever a school may do to give pupils a love for classical music, the fact remains that (I am guessing here) the records of the rock 'n' roll singers far exceed in volume and sale those of all the classics lumped together.

Given freedom from examinations I should aim at catching the children's interests and following them. Rock 'n' roll? Good, the music of the school would start with Elvis Presley and Tommy Steele. Reading would be all the whodunnits the school could procure. I should reverse the process by which the school begins with Addison and goes on to the post-graduate *News of the World*, feeling uneasily that my pupils' daily perusal of the *News of the World* might not automatically lead later to the reading of Addison.

But perhaps I should teach nothing at all on the ground that you cannot teach anything of importance. I know of no school that has been free enough to follow in its teaching the dictates of child nature; every school is to some extent divorced from outside life and interest; that follows the pre-psychology period that treated children as small adults. Adults must work and therefore children must be taught to work. Since the importance of play in a child's life has been recognized no fundamental alteration has been made to the timetable. I can fantasy a non-exam school which would be a large playground —not playing fields which are not really play at all. Play with books and tools and music and dance and—in Utopia—play with love. I doubt if the adage that tells that the hard way forms character has any validity in psychology. I see rock 'n' roll as a flight from the hard way of schooling with its insane demand for homework, yet to be honest I do not think that is the whole truth, for my pupils who are as free as can be in a school today love rock 'n' roll records, but to be honest again they do not seem to carry on the interest into the later teen age. Nor are my own pupils free from the G.C.E. obstacle to real education.

## FORMING CHARACTER

I ask: What does it matter what we teach? The only importance in education lies in character formation, and here many a teacher will agree. But not many will agree that character formation must come from inside. No study will form a good character. Indeed character is seldom mentioned by teachers; the cry today is not for better science, better science in an era in which knowing has run far ahead of emotion, and science has almost become synonymous with keeping up with the Joneseskis.

This insistence on the importance of playhood may sound mad to many a teacher. Maybe it is mad, but it is at least a tentative suggestion for coping with a most dangerous situation, that of a sick world whose values have little or nothing to do with schooling, and I do not mean Britain alone; the news of anti-social rebellious youth in Sweden, America, Russia shows that schooling is failing in many lands. Personally I think that conscious or more probably unconscious fear is at the bottom of youth's revolt. . . . Let us eat, drink, and be merry, for to-morrow we die. Sex repression is not enough to account for it; we had sex repression long before the H-bomb appeared and it did not seem to go so far as flick knives and cycle chains.

## REVOLT AGAINST SCHOOL

The question is this: Is youth rebelling because of its education or in spite of it? I suggest the former. I question if a lessonless school would produce any anti-social, any criminal products; I feel sure that most hateful coshings and stabbings are the result of unlived-out play, but again that cannot be the whole truth, for children of the upper and middle classes are not usually teddy boys. I am not wise enough to pose as an authority, but in the days when I had to deal with many anti-social adolescents, I saw most of them go out cured, not by lessons, not by my analyses, but cured because they had freedom to live out their playhood, cured because allowed to be themselves. And of moment, cured because relieved of guilt about sex. An odd thought to end up with: When any madman or fool of a statesman can press the button that could kill us all, why does such a small thing as sex retain its Victorian significance? Until the guilt complex of youth is relieved all or nearly all of our school subject teaching will remain useless and a matter of indifference to the young.

Fred M. Hechinger

# 15. SUMMERHILL: FOR AND AGAINST

Summerhill is not a school but a religion. That is why one can be intrigued by it—can even admire it—without being converted to it. To derive benefits from it for one's children requires religious faith in the efficacy of its myths. As with every religion, faith distilled into fanaticism can be dangerous. But there is so much essential goodness of intent and spirit in Summerhill that its doctrine may—in modified form—be most beneficial to ordinary parents who send their children to a variety of ordinary schools.

The underlying dogma of the Summerhill faith is that children, if not subjected to any adult pressures or influences, are perfect seeds that will turn into beings of predestined goodness. A. S. Neill actually goes beyond this when he says: "My view is that a child is innately wise and realistic. If left to himself without adult suggestion of any kind, he will develop as far as he is capable of developing."

This is not unlike the idea of Rousseau's Noble Savage, only presumably without the savagery. It is a difficult theory for parents to subscribe to when they have in fact experienced mean and contrary traits in their children; but Neill would (probably with much justification) dismiss such objections by pointing to the mean and contrary

Fred M. Hechinger, Education Editor of the *New York Times*, presents a sympathetic but critical appraisal of Summerhill and the educational significance of Neill's work. Long known for his perceptive commentaries on education, Mr. Hechinger has won the Fairbanks Award and has twice been recipient of the George Power Memorial Award. His books include *An Adventure in Education: Connecticut Points the Way, The Big Red Schoolhouse,* and *Teen-Age Tyranny.*

Source: Fred M. Hechinger, essay from *Summerhill: For and Against,* copyright © 1970 Hart Publishing Company, Inc., New York. Essay appears on pp. 35–46.

streaks in the parents and other adults and to the mean and contrary treatment to which the children have been subjected.

The holy writ of Summerhill says that if the mean and repressive influences could only be removed, the child would flower into a good adult according to his capacity. Whatever his accomplishments might turn out to be, he would be happy, and happiness is Summerhill's holy grail. It is not off in some distant promised land; it is attainable.

True to this belief, the original Summerhill therefore has been made into a place in which the mean and repressive influences have been removed, to the best human ability. It is not something that can be totally accomplished, any more than church or temple can be purged of human corruption and made into the original Eden; but it is fair to say that Summerhill has been startlingly successful in approaching its own ideal. Neill, by admitting that not all teachers nor even all children work out, and some have to be let go, defines the limitations of the experiment with characteristic honesty. But on the whole, Summerhill has created an oasis in which the children are left to develop without pressure and repression.

But even if it were not a religion and Neill its prophet and patron saint Summerhill would not be a school. It is really a family —an ideal family, to be sure, without overly possessive attachments —with an option to learn, but no compulsion to do so.

Size and arrangements alone make it a family rather than a school. It is very doubtful whether Summerhill, even given the funds and the facilities, could remain intact if it had many more than the 45 youngsters, subdivided into many smaller living and playing units.

It is more than doubtful—it is inconceivable—that Summerhill could exist without Neill. Whether one agrees or disagrees with him (and only the most computerized misanthrope could totally disagree with him) the fact is that he is a man of saintly strength and force. His intertwined belief in the child and the idea becomes, in the sweep of his eloquence, virtually irresistible. And this is so simply because all reservations are easily rejected by his conviction: it is the corruption of the world around, not any seed in body or soul, that corrupts the child. It is a conviction, unshakably held by Neill (without any shred of truculence), that can never be disproven. Unfortunately, in the face of continuing corruption, it cannot be proven either.

The rub is that—however some of the disciples and imitators are sure to dispute this—Summerhill cannot be reproduced. It is doubtful that even the original Summerhill will be able long to survive its founder. Indeed, the occasional playful exercise described by

Neill in which he pretends that he has died and is succeeded by some dictatorial school master almost seems like a subconscious premonition. Neill's successor, of course, will not be a martinet or scoundrel, although he may seem so to the children, but he will at best be a disciple. Disciples rarely save any enterprise or idea.

But with or without Neill, Summerhill, not being a school, cannot be turned into the prototype of anything but an occasional small reproduction—private, selective, special.

This is inherently so because—as Neill makes unmistakably clear —the great majority of the world's parents do not believe in his basic concepts. They do not believe that children can be brought up without the customary restraints; that children can be groomed for a competitive world without competition in school; that children can be left to go about their growing up without being made to attend class or study certain subjects and learn certain skills.

As long as this is so, there is no way of setting up Summerhills for great numbers—or for any more than the occasional odd parents who march to Neill's drummer. Neill himself makes it quite clear that he cannot fight the realities outside. There is pathos in Neill's realization that, while he may write about what he feels is wrong with society and teach the children of the few who agree with him, if he tried to reform society by action, society would fight back. He even believes, perhaps a little too flamboyantly or pessimistically, that it would kill him "as a public danger."

"Hating compromise as I do, I have to compromise here, realizing that my primary job is not the reformation of society, but the bringing of happiness to some few children," he writes with disarming modesty.

And so, Summerhill remains, in his own words, "an island." (He would not even think of asking the local newspaper to publish success stories about his old pupils, and could you be more of an island in this age of the press agent, and expect to go into mass-production.)

Yet, despite its limitations as a model for mass-education, Summerhill is one of the world's most powerful ideas that is not likely ever to die. It has lived before Neill, although it has rarely been represented with such dynamic, charismatic power. It will outlast him—nuclear fission permitting—as long as men live and learn.

Parents who love their children should know about Summerhill. Even if they refuse to share Neill's total faith they should try to imagine how much happier their children might be if their natural childish drives, curiosities and creativity could be given their way.

Just as Freud opened the eyes of men and physicians to the terrible damage done by sterile repressions, those who bring up children need to question, day after day, whether many of the old restrictions and taboos are not in fact mental and physical chains which, though designed to shape them, actually weigh their children down and misshape their bodies and minds.

In an age when mothers worry about College Board test scores before their tots enter nursery school, the Summerhill contempt for the educational rat race—for the school that trains rather than liberates—is an antidote against a terrible pollution.

At a time of frantic affluence, the Summerhill contempt for educational upward mobility to material success is a reminder that parental ambition to shine through the accomplishments of one's children can be mental cruelty of tribal savagery.

To all but the most incorrigible reactionaries, it is clear that there is so much wrong with social and political values today that an affirmative appeal from the heart is a humanitarian service to all. Neill says:

"Most political newspapers are bristling with hate, hate all the time. Too many are socialistic because they hate the rich instead of loving the poor. . . . All the Greek and math and history in the world will not help to make the home more loving, the child free from inhibitions, the parent free from neurosis. . . . New generations must be given the chance to grow in freedom. The bestowal of freedom is the bestowal of love. And only love can save the world."

To Neill, the issue is simple, perhaps oversimplified in the view of some non-believers. He sees a civilization that is sick and unhappy, producing children who, being made unhappy, will grow into sick and oppressive adults. He is repelled by the ritual of stressing the negative—saying "don't" to children rather than "do"; relying on fear rather than love.

Unlike other reformers, Neill is not a man of bromides. Except when he lives at Summerhill, he is near despair, knowing that "the fight is an unequal one, for the haters control education, religion, the law, the armies, and the vile prisons."

To Neill, "it is a race between the believers in deadness and the believers in life." It is a race in which "no man dare remain neutral —the death side gives us the problem child; the life side will give us the healthy child."

Every parent and every teacher—whether he cares about the

arrangements and the dogma of Summerhill—ought to carry this warning with him to the nursery and to the classroom.

I recommend Summerhill to parents and teachers—but not without misgivings. It is a religion based on love for, and understanding of, children; but it carries with it a religious mysticism that should not be accepted without critical analysis.

There is, in Neill himself, a strange streak of anti-intellectualism, almost a frantic rejection of all academic value judgments. Whatever the child likes, whatever makes him happy, is equal to any other enterprise. Bach equals Elvis Presley.

Neill can get upset about a ruined chisel but refuses to fuss about a book carelessly left in the rain "for books have little value for me."

This, I think, is a flaw that affects the Summerhill religion and the Neill philosophy. It claims to be non-coercive; but the model and the life style of those who teach do, in fact, coerce, however gently. The priorities of Summerhill are so non-intellectual as to place the book, the literary masterpiece, the evolution of thought at a disadvantage.

Neill is undoubtedly right in objecting—almost as much as to John Dewey's "learning by doing" reliance on the pragmatic consumer lesson—to the sugar-coated abomination of learning by playing or French without tears; but I am not convinced that the way to correct the subversion of honest play is to give it unlimited parity with work. Neither the history of man nor that of pedagogy has offered convincing proof that the child, if left without adult suggestion will (as Neill insists), "develop as far as he is capable of developing" by his own initiative.

Neill claims, and his disciples make an important point of it, that children who have the innate ability and wish to be scholars will be scholars, just as those who are only fit to sweep the streets will sweep the streets—and are likely, if left to their devices, to be happy street sweepers.

This, it seems to me, is an over-extension of the Freudian principle. It does not follow that men, merely by being free of sexual repressions, will lead happy lives—even only sexually—unless they are also positively guided into the proper use of their potential. While innate scholarly ability is essential to the development of scholars, it is not realistic to expect the wish to be a scholar to be present in every academically gifted child. Surely, the sampling of the delights and possibilities of scholarship—the function of good teaching, in contrast to the sterile or rote approach to learning—is part of the process. If repression and coercion are wrong, is not the absence of exposure, or sampling under expert guidance, equally deficient?

"Whether a school has or has not a special method for teaching long division is of no significance, for long division is of no importance except to those who *want* to learn it," says Neill. I find no logic in this. Only the rare—even odd—child is likely to want to learn long division, ever, unless he is given to understand what intellectual purpose it may ultimately serve. This is true of so much initial intellectual endeavor that it is very unlikely that intellectual progress— or the life of the mind—would get a fair shake under Summerhill auspices. Neill appears willing to sacrifice brain to heart.

Neill's criticism of the conventional teachers is that they lack "the power to subordinate thinking to feeling." He is distressed by any schooling that "goes on separating the head from the heart."

This is an immensely attractive concept. It is attractive, in part, for very sound reasons—because there is, in truth, so much heartless use of brain power. Much of the suffering in the world and in any community is caused by the highly intelligent who act without feeling and conscience. Much of what pretends to be government planning— particularly in the area of national defense—is based on computerized data, without concern for the consequences to humanity or human priorities.

But concern about the downgrading of the intellect and the excessive reliance on feelings and emotions is that, in the end, the results tend to be just about equally damaging to the only constituency that counts—people. The history of reforms is strewn with wreckage caused by kindly emotions defeated by lack of intellectual rigor.

This, too, is what worries me about the similarity between the Summerhill ideology and the present student unrest. Nowhere does the Summerhill dogma have as much appeal as among young rebels who seek happiness in activism. It is in the revolutionary occupation of buildings and the fellowship of the sit-in that youth finds emotional satisfaction based on the subordination of brain to emotion. Unfortunately, it also often seems to be an extension of just the kind of playing to which Summerhill accords such a key role. Yet, it is the playful, happiness-seeking campus revolution that is likely, not only to fragment and undermine the academic community, but frustrate and, in the end, disappoint and alienate those who seek concrete redress of just grievances. To uplift the poor and the deprived

requires more than heart and sympathy; it calls for effective strategies of social and economic reforms. Perhaps the greatest risk of
heart without intellect is that it is so easily fooled, and those in search
of power inevitably know, and ruthlessly exploit, this.

There is natural appeal, too, in Neill's report that, no matter how
long some youngsters might have decided to skip academic preparation, they quickly make up for lost time when they suddenly decide
to aim for the university admissions examinations. This may offer
some useful commentary on the nature of those tests—and the excessive and long-range worry expended on them traditionally by many
parents and their children. On that score—if Summerhill manages
to question and perhaps demolish some sterile myths—much is to be
gained. But it does not answer my concern that much latent talent
remains undeveloped in the process and that indeed the occasional
decision to opt for the climb up the academic ladder is even more
likely to be made on the basis of irrational, extraneous influences than
under the system of more conventional pressures.

Her Majesty's Inspectors, who incidentally approached Summerhill with a model of understanding that might well be studied by those
who have power over school accreditation and standards in the United
States, in the end could not suppress some honest, professional doubts.

"To have created a situation in which academic education of the
most intelligent kind could flourish is an achievement; but in fact, it is
not flourishing and a great opportunity is being lost," the inspectors
said.

To Neill, this criticism meant that even the most sympathetic
education officials could not completely "rise above their academic
preoccupations" and that they overlooked the fact that the system
does flourish when a child wants an academic education. The question on which, not unlike the inspectors, I part ways with Summerhill
is whether tastes and wants need not be nourished, trained, acquired.
I often feel that, had I been permitted to benefit a little more from
the Neill philosophy in my schooling, I might have gained some of
his facility with, and enjoyment of, the chisel and the rake. But I
would not want to trade such tastes and wants for my greater concern
with books. While I agree with his contempt for desiccated bookish-
ness in the worst of traditional education, I cannot accept attitudes
which, as a matter of experience and observation, give the non-
intellectual drives a fast and clear track.

Summerhill is rightly opposed to fear as a pedagogical tool. But
Neill admits that the search for approval is a strong human drive, and

in the concern for lack of approval (even by Neill and the best, most saintly of his teachers) there is, of course, an element of fear.

The goal—and I think the Summerhill disciples might be persuaded to accept this revision of the absence-of-fear concept—ought to be to teach children to consider the consequences of their actions and inactions, and in the light of such considerations to curb their desires for instant gratification. What this calls for, however, is the abandonment of the search for immediate happiness in the hope of attaining greater happiness later—with lesser risks of creating unhappiness in others. Whether this can be expected of children, without more direct guidance and restraints than Summerhill admits (or without so much covert manipulation that it would make dishonest men and women of the faculty), seems to me highly questionable. Even if Neill, and an occasional genius like him, can bring it off, this seems to me the kind of success story that proves the exception rather than the rule.

There is a direct line from America's Progressive Education Movement of the 1920's to Summerhill. But in reality, there is nevertheless a fundamental difference. The old progressives believed fervently in what they thought of as life-adjustment education, and only the more radical among them also thought of the school as an instrument of social change or even revolution.

Neill clearly does not want to adjust children to the corruptions and sterile competition of a life that he sees around him. This is to his credit. Simply to train people to play the game, whatever it may be, and to aim for the jackpot under existing rules is surely a perversion of the educational process. It is not adjustment to life but to death-in-life, and I applaud Neill's refusal to have any part in such an enterprise.

But not to bring up children to understand, and cope with, the realities and the challenges of the competition "outside" is to offer them little more than an escape into their islands of happiness, impotent either to adjust to existing realities or to change them into better ones.

In the end, the impact of Summerhill is—as it ought to be—in the needs of the beholder. Much depends on the society in which the schools exist which Summerhill wants to reform. If it is true in Britain, for instance, as Neill indicated, that many babies are still subjected to the tyranny of a rigid feeding schedule, then the need to remove these irrational restraints from child care is great. Her Majesty's Inspectors may have been surprised (and, I hope, pleased) not to find youngsters at Summerhill jumping to attention as they entered the classroom; but most sensible American schools have long since abandoned this disruptive Teutonic ersatz respect.

At a time when permissiveness in the American home and school has often become a mindless exercise in the abolition of all value judgments and standards of conduct, the Summerhill lesson should be read with caution and discrimination; it should be read particularly with the clear understanding that Neill would never expect any part of his religion to work without an abiding faith in the joint enterprise—adults and children together—of the search for what is good and right and peaceful. He seeks, as a result of the removal of restraints, not orgiastic license but self-discipline.

Unless Summerhill is considered in such a light, it can be very potent poison, encouraging parents and teachers in a hands-off policy, without the compelling dedication and love and, even more important, the essential adult example of righteousness and—I hesitate to use the word because of its chronic abuse—goodness. Without these ingredients, the free-style approach is dynamite. It may well turn children (even if they are indeed Noble Savages, which I doubt) into Ignoble Savages when they grow up.

But taken with these cautions an infusion of Summerhill into the minds of those who rear or educate children and into educational institutions is an important antidote against the suspicions and rigidities that creep into the brains of adults and into the policies of schools.

I recoil when Neill says: "The child should not do anything until he comes to the opinion—his own opinion—that it should be done."

But then I realize that Neill and his handpicked staff intend to be molders of opinion, though they would deny this, by way of demonstrated love and understanding—and with the added caveat that nobody's freedom must interfere with anybody else's.

This is why I agree with Neill that the future of Summerhill itself is of little import, while the future of the Summerhill idea is "of the greatest importance to humanity." My reservations about it are comparable to those I hold about many religious faiths and rituals in whose moral and ethical foundations I urgently concur.

1. Why are things outside of school, according to Neill, much more interesting than the activities in school? List some examples from your own experience. If you fail to find joy in school experiences, can you identify some of the reasons, inside you as well as around you?

2. Is it true that schools have failed to give children culture? Analyze Neill's argument.

3. Neill cites a wide range of subjects which schools teach and then questions whether these subjects are really worth teaching. Evaluate his reasons.

4. What would Neill begin with that children are interested in? Would he then seek to entice them to widen their interests to include the basic subjects?

5. Neill wants schools to follow "the dictates of child nature." What is Neill's underlying concept of "child nature?" Give evidence for or against his concept.

6. What role does Neill believe that play has in education?

7. What does Neill believe to be the purpose of education? Give reasons why you would accept or reject his statement of purpose.

8. What does Hechinger consider to be the "underlying dogma" and the "holy grail" of Summerhill? Is this a fair assessment? Give specific reasons for your answer.

9. Why does the author believe that Summerhill is more like a family than a school? If true, what is the significance of this feature?

10. Is it an exaggeration to say that Summerhill cannot be reproduced? That the original Summerhill will not long be able to survive its founder?

11. Hechinger criticizes Neill for a streak of anti-intellectualism. Is this charge warranted, and, if so, is it also mitigated by other factors?

12. Will the child, as Neill claims, if left without adult suggestion, "develop as far as he is capable of developing" by his own initiative?

13. "Neill appears willing to sacrifice brain to heart," says Hechinger. Is this a dangerous sacrifice? What place

should affective education have in the curriculum? Use what you know about psychology and your own experience to answer these questions.

14. Would you agree with the author that tastes and wants need to be "nourished, trained, and acquired"? Develop your position.

15 Should students curb their desires for instant gratification in the hope of attaining greater happiness later? How would the different schools of psychology answer this question?

16 By not preparing children to understand and cope with the realities and the competitive nature of society, Hechinger asserts, Summerhill makes them incapable either of adjusting to the realities or changing them. Is it a fact that competition is a learned trait? Should one be taught to compete only with himself? List what you think schools might do to eliminate unhealthy competition among students.

17. Organize a panel to discuss the merits and limitations of Neill's ideas.

# VIII. *Compulsory Mis-Education* and Paul Goodman

*Many people accept the world as they find it, rarely questioning the arrangement of our institutions or considering the possibility that the present social structure is not inevitable and that an entirely different one would not necessarily be immoral or unjust —in fact, such a system might constitute a substantial improvement. Paul Goodman was a different breed altogether. "Fundamentally, there is no right education," he said, "except growing up in a worthwhile world. Indeed, our excessive concern with problems of education at present simply means that the grown-ups do not have such a world."*

*A society that alternately fears and admires its youth, a society which establishes artificial selective criteria for the world of work through formal schooling when a youth can be trained on the job in a fraction of the time, is a society in need of self-reassessment. Paul Goodman believes that schools "pressure and bribe" bright youth and attempt to "subdue" the majority of students. He questions compulsory education, the job market, the types of goals that we encourage the young to seek, and, most of all, how they can gain a genuine education in the type of society which they have inherited. As a result, he offers his own proposals on how our entire way of educating youth can take on greater meaning and purpose.*

*In his essay, Vaughan offers a sympathetic critique explaining Goodman's peculiar style and his holistic conception of man. He also indicates why many of those not already in sympathy with Goodman's indictment may not necessarily be persuaded by the evidence presented. The essay serves to point up the more radical way Goodman had of seeing the world and why he could not be satisfied with just another system to replace the present one.*

Paul Goodman

# 16. COMPULSORY MIS-EDUCATION

It is claimed that society needs more people who are technically trained. But informed labor people tell me that, for a job requiring skill but no great genius, a worker can be found at once, or quickly trained, to fill it. For instance, the average job in General Motors' most automated plant requires three weeks of training for those who have no education whatever. It used to require six weeks; for such jobs, automation has diminished rather than increased the need for training. In the Army and Navy, fairly complicated skills, e.g., radar operation and repair, are taught in a year *on the job,* often to practical illiterates.

Naturally, if diplomas are pre-requisite to hiring a youngster, the correlation of schooling and employment is self-proving. Because of this fad, there is a fantastic amount of mis-hiring, hiring young people far too school-trained for the routine jobs they get. I was struck by a recent report in the *Wall Street Journal* of firms philanthropically deciding to hire *only* drop-outs for certain categories of jobs, since the diploma made no difference in performance.

Paul Goodman studied at City University of New York and took his doctorate in humanities at the University of Chicago. One of the most versatile and prolific writers in America today, he has written for *Commentary, New York Review of Books, Politics, Kenyon Review, Resistance, Liberation, Partisan Review,* and other journals. His fiction includes *The Facts of Life, The Break-Up of Our Camp, Parent's Day, The Empire City,* and his verse includes *The Lordly Hudson. The Structure of Literature* and *Kafka's Prayer* are books of criticism. He is also the co-author of *Gestalt Therapy* and *Communitas,* and has written *Art and Social Nature, Growing Up Absurd, Utopian Essays and Political Proposals, People or Personnel,* and *New Reformation: Notes of a Neolithic Conservative.* Paul Goodman's important work was cut short when he died in 1972 at the age of sixty.
Source: Reprinted from *Compulsory Mis-Education* by Paul Goodman. Copyright © 1964 by Horizon Press, New York. Reprinted with permission. Excerpt from pp. 66–77.

Twist it and turn it how you will, there is no logic to the proposal to extend compulsory schooling *except* as a device to keep the unemployed off the streets by putting them into concentration camps called schools. The Continuation branch of Milwaukee Vocational is, then, typical of what we can expect. (By the way, Milwaukee Vocational is otherwise a justly famous school, a fine product of Populism and right-wing Socialism.)

As an academic, I am appalled by this motivation for schooling. As a citizen and human being, I am appalled by this waste of youthful vitality. It is time that we stopped using the word "education" honorifically. We must ask, education how? where? for what? and under whose administration? Certainly every youth should get the best possible education, but, in my opinion, the present kind of compulsory schooling under the present administrators, far from being extended, should be sharply curtailed.

## IV

As I have been saying, by and large primary schooling is, and should be, mainly baby-sitting. It has the great mission of democratic socialization—it certainly must not be segregated by race and income; apart from this, it should be happy, interesting, not damaging. The noise about stepping-up the primary curriculum is quite uncalled for; I have seen no convincing evidence—not by progressive educators either—that early schooling makes much academic difference in the long run. But in the secondary schools, after puberty, the tone of the baby-sitting must necessarily turn to regimentation and policing, and it is at peril that we require schooling; it fits some, it hurts others. A recent study by Edgar Friedenberg concludes that spirit-breaking is the *principal* function of typical lower-middle-class schools.

I wonder whether the Secretary of Labor thought through the constitutionality, not to speak of the morals, of his compulsory proposal. The legal justifications for compulsory schooling have been to protect children from exploitation by parents and employers, and to ensure the basic literacy and civics necessary for a democratic electorate. It is quite a different matter to deprive adolescents of their freedom in order to alleviate the difficulties of a faulty economic and political system. Is this constitutional?

We are back, in another context, to Dr. Conant's intolerable distinction between "individual development" and "national needs"; Dr. Conant was talking about the post-Sputnik putative need for scientists, Secretary Wirtz was talking about unemployment. So let us go over the ground again and look at the picture squarely. At present, in most states, for 10 to 13 years every young person is obliged to sit the better part of his day in a room almost always too crowded, facing front, doing lessons predetermined by a distant administration at the state capital and that have no relation to his own intellectual, social, or animal interests, and not much relation even to his economic interests. The overcrowding precludes individuality or spontaneity, reduces the young to ciphers, and the teacher to a martinet. If a youth tries to follow his own bent, he is interrupted and even jailed. If he does not perform, he is humiliated and threatened, but he is *not allowed to fail and get out.* Middle-class youth go through this for at least four more years—at the college level, the overcrowding has become an academic scandal—but they are steeled to it and supported by their middle-class anxiety and middle-class perquisites, including money to spend. Secretary Wirtz now wants poor youth, not thus steeled and supported, to get two more years of it. What will this 17-year-old do for spending money?

In his speech the Secretary referred to the admirable extension of free education from 1850 to, say, 1930. But this is again entirely misleading with regard to our present situation. To repeat, that opening of opportunity took place in an open economy, with an expanding market for skills and cultural learning. Young people took advantage of it *of their own volition*; therefore there were no blackboard jungles and endemic problems of discipline. Teachers taught those who wanted to learn; therefore there was no especial emphasis on grading. What is the present situation? The frantic competitive testing and grading means that the market for skills and learning is *not* open, it is tight. There are relatively few employers for those who score high; and almost none of the high-scorers become independent enterprisers. This means, in effect, that a few great corporations are getting the benefit of an enormous weeding-out and selective process—all children are fed into the mill and everybody pays for it.

If our present high schools, junior colleges, and colleges reflected the desire, freedom, and future of opportunity of the young, there would be no grading, no testing except as a teaching method, and no blackboard jungles. In fact, we are getting lockstep scheduling and grading to the point of torture. The senior year of high school is sacrificed to batteries of national tests, and policemen are going to stand in the corridors. Even an elite school such as Bronx Science— singled out by Dr. Conant as the best school in the country—is run as if for delinquents, with corridor passes and a ban on leaving the building. The conclusion is inevitable: The scholastically bright are not following their aspirations but are being pressured and bribed; the majority—those who are bright but not scholastic, and those who are not especially bright but have other kinds of vitality—are being subdued.

# V

This is the schooling that Secretary Wirtz says we "ought to make the biggest industry in the country." I thought it already was! As one observes the sprawling expansion of the universities and colleges, eating up their neighborhoods, dislocating the poor, dictating to the lower schools, battening on Federal billions for research and development, and billions for buildings, and billions through the National Defense Education Act, and billions from foundations and endowments—one suddenly realizes that here again is the Dead Hand of the medieval church, that inherits and inherits and never dies. The University, which should be dissident and poor, has become the Establishment. The streets are full of its monks.

What a bad scene! Its spirit pervades all of society. Let me quote from a man in Secretary Wirtz's own department, in charge of retraining: "We retrain him, but before the course is finished, that job too has vanished. So we begin again. But after the fourth or fifth retraining, he has a job that doesn't vanish: he becomes a Teacher of Retraining." We must remember that, whatever the motive, *pouring money into the school-and-college system and into the academic social-work way of coping with problems, is strictly class legislation that confirms the inequitable structure of the economy.* I have mentioned how the professor-ridden Peace Corps needs $15,000 to get a single youngster in the field for a year, whereas the dedicated Quakers achieve almost the same end for $3,500. Again, when $13 millions are allotted for a local Mobilization for Youth program, it is soon found that nearly $12 millions have gone for sociologists doing "research," diplomated social workers, the N.Y. school system, and administrators, but only one million to field workers and the youths themselves.

## VI

In my opinion, the public buys this unexamined "education" because of the following contradiction: The Americans are guilty because these youth *are* useless in the present set-up, so they spend money on them (though they get oddly stingy at crucial moments) ; on the other hand, they insist that the youth work hard at something "useful"—namely useless training. One can't just let them play ball; they must compete and suffer.

I agree that we ought to spend more public money on education. And where jobs exist and there is need for technical training, the corporations ought to spend more money on apprenticeships. We are an affluent society and can afford it. And the conditions of modern life are far too complicated for independent young spirits to get going on their own. They need some preparation, though probably not as much as is supposed; but more important, they need various institutional frameworks in which they can try out and learn the ropes.

Nevertheless, I would not give a penny more to the present school administrators. The situation is this: to make the present school set-up even *tolerable*, not positively damaging—e.g., to cut the elementary class size to 20 or to provide colleges enough to diminish the frantic competition for places—will require at least *doubling* the present school budgets. I submit that this kind of money should be spent in other ways.

## VII

What, then, ought the education of these youth to be? We are back to our fundamental question: what are the alternatives?

Fundamentally, there is no right education except growing up into a worthwhile world. Indeed, our excessive concern with problems of education at present simply means that the grown-ups do not have such a world. The poor youth of America will *not* become equal by rising through the middle class, going to middle-class schools. By plain social justice, the Negroes and other minorities have the right to, and must get, equal opportunity for schooling with the rest, but the exaggerated expectation from the schooling is a chimera—and, I fear, will be shockingly disappointing. But also the middle-class youth will not escape their increasing exploitation and *anomie* in such schools. A decent education aims at, prepares for, a more worthwhile future, with a different community spirit, different occupations, and more real utility than attaining status and salary.

We are suffering from a bad style, perhaps a wrong religion. Although it is pretty certain, as I have said, that the automated future will see less employment in the manufacture of hardware and more employment in service occupations, as well as more leisure, yet astoundingly the mass-production and cash-accounting attitude toward the hardware is carried over unchanged into the thinking about the services and leisure! The lockstep regimentation and the petty-bourgeois credits and competitive grading in the schooling are typical of all the rest. (For a charming, and grim, study of the spread of "business methods" to schooling, from 1900 to 1930, let me refer the reader to Callahan's *The Cult of Efficiency in American Education.*)

My bias is that we should maximize automation as quickly as possible, *where it is relevant*—taking care to cushion job dislocation and to provide adequate social insurance. But the spirit and method of automation, logistics, chain of command, and clerical work are *entirely irrelevant* to humane services, community service, communications, community culture, high culture, citizenly initiative, education, and recreation. To give a rather special but not trivial example of what I mean, TV sets should be maximum-mass-produced with maximum automation, in a good standard model, as cheaply as possible; but TV programming should, except for a few national services, be as much decentralized, tailor-made, and reliant on popular and free-artist initiative as possible.

The dangers of the highly technological and automated future are obvious: We might become a brainwashed society of idle and frivolous consumers. We might continue in a rat race of highly competitive, unnecessary busy-work with a meaninglessly expanding Gross National Product. In either case, there might still be an outcast group that must be suppressed. To countervail these dangers and make active, competent, and initiating citizens who can produce a community culture and a noble recreation, we need a very different education than the schooling that we have been getting.

Large parts of it must be directly useful, rather than useless and merely aiming at status. Here we think of the spending in the public sector, advocated by Myrdal, Keyserling, Galbraith, and many others. E.g., the money spent on town improvement, community service, or rural rehabilitation can also provide educational occasions. (When these economists invariably list schooling as high—and often first—in the list of public expenditures, they fail to realize that such expense is probably wasted and perhaps even further dislocates the economy. I would say the same about Galbraith's pitch for new highways.)

On the whole, the education must be voluntary rather than compulsory, for no growth to freedom occurs except by intrinsic motivation. Therefore the educational opportunities must be various and variously administered. We must diminish rather than expand the present monolithic school system. I would suggest that, on the model of the GI-Bill, we experiment, giving the school money directly to the high-school-age adolescents, for any plausible self-chosen educational proposals, such as purposeful travel or individual enterprise. This would also, of course, lead to the proliferation of experimental schools.

Unlike the present inflexible lockstep, our educational policy must allow for periodic quitting and easy return to the scholastic ladder, so that the young have time to find themselves and to study when they are themselves ready. This is Eric Erickson's valuable notion of the need for *moratoria* in the life-career; and the anthropological insistence of Stanley Diamond and others, that our society neglects the crises of growing up.

Education must foster independent thought and expression, rather than conformity. For example, to countervail the mass communications, we have an imperative social need, indeed a constitutional need to protect liberty, for many thousands of independent media: local newspapers, independent broadcasters, little magazines, little theaters; and these, under professional guidance, could provide remarkable occasions for the employment and education of adolescents of brains and talent. (I have elsewhere proposed a graduated tax on the audience-size of mass-media, to provide a Fund to underwrite such new independent ventures for a period, so that they can try to make their way.)

Finally, contemporary education must inevitably be heavily weighted toward the sciences. But this does not necessarily call for school-training of a relatively few technicians, or rare creative scientists (if such can indeed be trained in schools). Our aim must be to make a great number of citizens at home in a technological environment, not alienated from the machines we use, not ignorant as consumers, who can somewhat judge governmental scientific policy, who can enjoy the humanistic beauty of the sciences, and above all, who can understand the morality of a scientific way of life. I try to spell out the meaning of this below. (See Chapter 7.)

When Secretary Wirtz means by education something like this, and not compulsory junior college for delinquents, we can think of extending education as a device for diminishing youth unemployment. Because it will then be more useful employment than most of the available, or non-available, jobs. It will be relevant to a good future rather than a morally-bankrupt past.

William Vaughan

# 17. PAUL GOODMAN: CRITIC AND REFORMER

"Anarchistic," "utopian," "romantic"—these and similar labels attached to the social and educational thought of Paul Goodman have overshadowed the positive and constructive dimensions to be found in his works. While Goodman has been generally acknowledged as a significant critic of contemporary society and education, he is also, and perhaps most importantly, a serious social and educational reformer with definite ideas on how we ought to reconstitute our society and educate our young. Indeed, Goodman's most poignant and reoccurring social and educational critiques can only be fully understood in light of his positive vision of a free and open society, a central feature of that "worthwhile world" needed for a "right education."[1] A valid assessment of Goodman's educational thought

William H. Vaughan recently obtained his doctorate from the University of Kentucky. A leading authority on the educational and social ideas of Paul Goodman, William H. Vaughan is a member of the faculty at Glassboro State College, Glassboro, New Jersey. "Paul Goodman: Critic and Reformer" was written especially for this book and is here published for the first time.
[1] Paul Goodman, *Compulsory Mis-Education* (New York: Horizon Press, 1964), p. 51.

calls for an examination of both of these critical and constructive dimensions.

The preceding selection taken from *Compulsory Mis-Education* reflects Goodman's fundamental moral concern with contemporary educational policies and practices. This concern gives rise to several practical proposals, elaborated in more detail in other works, for changing the structure and content of public education. Evident also is Goodman's inimitable "style," a style which distresses, excites, prods, and, finally, provokes the reader to come to terms with the issues at hand. Goodman's style mirrors on a deeper level of meaning a dynamic conception of human reality and an approach to understanding and dealing with that reality. Goodman's critiques and proposals for educational reform must be understood in terms of this "philosophic backdrop."

The reader who approaches the educational thought of Paul Goodman looking for a systematic and analytic treatment of pedagogical questions will not find it. Goodman's holistic, Gestaltist conception of human reality as a functional, unified whole does not admit such treatment. The reference for any "theorizing" about the individual, for Goodman, is the dynamic organism/environmental interaction.[2] Intrinsic to any question of human association is a composite of interacting socio-cultural, historical, physical, and animal forces. Human growth and learning emerge as a central dimension of the pushes and pulls of such a dynamic Gestalt. The critical concern for Goodman is that the analytic approach dominant in the various socio-scientific disciplines separates and isolates specific elements for study and, in so doing, loses the interrelationships, the unity, the wholeness of that which is being studied.[3] While Goodman does not completely reject analytic inquiry, his interest in maintaining the wholeness of the subjects he treats leads him to choose a "Man of Letters" style, that is, "a blending of memory, observation, criticism, reasoning, imagination, and reconstruction."[4]

Goodman's holistic conception of human reality and Man of Letters style is easily discernible in his writing. Sociological, psychological, political, economic, and moral issues within the context of a particular educational problem being considered are not given

[2] Paul Goodman, Ralph F. Hefferline, and Frederick Perls, *Gestalt Therapy* (New York: Dell Publishing Company, 1951), p. 288.
[3] Paul Goodman, *Utopian Essays and Practical Proposals*, ed. Paul Goodman (New York: Random House, 1964), p. xiii.
[4] Ibid., pp. xiii–xiv.

separate and isolated treatment. These elements, as they are found
in Goodman's arguments, often overlap and are interwoven in a
manner analogous to the threads in a multi-colored fabric. The
relevance of a particular line of reasoning, i.e., psychological, economic, moral, etc., is determined by whether or not it maintains the
integrity of the human problem under consideration. The Man of
Letters style enables Goodman to address these problems on a first-
person, existential level. The language he uses is, for the most part,
personal and practical, that is, ordinary language, rather than the
language of the psychologist, economist, etc.

Understanding Goodman, to go back to the previous analogy, is
comparable to seeing and discerning the intricate patterns and designs
of a multi-colored tapestry. While Goodman's educational thought
constitutes a significant element which can be "separated" and
examined apart, as a thread in the tapestry can be removed and
examined, a full and valid understanding of Goodman can be achieved
only by grasping the whole of which it is a part.

Goodman criticizes our mass-urban, technologically complex
society in general and our educational system in particular for doing
positive harm to human growth. Our social and educational institutions go beyond simply failing to protect and provide for the welfare
of the young; they stultify and diminish human existence. In the
preceding selection, for example, Goodman is "appalled" at the "waste
of youthful vitality" in compulsory schooling. He criticizes a classroom structure which humiliates and threatens while prohibiting
individuality and spontaneity. He questions the constitutionality of
depriving adolescents of their freedom. He concludes that the scholastically bright are being "pressured and bribed" while the majority
of students are simply being "subdued." The current state-of-affairs
is, for Goodman, a "bad scene."

Goodman's basic critique is moral in both tone and intent. Few
would disagree with moral judgments condemning the waste of youthful vitality, practices which humiliate, threaten, bribe, and subdue the
young, and situations which prohibit individuality and spontaneity.
Few, moreover, would morally condone reducing children and adolescents to "ciphers." The critical question is whether or not such
states-of-affairs exist and, if they do, the extent to which they characterize contemporary education. It is in response to this question
that radical disagreements occur.

Goodman provides little by way of evidence to convince those
who are not already convinced that such states-of-affairs not only exist

but are the distinguishing traits of contemporary public education. For example, Goodman looks at Bronx Science High School, noted by James B. Conant as outstanding, and observes the corridor passes and ban on leaving the building. This, coupled with the standard educational procedures of scheduling, grading, and the batteries of national tests, is enough for Goodman to draw a conclusion which he deems "inevitable," i.e., that the scholastically bright are not following their aspirations and are being pressured and bribed. Is this conclusion inevitable given the "meager" evidence provided? The corridor passes and ban on leaving the building are certainly restrictive measures. The educational practices of scheduling, grading, and testing might well introduce pressures. But—for Goodman the conclusion is self-evident. For those who "see" and "feel" with him, drawing on their life-experiences and sensitivities, it is also self-evident. For those who do not see what Goodman sees and feel what he feels, the conclusion is far from being established. Goodman, however, goes no further in "building a case" to convince those who perceive the situation differently. He moves on to make another point, in much the same fashion, focusing on what he sees as the central and underlying reality of the situation.

For Goodman there is no need to "pile up" mounds of evidence to support what in many instances may appear to be a hastily drawn conclusion. In dealing with "basic issues" the evidence, according to Goodman, is "everywhere" and "will be noticed unless one will not or cannot notice it."[5] Goodman's approach is to draw attention to what the basic evidence is and where it is rather than to give a complete and detailed explication. If the obvious is not noticed it is "the result of a neurotic failure of perception, feeling, or action."[6] In such cases it is pointless to introduce more detailed evidence for the individual "does not see what you see, it slips his mind, it seems irrelevant, he explains it away, etc."[7] Goodman's critiques, then, move on in the hope of striking a responsive chord and initiating, as far as possible through the written medium, a therapeutic dialogue with the recalcitrant reader.

The fact remains, however, that there are many who do not see the obvious and who might possibly be rationally persuaded of the injustices and inadequacies of public schooling if more evidence were

[5] Goodman, *Gestalt Therapy*, p. 243.

[6] Ibid.

[7] Ibid.

provided. This evidence is needed and, indeed, is demanded by and from those responsible for the development and implementation of educational policy. Goodman's critiques of educational policies and practices need in many instances further substantiation to be introduced into serious policy discourse. Goodman's response might well be that he is not interested in changing particular educational policies and practices. The "enemy" is the "System" as a whole and reforming that System, including what the System accepts as evidence, requires a global attack.

Goodman's educational critiques are followed by positive statements of educational purpose and practical proposals for alternative ways of educating the young. For Goodman, the basic purpose of education, as noted in the preceding selection, is to "make active, competent, initiating citizens who can produce a community culture and a noble recreation." It is necessary in realizing this overriding purpose that education foster independent thought and expression, make citizens at home in a technological environment, enable people to judge governmental scientific policy and to enjoy the humanistic beauty of the sciences, and create an understanding of the morality of a scientific way of life. This basic purpose and examples of attendant aims emerge time and again in Goodman's educational thought.

A central concept in Goodman's statement of purpose is "initiative." Goodman defines freedom as "the condition of initiating activity."[8] This positive notion of freedom goes beyond a negative sense of freedom, i.e., freedom from interference, to focus on the conditions of modern society which effectively hem in and impose on an individual. While there may be no laws preventing an individual from undertaking a particular course of action, the conditions surrounding that action may pre-empt needed resources or simply overwhelm the individual. The result in such a situation would be a "decision" not to act. Such a decision, however, is not a decision at all inasmuch as the individual is unable to get the resources he needs to act or does not understand the complexities of the situation enough to act. The basic educational purpose of making active, competent, initiating citizens, then, is that of making free citizens, citizens who know how to obtain needed resources and are able to manage the complexities of a technological society. The young are

[8] Paul Goodman, "Reply on Pornography and Censorship," *Patterns of Anarchy*, eds. Leonard I. Krimerman and Lewis Perry (Garden City, New York: Doubleday & Company, Inc., 1966), p. 55.

to be brought up as new centers of initiative. The educational task of
the young, more specifically, is to grow up by identifying with adult
society and culture, taking it over, renewing it, and transforming it to
reflect their own powers and resources.[9]

Achieving this basic purpose requires, according to Goodman,
a radically different approach to educating the young than the compulsory schooling now in effect. In the preceding selection Goodman
makes brief reference to several educational needs of the child and
adolescent. More specifically, Goodman notes that primary schooling
should be "mainly baby-sitting." It should be integrated and "happy,
interesting, and not damaging." Adolescents, in turn, might well be
given money directly for "self-chosen educational proposals." Such
brief proposals as these seem to characterize Goodman's writing. In
a later work, however, Goodman draws together the common threads
running through his proposals for educating the child to outline in
more comprehensive terms "Mini-Schools" as a model for elementary
education.[10] "Youth Work Camps" emerge as the educative environment for adolescents[11] and a "Community of Scholars" is outlined
for young adults.[12] Each of these proposed alternatives is directed
toward providing the child, adolescent, and young adult with the environment Goodman depicts as necessary for growth, i.e., community.

Goodman's proposals for reforming education have been criticized for the vagueness and overall inadequacy in dealing with the
practical problems which arise in the daily conduct of education.
If Goodman's purpose was to provide a comprehensive educational
plan, then such criticisms would be valid. The major thrust of
Goodman's practical proposals for reforming our educational system,
however, is not to provide or create another "System."[13] The practical
dimensions in the education of the young must be developed from
within the social and physical context of a given community if these
dimensions are to make use of and reflect the needs, interests, resources, and eccentricities of the individuals in the situation.

Goodman sees his proposals serving a "pragmatic" function in

[9] Paul Goodman, *The Community of Scholars* (New York: Random House,
1964), p. 257.

[10] Paul Goodman, *New Reformation: Notes of a Neolithic Conservative* (New
York: Random House, 1970), pp. 95–99.

[11] Paul Goodman, "Youth Work Camps," *Utopian Essays and Practical Proposals*, pp. 263–273.

[12] Goodman, *The Community of Scholars.*

[13] Paul Goodman, *People or Personnel* (New York: Random House, 1968),
p. 27.

the search for viable alternatives to contemporary education.[14] Goodman's proposals for educational reform such as Mini-Schools and Youth Work Camps are to be considered in one sense as practical hypotheses calling for action research. The educational value of such ideas needs to be explored and determined in an experimental context. In a second, related sense such proposals are intended to function as "intellectual tools" for initiating dialogue revolving around the reconceptualization and restructuring of contemporary education. Both of these functions place the responsibility for initiating educational reform on the shoulders of those who are to be involved.

While Goodman would structure all of society as educative as part of his vision of a better world, he settles for much less initially. The first step, given the resources in and conditions of modern society, is to loosen up the System and establish more alternatives. This would make society at least livable. Perhaps a reader wants more and, indeed, has a right to expect more. Goodman, I am sure, would have been open to suggestions.

[14] Paul Goodman, "Utopian Thinking," *Utopian Essays and Practical Proposals*, pp. 19–20.

# Discussion Questions
# and Activities

1. Are many workers getting more formal education than they need for the jobs they take? Is this true for today's college students? If so, what is the cause of this condition? What consequences does it have for both the worker and society?

2. Explain Goodman's attitude toward compulsory education. Is he opposed to more "education" in general or just certain types? What is your position on compulsory education?

3. Is Goodman correct when he says that secondary youth is "not allowed to fail and get out"? In what context would it be better "to fail and get out"?

4. Is it true that the scholastically bright are being "pressured and bribed," and the other students are being "subdued"? Is Goodman guilty of overstatement? If not, give some examples from your own experience.

5. What does Goodman mean by "there is no right education except growing up into a worthwhile world"? What are the implications of this statement for education?

6. Suppose you were the state superintendent of public instruction. Would you recommend to the state board and to the legislature that compulsory education laws should be cut back or even abolished?

7. Imagine that there were no compulsory attendance laws, your parents or friends did not insist that you attend school, and that no diplomas or degrees were awarded. Would you then attend school of your own free will, if, in fact, you had to attend schools exactly like the ones you had attended up to this point in your life?

8. Was Goodman too severe in condemning the schools? Suppose you were a school superintendent with authority to implement some of his recommendations. Would you do so? If so, state your reasons.

9. Does Goodman provide evidence that the conditions which he condemns are actually widely prevalent? Is his evidence substantial?

10. Is Goodman basically interested in changing specific policies and practices, or does he aim to bring about larger goals?

11. From what you know about education, would you say that a radically different approach is needed in educating the young? State specifically what that approach would be.

# IX.  Deschooling Society

*A fundamental axiom about the social order that most people share is that formal school systems are necessary and essential institutions. The Western idea of inevitable progress, while subject to a loss of faith in recent years, rested at least in part upon a belief in the value of schooling for the improvement of society. Indeed a world without schools seemed incomprehensible to almost everyone—everyone, that is, except Ivan Illich.*

*Among the reformers of education, there are those who would reform teaching practices and the curriculum, some would favor the "free school" movement, and still others would exploit the media to bring about a worldwide classroom. While recognizing certain advantages in those proposals, Ivan Illich rejects them all in favor of deschooling society. By his analysis of what the schools stand for and the functions they serve, he rejects the idea of organized schooling and compulsory education in favor of a society of informal learning network where everyone will have free access to information and tools needed in their lives.*

*The startling impact of Ivan Illich's ideas have tended to polarize educators in their attack upon the articles of faith in the educational pantheon. Some have turned a deaf ear after the initial shock of incredulity; whereas certain reformers, such as John Holt and Neil Postman, have been sympathetic. Still a third group, while being critical of the schools and aware of the need for change, refuse to accept Illich's ideas. In this latter group is Arthur Pearl, too much of an individualist to be a follower and too skeptical to be uncritical. He points out in the fol-*

*lowing essay what he believes to be the weaknesses of Illich's position, while explaining why his own ideas would prove to be a more viable substitute.*

# 18. THE ALTERNATIVE TO
# SCHOOLING

For generations we have tried to make the world a better place by
providing more and more schooling, but so far the endeavor has
failed. What we have learned instead is that forcing all children to
climb an open-ended education ladder cannot enhance equality but
must favor the individual who starts out earlier, healthier, or better
prepared; that enforced instruction deadens for most people the will
for independent learning; and that knowledge treated as a commodity, delivered in packages, and accepted as private property once
it is acquired, must always be scarce.

In response, critics of the educational system are now proposing
strong and unorthodox remedies that range from the voucher plan,
which would enable each person to buy the education of his choice
on an open market, to shifting the responsibility for education from
the school to the media and to apprenticeship on the job. Some
individuals foresee that the school will have to be disestablished just
as the church was disestablished all over the world during the last
two centuries. Other reformers propose to replace the universal

Ivan D. Illich, internationally known educator and social reformer, was born
in Vienna in 1926. He was educated in Vienna, Salzburg, and Rome (where
he was ordained). He came to the United States in 1951 and served as assistant pastor in an Irish-Puerto Rican parish. From 1956 to 1960 he was
assigned as vice chancellor of the Catholic University of Puerto Rico. Since
then he has served as director of the Center for Intercultural Documentation
(CIDOC) in Cuernavaca, Mexico, an educational organization devoted to improving the social and cultural conditions of the Latin American people. His
commitment to radical humanism has caused him to be interdicted as a rebel and
heretic by the church. Illich's writings include *Celebration of Awareness* and
*Deschooling Society*.
Source: Ivan Illich, "An Alternative to Schooling," *Saturday Review* (June
19, 1971), pp. 44–48, 59–60.

school with various new systems that would, they claim, better prepare everybody for life in modern society. These proposals for new educational institutions fall into three broad categories: the reformation of the classroom within the school system; the dispersal of free schools throughout society; and the transformation of all society into one huge classroom. But these three approaches—the reformed classroom, the free school, and the worldwide classroom—represent three stages in a proposed escalation of education in which each step threatens more subtle and more pervasive social control than the one it replaces.

I believe that the disestablishment of the school has become inevitable and that this end of an illusion should fill us with hope. But I also believe that the end of the "age of schooling" could usher in the epoch of the global schoolhouse that would be distinguishable only in name from a global madhouse or global prison in which education, correction, and adjustment become synonymous. I therefore believe that the breakdown of the school forces us to look beyond its imminent demise and to face fundamental alternatives in education. Either we can work for fearsome and potent new educational devices that teach about a world which progressively becomes more opaque and forbidding for man, or we can set the conditions for a new era in which technology would be used to make society more simple and transparent, so that all men can once again know the facts and use the tools that shape their lives. In short, we can disestablish schools or we can deschool culture.

In order to see clearly the alternatives we face, we must first distinguish education from schooling, which means separating the humanistic intent of the teacher from the impact of the invariant structure of the school. This hidden structure constitutes a course of instruction that stays forever beyond the control of the teacher or of his school board. It conveys indelibly the message that only through schooling can an individual prepare himself for adulthood in society, that what is not taught in school is of little value, and that what is learned outside of school is not worth knowing. I call it the hidden curriculum of schooling, because it constitutes the unalterable framework of the system, within which all changes in the curriculum are made.

The hidden curriculum is always the same regardless of school or place. It requires all children of a certain age to assemble in groups of about thirty, under the authority of a certified teacher, for some 500 to 1,000 or more hours each year. It doesn't matter whether the curriculum is designed to teach the principles of fascism, liberalism, Catholicism, or socialism; or whether the purpose of the school is to produce Soviet or United States citizens, mechanics, or doctors. It makes no difference whether the teacher is authoritarian or permissive, whether he imposes his own creed or teaches students to think for themselves. What is important is that students learn that education is valuable when it is acquired in the school through a graded process of consumption; that the degree of success the individual will enjoy in society depends on the amount of learning he consumes; and that learning *about* the world is more valuable than learning *from* the world.

It must be clearly understood that the hidden curriculum translates learning from an activity into a commodity—for which the school monopolizes the market. In all countries knowledge is regarded as the first necessity for survival, but also as a form of currency more liquid than rubles or dollars. We have become accustomed, through Karl Marx's writings, to speak about the alienation of the worker from his work in a class society. We must now recognize the estrangement of man from his learning when it becomes the product of a service profession and he becomes the consumer.

The more learning an individual consumes, the more "knowledge stock" he acquires. The hidden curriculum therefore defines a new class structure for society within which the large consumers of knowledge—those who have acquired large quantities of knowledge stock—enjoy special privileges, high income, and access to the more powerful tools of production. This kind of knowledge-capitalism has been accepted in all industrialized societies and establishes a rationale for the distribution of jobs and income. (This point is especially important in the light of the lack of correspondence between schooling and occupational competence established in studies such as Ivar Berg's *Education and Jobs: The Great Training Robbery.*)

The endeavor to put all men through successive stages of enlightenment is rooted deeply in alchemy, the Great Art of the waning Middle Ages. John Amos Comenius, a Moravian bishop, self-styled Pansophist, and pedagogue, is rightly considered one of the founders of the modern schools. He was among the first to propose seven or twelve grades of compulsory learning. In his *Magna Didactica*, he described schools as devices to "teach everybody everything" and outlined a blueprint for the assembly-line production of knowledge, which according to his method would make education cheaper and better and make growth into full humanity possible for all. But

Comenius was not only an early efficiency expert, he was an alchemist who adopted the technical language of his craft to describe the art of rearing children. The alchemist sought to refine base elements by leading their distilled spirits through twelve stages of successive enlightenment, so that for their own and all the world's benefit they might be transmuted into gold. Of course, alchemists failed no matter how often they tried, but each time their "science" yielded new reasons for their failure, and they tried again.

Pedagogy opened a new chapter in the history of Ars Magna. Education became the search for an alchemic process that would bring forth a new type of man, who would fit into an environment created by scientific magic. But, no matter how much each generation spent on its schools, it always turned out that the majority of people were unfit for enlightenment by this process and had to be discarded as unprepared for life in a man-made world.

Educational reformers who accept the idea that schools have failed fall into three groups. The most respectable are certainly the great masters of alchemy who promise better schools. The most seductive are popular magicians, who promise to make every kitchen into an alchemic lab. The most sinister are the new Masons of the Universe, who want to transform the entire world into one huge temple of learning. Notable among today's masters of alchemy are certain research directors employed or sponsored by the large foundations who believe that schools, if they could somehow be improved, could also become economically more feasible than those that are now in trouble, and simultaneously could sell a larger package of services. Those who are concerned primarily with the curriculum claim that it is outdated or irrelevant. So the curriculum is filled with new packaged courses on African Culture, North American Imperialism, Women's Lib, Pollution, or the Consumer Society. Passive learning is wrong—it is indeed—so we graciously allow students to decide what and how they want to be taught. Schools are prison houses. Therefore, principals are authorized to approve teach-outs, moving the school desks to a roped-off Harlem street. Sensitivity training becomes fashionable. So, we import group therapy into the classroom. School, which was supposed to teach everybody everything, now becomes all things to all children.

Other critics emphasize that schools make inefficient use of modern science. Some would administer drugs to make it easier for the instructor to change the child's behavior. Others would transform school into a stadium for educational gaming. Still others would electrify the classroom. If they are simplistic disciples of McLuhan, they replace blackboards and textbooks with multimedia happenings; if they follow Skinner, they claim to be able to modify behavior more efficiently than old-fashioned classroom practitioners can.

Most of these changes have, of course, some good effects. The experimental schools have fewer truants. Parents do have a greater feeling of participation in a decentralized district. Pupils, assigned by their teacher to an apprenticeship, do often turn out more competent than those who stay in the classroom. Some children do improve their knowledge of Spanish in the language lab because they prefer playing with the knobs of a tape recorder to conversations with their Puerto Rican peers. Yet all these improvements operate within predictably narrow limits, since they leave the hidden curriculum of school intact.

Some reformers would like to shake loose from the hidden curriculum, but they rarely succeed. Free schools that lead to further free schools produce a mirage of freedom, even though the chain of attendance is frequently interrupted by long stretches of loafing. Attendance through seduction inculcates the need for educational treatment more persuasively than the reluctant attendance enforced by a truant officer. Permissive teachers in a padded classroom can easily render their pupils impotent to survive once they leave.

Learning in these schools often remains nothing more than the acquisition of socially valued skills defined, in this instance, by the consensus of a commune rather than by the decree of a school board. New presbyter is but old priest writ large.

Free schools, to be truly free, must meet two conditions: First, they must be run in a way to prevent the reintroduction of the hidden curriculum of graded attendance and certified students studying at the feet of certified teachers. And, more importantly, they must provide a framework in which all participants—staff and pupils—can free themselves from the hidden foundations of a schooled society. The first condition is frequently incorporated in the stated aims of a free school. The second condition is only rarely recognized, and is difficult to state as the goal of a free school.

It is useful to distinguish between the hidden curriculum, which I have described, and the occult foundations of schooling. The hidden curriculum is a ritual that can be considered the official initiation into modern society, institutionally established through the school. It is the purpose of this ritual to hide from its participants the contraditions between the myth of an egalitarian society and the class-conscious reality it certifies. Once they are recognized as such, rituals lose their power, and this is what is now beginning to happen to schooling. But there are certain fundamental assumptions about growing up—the occult foundations—which now find their expression in the ceremonial of schooling, and which could easily be reinforced by what free schools do.

Among these assumptions is what Peter Schrag calls the "immigration syndrome," which impels us to treat all people as if they were newcomers who must go through a naturalization process. Only certified consumers of knowledge are admitted to citizenship. Men are not born equal, but are made equal through gestation by Alma Mater.

The rhetoric of all schools states that they form a man for the future, but they do not release him for his task before he has developed a high level of tolerance to the ways of his elders: education *for* life rather than *in* everyday life. Few free schools can avoid doing precisely this. Nevertheless they are among the most important centers from which a new life-style radiates, not because of the effect their graduates will have but, rather, because elders who choose to bring up their children without the benefit of properly ordained teachers frequently belong to a radical minority and because their preoccupation with the rearing of their children sustains them in their new style.

The most dangerous category of educational reformer is one who argues that knowledge can be produced and sold much more effectively on an open market than on one controlled by school. These people argue that most skills can be easily acquired from skill-models if the learner is truly interested in their acquisition; that individual entitlements can provide a more equal purchasing power for education. They demand a careful separation of the process by which knowledge is acquired from the process by which it is measured and certified. These seem to me obvious statements. But it would be a fallacy to believe that the establishment of a free market for knowledge would constitute a radical alternative in education.

The establishment of a free market would indeed abolish what I have previously called the hidden curriculum of present schooling—its age-specific attendance at a graded curriculum. Equally, a free market would at first give the appearance of counteracting what I have called the occult foundations of a schooled society: the "immigration syndrome," the institutional monopoly of teaching, and the ritual of linear initiation. But at the same time a free market in education would provide the alchemist with innumerable hidden hands to fit each man into the multiple, tight little niches a more complex technocracy can provide.

Many decades of reliance on schooling has turned knowledge into a commodity, a marketable staple of a special kind. Knowledge is now regarded simultaneously as a first necessity and also as society's most precious currency. (The transformation of knowledge into a commodity is reflected in a corresponding transformation of language. Words that formerly functioned as verbs are becoming nouns that designate possessions. Until recently dwelling and learning and even healing designated activities. They are now usually conceived as commodities or services to be delivered. We talk about the manufacture of housing or the delivery of medical care. Men are no longer regarded fit to house or heal themselves. In such a society people come to believe that professional services are more valuable than personal care. Instead of learning how to nurse grandmother, the teen-ager learns to picket the hospital that does not admit her.) This attitude could easily survive the disestablishment of school, just as affiliation with a church remained a condition for office long after the adoption of the First Amendment. It is even more evident that test batteries measuring complex knowledge-packages could easily survive the disestablishment of school—and with this would go the compulsion to obligate everybody to acquire a minimum package in the knowledge stock. The scientific measurement of each man's worth and the alchemic dream of each man's "educability to his full humanity" would finally coincide. Under the appearance of a "free" market, the global village would turn into an environmental womb where pedagogic therapists control the complex navel by which each man is nourished.

At present schools limit the teacher's competence to the classroom. They prevent him from claiming man's whole life as his domain. The demise of school will remove this restriction and give a semblance of legitimacy to the life-long pedagogical invasion of everybody's privacy. It will open the way for a scramble for "knowledge" on a free market, which would lead us toward the paradox of a vulgar, albeit seemingly egalitarian, meritocracy. Unless the concept of knowledge is transformed, the disestablishment of school will lead to a wedding between a growing meritocratic system that separates learning from certification and a society committed to provide therapy for each man until he is ripe for the gilded age.

For those who subscribe to the technocratic ethos, whatever is technically possible must be made available at least to a few whether they want it or not. Neither the privation nor the frustration of the majority counts. If cobalt treatment is possible, then the city of Tegucigalpa needs one apparatus in each of its two major hospitals, at a cost that would free an important part of the population of Honduras from parasites. If supersonic speeds are possible, then it must speed the travel of some. If the flight to Mars can be conceived, then a rationale must be found to make it appear a necessity. In the technocratic ethos poverty is modernized: Not only are old alternatives closed off by new monopolies, but the lack of necessities is also compounded by a growing spread between those services that are technologically feasible and those that are in fact available to the majority.

A teacher turns "educator" when he adopts this technocratic ethos. He then acts as if education were a technological enterprise designed to make man fit into whatever environment the "progress" of science creates. He seems blind to the evidence that constant obsolescence of all commodities comes at a high price: the mounting cost of training people to know about them. He seems to forget that the rising cost of tools is purchased at a high price in education: They decrease the labor intensity of the economy, make learning on the job impossible or, at best, a privilege for a few. All over the world the cost of educating men for society rises faster than the productivity of the entire economy, and fewer people have a sense of intelligent participation in the commonweal.

A revolution against those forms of privilege and power, which are based on claims to professional knowledge, must start with a transformation of consciousness about the nature of learning. This means, above all, a shift of responsibility for teaching and learning. Knowledge can be defined as a commodity only as long as it is viewed as the result of institutional enterprise or as the fulfillment of institutional objectives. Only when a man recovers the sense of personal responsibility for what he learns and teaches can this spell be broken and the alienation of learning from living be overcome.

The recovery of the power to learn or to teach means that the teacher who takes the risk of interfering in somebody else's private affairs also assumes responsibility for the results. Similarly, the student who exposes himself to the influence of a teacher must take responsibility for his own education. For such purposes educational institutions—if they are at all needed—ideally take the form of facility centers where one can get a roof of the right size over his head, access to a piano or a kiln, and to records, books, or slides. Schools, TV stations, theaters, and the like are designed primarily for use by professionals. Deschooling society means above all the denial of professional status for the second-oldest profession, namely teaching. The certification of teaching now constitutes an undue restriction of the right to free speech: the corporate structure and professional pretensions of journalism an undue restriction on the right to free press. Compulsory attendance rules interfere with free assembly. The deschooling of society is nothing less than a cultural mutation by which a people recovers the effective use of its Constitutional freedoms: learning and teaching by men who know that they are born free rather than treated to freedom. Most people learn most of the time when they do whatever they enjoy; most people are curious and want to give meaning to whatever they come in contact with; and most people are capable of personal intimate intercourse with others unless they are stupefied by inhuman work or turned off by schooling.

The fact that people in rich countries do not learn much on their own constitutes no proof to the contrary. Rather it is a consequence of life in an environment from which, paradoxically, they cannot learn much, precisely because it is so highly programed. They are constantly frustrated by the structure of contemporary society in which the facts on which decisions can be made have become elusive. They live in an environment in which tools that can be used for creative purposes have become luxuries, an environment in which channels of communication serve a few to talk to many.

A modern myth would make us believe that the sense of impotence with which most men live today is a consequence of technology that cannot but create huge systems. But it is not technology that makes systems huge, tools immensely powerful, channels of communication one-directional. Quite the contrary: Properly controlled, technology could provide each man with the ability to understand his environment better, to shape it powerfully with his own hands, and to permit him full intercommunication to a degree never before possible. Such an alternative use of technology constitutes the central alternative in education.

If a person is to grow up he needs, first of all, access to things, to places and to processes, to events and to records. He needs to see, to touch, to tinker with, to grasp whatever there is in a meaningful setting. This access is now largely denied. When knowledge became a commodity, it acquired the protections of private property, and thus a principle designed to guard personal intimacy became a rationale for declaring facts off limits for people without the proper credentials. In school teachers keep knowledge to themselves unless it fits into the day's program. The media inform, but exclude those things they regard as unfit to print. Information is locked into special languages, and specialized teachers live off its retranslation. Patents are protected by corporations, secrets are guarded by bureaucracies, and the power to keep others out of private preserves—be they cockpits, law offices, junkyards, or clinics—is jealously guarded by professions, institutions, and nations. Neither the political nor the professional structure of our societies, East and West, could withstand the elimination of the power to keep entire classes of people from facts that could serve them. The access to facts that I advocate goes far beyond truth in labeling. Access must be built into reality, while all we ask from advertising is a guarantee that it does not mislead. Access to reality constitutes a fundamental alternative in education to a system that only purports to teach *about* it.

Abolishing the right to corporate secrecy—even when professional opinion holds that this secrecy serves the common good—is, as shall presently appear, a much more radical political goal than the traditional demand for public ownership or control of the tools of production. The socialization of tools without the effective socialization of know-how in their use tends to put the knowledge-capitalist into the position formerly held by the financier. The technocrat's only claim to power is the stock he holds in some class of scarce and secret knowledge, and the best means to protect its value is a large and capital-intensive organization that renders access to know-how formidable and forbidding.

It does not take much time for the interested learner to acquire almost any skill that he wants to use. We tend to forget this in a society where professional teachers monopolize entrance into all fields, and thereby stamp teaching by uncertified individuals as quackery. There are few mechanical skills used in industry or research that are as demanding, complex, and dangerous as driving cars, a skill that most people quickly acquire from a peer. Not all people are suited for advanced logic, yet those who are make rapid progress if they are challenged to play mathematical games at an early age. One out of twenty kids in Cuernavaca can beat me at Wiff 'n' Proof after a couple of weeks' training. In four months all but a small percentage of motivated adults at our CIDOC center learn Spanish well enough to conduct academic business in the new language.

A first step toward opening up access to skills would be to provide various incentives for skilled individuals to share their knowledge. Inevitably, this would run counter to the interest of guilds and professions and unions. Yet, multiple apprenticeship is attractive: It provides everybody with an opportunity to learn something about almost anything. There is no reason why a person should not combine the ability to drive a car, repair telephones and toilets, act as a midwife, and function as an architectural draftsman. Special-interest groups and their disciplined consumers would, of course, claim that the public needs the protection of a professional guarantee. But this argument is now steadily being challenged by consumer protection associations. We have to take much more seriously the objection that economists raise to the radical socialization of skills: that "progress" will be impeded if knowledge—patents, skills, and all the rest—is democratized. Their argument can be faced only if we demonstrate to them the growth rate of futile diseconomies generated by any existing educational system.

Access to people willing to share their skills is no guarantee of learning. Such access is restricted not only by the monopoly of educational programs over learning and of unions over licensing but also by a technology of scarcity. The skills that count today are know-how in the use of highly specialized tools that were designed to be scarce. These tools produce goods or render services that everybody wants but only a few can enjoy, and which only a limited number of people know how to use. Only a few privileged individuals out of the total number of people who have a given disease ever benefit from the results of sophisticated medical technology, and even fewer doctors develop the skill to use it.

The same results of medical research have, however, also been employed to create a basic medical tool kit that permits Army and Navy medics, with only a few months of training, to obtain results, under battlefield conditions, that would have been beyond the expectations of full-fledged doctors during World War II. On an even simpler level any peasant girl could learn how to diagnose and treat most infections if medical scientists prepared dosages and instructions specifically for a given geographic area.

All these examples illustrate the fact that educational considerations alone suffice to demand a radical reduction of the professional structure that now impedes the mutual relationship between the scientist and the majority of people who want access to science. If this demand were heeded, all men could learn to use yesterday's tools, rendered more effective and durable by modern science, to create tomorrow's world.

Unfortunately, precisely the contrary trend prevails at present. I know a coastal area in South America where most people support themselves by fishing from small boats. The outboard motor is certainly the tool that has changed most dramatically the lives of these coastal fishermen. But in the area I have surveyed, half of all outboard motors that were purchased between 1945 and 1950 are still kept running by constant tinkering, while half the motors purchased in 1965 no longer run because they were not built to be repaired. Technological progress provides the majority of people with gadgets they cannot afford and deprives them of the simpler tools they need.

Metals, plastics, and ferro cement used in building have greatly improved since the 1940s and ought to provide more people the opportunity to create their own homes. But while in the United States, in 1948, more than 30 per cent of all one-family homes were owner-built, by the end of the 1960s the percentage of those who acted as their own contractors had dropped to less than 20 per cent.

The lowering of the skill level through so-called economic development becomes even more visible in Latin America. Here most people still build their own homes from floor to roof. Often they use mud, in the form of adobe, and thatchwork of unsurpassed utility in the moist, hot, and windy climate. In other places they make their dwellings out of cardboard, oildrums, and other industrial refuse. Instead of providing people with simple tools and highly standardized, durable, and easily repaired components, all governments have gone in for the mass production of low-cost buildings. It is clear that not one single country can afford to provide satisfactory modern dwelling units for the majority of its people. Yet, everywhere this policy makes it progressively more difficult for the majority to acquire the knowledge and skills they need to build better houses for themselves.

Educational considerations permit us to formulate a second fundamental characteristic that any post-industrial society must possess: a basic tool kit that by its very nature counteracts technocratic control. For educational reasons we must work toward a society in which scientific knowledge is incorporated in tools and components that can be used meaningfully in units small enough to be within the reach of all. Only such tools can socialize access to skills. Only such tools favor temporary associations among those who want to use them for a specific occasion. Only such tools allow specific goals to emerge in the process of their use, as any tinkerer knows. Only the combination of guaranteed access to facts and of limited power in most tools renders it possible to envisage a subsistence economy capable of incorporating the fruits of modern science.

The development of such a scientific subsistence economy is unquestionably to the advantage of the overwhelming majority of all people in poor countries. It is also the only alternative to progressive pollution, exploitation, and opaqueness in rich countries. But, as we have seen, the dethroning of the GNP cannot be achieved without simultaneously subverting GNE (Gross National Education—usually conceived as manpower capitalization). An egalitarian economy cannot exist in a society in which the right to produce is conferred by schools.

The feasibility of a modern subsistence economy does not depend on new scientific inventions. It depends primarily on the ability of a society to agree on fundamental, self-chosen anti-bureaucratic and anti-technocratic restraints.

These restraints can take many forms, but they will not work unless they touch the basic dimensions of life. (The decision of Congress against development of the supersonic transport plane is one of the most encouraging steps in the right direction.) The substance of these voluntary social restraints would be very simple matters that can be fully understood and judged by any prudent man. The issues at stake in the SST controversy provide a good example. All such restraints would be chosen to promote stable and equal enjoyment of scientific know-how. The French say that it takes a thousand years to educate a peasant to deal with a cow. It would not take two generations to help all people in Latin America or Africa to use and repair outboard motors, simple cars, pumps, medicine kits, and ferro cement machines if their design does not change every few years. And since a joyful life is one of constant meaningful intercourse with others in a meaningful environment, equal enjoyment does translate into equal education.

At present a consensus on austerity is difficult to imagine. The reason usually given for the impotence of the majority is stated in terms of political or economic class. What is not usually understood is that the new class structure of a schooled society is even more powerfully controlled by vested interests. No doubt an imperialist and capitalist organization of society provides the social structure within which a minority can have disproportionate influence over the effective opinion of the majority. But in a technocratic society the power of a minority of knowledge capitalists can prevent the formation of true public opinion through control of scientific know-how and the media of communication. Constitutional guarantees of free speech, free press, and free assembly were meant to ensure government by the people. Modern electronics, photo-offset presses, time-sharing computers, and telephones have in principle provided the hardware that could give an entirely new meaning to these freedoms. Unfortunately, these things are used in modern media to increase the power of knowledge-bankers to funnel their program-packages through international chains to more people, instead of being used to increase true networks that provide equal opportunity for encounter among the members of the majority.

Deschooling the culture and social structure requires the use of technology to make participatory politics possible. Only on the basis of a majority coalition can limits to secrecy and growing power be determined without dictatorship. We need a new environment in which growing up can be classless, or we will get a brave new world in which Big Brother educates us all.

Arthur Pearl

# 19. THE CASE FOR
# SCHOOLING AMERICA

Ivan Illich refuses to define his "desirable society" or to defend its
feasibility. Instead of setting forth a set of goals and the logic for
same, and a strategy that at least offers a promissory note for payoff,
he parades before us metaphor and hyperbole that are—when analyzed—either contradictory or trivial. Any dream of a good life
offered by a responsible critic should have at least: (1) its attributes
sufficiently spelled out so that advocates and opponents know what
they are arguing about; (2) its essence analyzed for ecological,
political, psychological, and economic reality (which, of course, could
then be debated); and (3) its political course laid out so that we
are alerted to the tactics and strategy needed to get us from where we
are to where we ought to be.

Illich doesn't come close. He is fuzzy about his "desirable society." He touches on freedom of the individual to learn whatever
he desires to learn; he touches on the question of universal and
unlimited access to the secrets and tools of the society. But he never
discusses the feasibility of his good society. He believes that by the
elimination of compulsory education, the good society will somehow
emerge.

Illich never tells us how his improved society will function
without institutions. Indeed, he in no way challenges my own belief
that no steps toward what he and I might well agree are the goals of
a "desirable society" can be taken without institutions. Public

Biographical information on Arthur Pearl has been given on page 69.

Source: Arthur Pearl, "The Case for Schooling America," *Social Policy* 2
(March–April 1972), pp. 51–52. Reprinted by permission. *Social Policy* is
published by Social Policy Corporation, New York, New York 10010.

schools will be basic to this institutional infrastructure directed toward widescale social benefits. Illich's call for deinstitutionalized schools in a deinstitutionalized society is nonsense, and dangerous to the extent that its simplicity is attractive.

> Deinstitutionalize a city and within a month that city will literally be buried in its garbage. To have a deinstitutionalized natural society in which man maintained himself through self-sufficient primitive hunting, fishing or gathering would require that we reduce the world's population to something less than 200 million people.

It remains true, however, that although schools do not run society, they are more resistant to society's attempt to run them than are most other institutions. The fact is that our schools are not monolithic; people do not emerge from them as sausages out of a meatpacking plant.

True educational reform inside and outside schools is really possible, then, because the schools themselves do not have an already established or predetermined monopolistic role. They offer a variety of experiences and interests and provide a place for increasing numbers of "radical" teachers to function. It is, after all, only among persons with many years of compulsory education that Ivan Illich has any following—and that is not an accidental occurrence. Schools develop intellectual opponents to injustice not because they are designed to, but because once a group of inquiring youths are compelled to interact with each other, a percentage will begin to question the values and direction of their society. Thus it was the students and teachers in public institutions who first questioned the war in Vietnam; and efforts to restrict them, though powerful, cannot succeed.

## OH, FOR A SCHOOLED SOCIETY!

It will not be easy to create schools with a democratically-oriented leadership that convinces rather than coerces people to acknowledge the importance of education. And yet that challenge cannot be avoided either by the dehumanizing experts of education (B. F. Skinner and the like) or the humanely oriented romanticists (Illich and his buddies). Universal education is necessary and must be organized because the threats to man's existence are universal. What we have come to regard as human rights can be guaranteed only within an institutional structure—societies with primitive institutions never even considered individual rights.

The rights of students must be considered within a context of social responsibility. If the student chooses to be in a classroom rather than a library, laboratory, park, museum, home, or pool hall, he must justify that or the other choices within the context of the goals of a desirable society. He must make a case, with logic and evidence, that he has fulfilled his obligations to other human beings; he has equal rights to require that teachers and colleagues justify their actions to him.

But when Illich speaks with the voice of pure freedom, he masks a conservative message: ". . . protect the autonomy of the learner— his private initiative to decide what he will learn and his inalienable right to learn what he likes rather than what is useful to somebody else." To learn what one likes is to learn prejudices. If there is one thing we know about human beings it is that they don't want to know what they don't want to know. Erich Fromm tried to get that truth across to us twenty years ago in *Escape from Freedom*. The important truths of today are painful truths. People will do everything they can to avoid them. Important truths will require enormous changes in attitudes and life-style. Education self-selected will be no education—we have such education currently available to us (it comes to us on half a dozen simultaneous channels on television), and there we find a Gresham's law of culture: bad drives out good, and the frivolous outdraws the serious.

The institutional school has not, of course, been relevant to producing a "desirable world"; that is why it must be reformed. Schools must go beyond merely raising the problems; instead they must begin to suggest real solutions—describe models and plans for peace, a universal quality of life, and equal opportunity, within the context of life styles that are ecologically sane. Rather than eradicate the public school, then, Illich ought to be directing his fire against the powerful institutions—the ones C. Wright Mills identified as military, industrial, and political—that block the progressive potential of the schooling process.

The public schools are clearly in desperate shape. Reform won't come easily, and we have a long way to go. Illich and other critics provide a useful function when they hammer away at the schools' inhumanity; but they become counterproductive when they offer nonsolutions and lose sight of the Gideon's army of radical public-school leaders whose growing number has greatly contributed to the clamor to do something about war, racism, poverty, and the destruction of earth during the past decade. Try to deinstitutionalize education as a symbol and the beginning of the deinstitutionalization of everything and you *reinstitute the law of the jungle*—which quickly breaks down into a new set of oppressive institutions. The same unfortunate situation holds true for attaining any of the other goals of a desirable society. Politics learned at the hands of Richard Daley, culture picked up at the feet of Johnny Carson, and interpersonal relations gleaned from gropings in the street are the alternatives to school. That these alternatives are already too characteristic of contemporary American society is not a reason for removing schools, but for reforming them.

# Discussion Questions and Activities

1. According to Illich, why have the schools failed? Explain why you accept or reject his diagnosis of the problem and his conclusions.

2. Illich rejects the three proposals for new educational institutions. If you do not see his viewpoint, state specific reasons.

3. What does he mean by the "hidden curriculum of the schools"? Do you think it actually has the pernicious effect that he attributes to it? Can you cite any examples of it from your own experience?

4. State your understanding of what Illich means by the statement that the hidden curriculum "translates learning from an activity into a commodity"?

5. While noting some limited benefits accruing from the work of educational reformers, Illich essentially rejects their approach to education. In what respect is his stance warranted?

6. How do today's schools deny the egalitarian society? What specific practices have you found which support this assertion?

7. Establishing a "free market" for education has, for Illich, certain advantages over the old system but also certain dangers. Explain his position on the "free market."

8. Why does deschooling society mean a denial of the professional status of teaching? Do you consider this to be a weakness of the deschooling position?

9. Is it true that society and its professionals do not allow the free access to information and tools that people need for their educational development? If so, is this lack of access as serious as Illich would have us believe? What do you believe could be done, short of deschooling society, to overcome this problem?

10. Does the evidence presented warrant the demand for a "radical reduction of the professional structure"? What would be your role in Illich's deschooled society?

11. Poll the students in class to determine who supports

and opposes Illich's position. Organize a debate among those who feel most strongly about his ideas.

12. Pearl states that every reformer's conception of the good life he hopes to bring about should fulfill three requirements. Is it actually the responsibility of the reformer to fulfill these three requirements, or only to state the general contours of the good life as he sees it? Should all reformers, in other words, provide a detailed blueprint?

13. Does Illich believe that "by the elimination of compulsory education, the good society will somehow emerge"? If so, what, if anything, is wrong with the belief?

14. Does Illich call for a deschooled society or a totally deinstitutionalized society? What is the difference between the two?

15. Is the argument sound that schools are not monopolistic, otherwise Illich's followers, and opponents of the Vietnam war, could not have been produced by them?

16. Human rights can only be guaranteed within an institutional structure. Is this a sound argument against Illich's position? What is your view of the relationship between institutions and human rights?

17. Pearl disagrees with Illich that students have an inalienable right to learn what they like, because, Pearl asserts, "to learn what one likes is to learn prejudices." Note the supporting reasons that Pearl gives and then determine which of the two positions is more sound.

18. Rather than eradicate public schools, Illich should direct his attention to the social institutions that impede the schools from realizing their full potential. State reasons to either accept or reject this statement.

# X.  The Pedagogy of Liberation

*Viewing education in an international perspective, we find that most of the world's peoples are destitute —ill-clothed, ill-fed, and ill-housed, and vast numbers have scarcely received the rudiments of an education.  These people frequently are unable to rise out of the condition, not only as a result of apathy and torpor that crushes their spirit but also because of exploitation by those in power.  Paulo Freire worked with the peasants of Brazil and fostered literacy by using materials that taught them the nature of their oppression and how it could best be overcome so that a new society could be created. His philosophy is a remarkable admixture of Marx and Marcuse, Mao and Che Guevara, Fromm and Christian love, all welded into an instrument for the transformation of the human condition.*

*By means of Egerton's notes we listen to conversations of workshop participants and observe how they project onto Freire their own hopes and fears. We overhear Freire as the man in dialogue with eager teachers—some frustrated, others seeking panaceas, and some who are open-minded.*

Paulo Freire

# 20. PEDAGOGY OF THE OPPRESSED

The pedagogy of the oppressed, as a humanist and libertarian pedagogy, has two distinct stages. In the first, the oppressed unveil the world of oppression and through the praxis commit themselves to its transformation. In the second stage, in which the reality of oppression has already been transformed, this pedagogy ceases to belong to the oppressed and becomes a pedagogy of all men in the process of permanent liberation. In both stages, it is always through action in depth that the culture of domination is culturally confronted.[10] In the first stage this confrontation occurs through the change in the way the oppressed perceive the world of oppression; in the second stage, through the expulsion of the myths created and developed in the old order, which like specters haunt the new structure emerging from the revolutionary transformation.

The pedagogy of the first stage must deal with the problem of the oppressed consciousness and the oppressor consciousness, the problem of men who oppress and men who suffer oppression. It must take into account their behavior, their view of the world, and their ethics. A particular problem is the duality of the oppressed: they are con-

Paulo Freire devoted seventeen years in devising and refining a program for basic literacy before he was imprisoned for several months after the military seized control of the Brazilian government in 1964. Leaving Brazil, he tested his program in Chile for the next five years. After a year at Harvard University, he became consultant to the World Council of Churches in Geneva. He is best known in English for his *Pedagogy of the Oppressed*.

[10] This appears to be the fundamental aspect of Mao's Cultural Revolution.

tradictory, divided beings, shaped by and existing in a concrete situation of oppression and violence.

Any situation in which "A" objectively exploits "B" or hinders
his pursuit of self-affirmation as a responsible person is one of oppression.  Such a situation in itself constitutes violence, even when
sweetened by false generosity, because it interferes with man's onto-
logical and historical vocation to be more fully human.  With the
establishment of a relationship of oppression, violence has *already*
begun.  Never in history has violence been initiated by the oppressed.
How could they be the initiators, if they themselves are the result of
violence?  How could they be the sponsors of something whose
objective inauguration called forth their existence as oppressed?
There would be no oppressed had there been no prior situation of
violence to establish their subjugation.

Violence is initiated by those who oppress, who exploit, who fail
to recognize others as persons—not by those who are oppressed,
exploited, and unrecognized.  It is not the unloved who initiate
disaffection, but those who cannot love because they love only themselves.  It is not the helpless, subject to terror, who initiate terror,
but the violent, who with their power create the concrete situation
which begets the "rejects of life."  It is not the tyrannized who
initiate despotism, but the tyrants.  It is not the despised who initiate
hatred, but those who despise.  It is not those whose humanity is
denied them who negate man, but those who denied that humanity
(thus negating their own as well).  Force is used not by those who
have become weak under the preponderance of the strong but by the
strong who have emasculated them.

For the oppressors, however, it is always the oppressed (whom
they obviously never call "the oppressed" but—depending on whether
they are fellow countrymen or not—"those people" or "the blind and
envious masses" or "savages" or "natives" or "subversives") who are
disaffected, who are "violent," "barbaric," "wicked," or "ferocious"
when they react to the violence of the oppressors.

Yet it is—paradoxical though it may seem—precisely in the
response of the oppressed to the violence of their oppressors that a
gesture of love may be found.  Consciously or unconsciously, the act
of rebellion by the oppressed (an act which is always, or nearly
always, as violent as the initial violence of the oppressors) can initiate
love.  Whereas the violence of the oppressors prevents the oppressed
from being fully human, the response of the latter to this violence is
grounded in the desire to pursue the right to be human.  As the

oppressors dehumanize others and violate their rights, they themselves also become dehumanized. As the oppressed, fighting to be human, take away the oppressors' power to dominate and suppress, they restore to the oppressors the humanity they had lost in the exercise of oppression.

It is only the oppressed who, by freeing themselves, can free their oppressors. The latter, as an oppressive class, can free neither others nor themselves. It is therefore essential that the oppressed wage the struggle to resolve the contradiction in which they are caught; and the contradiction will be resolved by the appearance of the new man: neither oppressor nor oppressed, but man in the process of liberation. If the goal of the oppressed is to become fully human, they will not achieve their goal by merely reversing the terms of the contradiction, by simply changing poles.

This may seem simplistic; it is not. Resolution of the oppressor-oppressed contradiction indeed implies the disappearance of the oppressors as a dominant class. However, the restraints imposed by the former oppressed on their oppressors, so that the latter cannot reassume their former position, do not constitute *oppression*. An act is oppressive only when it prevents men from being more fully human. Accordingly, these necessary restraints do not *in themselves* signify that yesterday's oppressed have become today's oppressors. Acts which prevent the restoration of the oppressive regime cannot be compared with those which create and maintain it, cannot be compared with those by which a few men deny the majority their right to be human. . . .

Critical and liberating dialogue, which presupposes action, must be carried on with the oppressed at whatever the stage of their struggle for liberation.[24] The content of that dialogue can and should vary in accordance with historical conditions and the level at which the oppressed perceive reality. But to substitute monologue, slogans, and communiques for dialogue is to attempt to liberate the oppressed with the instruments of domestication. Attempting to liberate the oppressed without their reflective participation in the act of liberation is to treat them as objects which must be saved from a burning building; it is to lead them into the populist pitfall and transform them into masses which can be manipulated. . . .

[24] Not in the open, of course; this would only provoke the fury of the oppressor and lead to still greater repression.

Through dialogue, the teacher-of-the-students and the students-of-the-teacher cease to exist and a new term emerges: teacher-student with students-teachers. The teacher is no longer merely the-one-who-teaches, but one who is himself taught in dialogue with the students, who in turn while being taught also teach. They become jointly responsible for a process in which all grow. In this process, arguments based on "authority" are no longer valid; in order to function, authority must be *on the side of* freedom, not *against* it. Here, no one teaches another, nor is anyone self-taught. Men teach each other, mediated by the world, by the cognizable objects which in banking education are "owned" by the teacher.

The banking concept (with its tendency to dichotomize everything) distinguishes two stages in the action of the educator. During the first, he cognizes a cognizable object while he prepares his lessons in his study or his laboratory; during the second, he expounds to his students about that object. The students are not called upon to know, but to memorize the contents narrated by the teacher. Nor do the students practice any act of cognition, since the object towards which that act should be directed is the property of the teacher rather than a medium evoking the critical reflection of both teacher and students. Hence in the name of the "preservation of culture and knowledge" we have a system which achieves neither true knowledge nor true culture.

The problem-posing method does not dichotomize the activity of the teacher-student: he is not "cognitive" at one point and "narrative" at another. He is always "cognitive," whether preparing a project or engaging in dialogue with the students. He does not regard cognizable objects as his private property, but as the object of reflection by himself and the students. In this way, the problem-posing educator constantly re-forms his reflections in the reflection of the students. The students—no longer docile listeners—are now critical co-investigators in dialogue with the teacher. The teacher presents the material to the students for their consideration, and re-considers his earlier considerations as the students express their own. The role of the problem-posing educator is to create, together with the students, the conditions under which knowledge at the level of the *doxa* is superseded by true knowledge, at the level of the *logos*.

Whereas banking education anesthetizes and inhibits creative power, problem-posing education involves a constant unveiling of reality. The former attempts to maintain the *submersion* of consciousness; the latter strives for the *emergence* of consciousness and *critical intervention* in reality.

Students, as they are increasingly posed with problems relating to themselves in the world and with the world, will feel increasingly challenged and obliged to respond to that challenge. Because they apprehend the challenge as interrelated to other problems within a total context, not as a theoretical question, the resulting comprehension tends to be increasingly critical and thus constantly less alienated. Their response to the challenge evokes new challenges, followed by new understandings; and gradually the students come to regard themselves as committed.

Education as the practice of freedom—as opposed to education as the practice of domination—denies that man is abstract, isolated, independent, and unattached to the world; it also denies that the world exists as a reality apart from men. Authentic reflection considers neither abstract man nor the world without men, but men in their relations with the world. In these relations consciousness and world are simultaneous: consciousness neither precedes the world nor follows it. . . .

Problem-posing education affirms men as beings in the process of *becoming*—as unfinished, uncompleted beings in and with a likewise unfinished reality. Indeed, in contrast to other animals who are unfinished, but not historical, men know themselves to be unfinished; they are aware of their incompletion. In this incompletion and this awareness lie the very roots of education as an exclusively human manifestation. The unfinished character of men and the transformational character of reality necessitate that education be an ongoing activity.

Education is thus constantly remade in the praxis. In order to *be*, it must *become*. Its "duration" (in the Bergsonian meaning of the word) is found in the interplay of the opposites *permanence* and *change*. The banking method emphasizes permanence and becomes reactionary; problem-posing education—which accepts neither a "well-behaved" present nor a predetermined future—roots itself in the dynamic present and becomes revolutionary.

Problem-posing education is revolutionary futurity. Hence it is prophetic (and, as such, hopeful). Hence, it corresponds to the historical nature of man. Hence, it affirms men as beings who transcend themselves, who move forward and look ahead, for whom immobility represents a fatal threat, for whom looking at the past must only be a means of understanding more clearly what and who they are so that they can more wisely build the future. Hence, it identifies with the movement which engages men as beings aware of their incompletion—an historical movement which has its point of departure, its Subjects and its objective.

The point of departure of the movement lies in men themselves. But since men do not exist apart from the world, apart from reality, the movement must begin with the men-world relationship. Accordingly, the point of departure must always be with men in the "here and now," which constitutes the situation within which they are submerged, from which they emerge, and in which they intervene. Only by starting from this situation—which determines their perception of it—can they begin to move. To do this authentically they must perceive their state not as fated and unalterable, but merely as limiting—and therefore challenging.

Whereas the banking method directly or indirectly reinforces men's fatalistic perception of their situation, the problem-posing method presents this very situation to them as a problem. As the situation becomes the object of their cognition, the naive or magical perception which produced their fatalism gives way to perception which is able to perceive itself even as it perceives reality, and can thus be critically objective about that reality.

A deepened consciousness of their situation leads men to apprehend that situation as an historical reality susceptible of transformation. Resignation gives way to the drive for transformation and inquiry, over which men feel themselves to be in control. If men, as historical beings necessarily engaged with other men in a movement of inquiry, did not control that movement, it would be (and is) a violation of men's humanity. Any situation in which some men prevent others from engaging in the process of inquiry is one of violence. The means used are not important; to alienate men from their own decision-making is to change them into objects.

This movement of inquiry must be directed towards humanization—man's historical vocation. The pursuit of full humanity, however, cannot be carried out in isolation or individualism, but only in fellowship and solidarity; therefore it cannot unfold in the antagonistic relations between oppressors and oppressed. No one can be authentically human while he prevents others from being so. . . .

Every thematic investigation which deepens historical awareness is thus really educational, while all authentic education investigates thinking. The more educators and the people investigate the people's thinking, and are thus jointly educated, the more they continue to investigate. Education and thematic investigation, in the problem-posing concept of education, are simply different moments of the same process.

In contrast with the antidialogical and non-communicative "deposits" of the banking method of education, the program content of the problem-posing method—dialogical par excellence—is constituted and organized by the students' view of the world, where their own generative themes are found. The content thus constantly expands and renews itself. The task of the dialogical teacher in an interdisciplinary team working on the thematic universe revealed by their investigation is to "re-present" that universe to the people from whom he first received it—and "re-present" it not as a lecture, but as a problem.

John Egerton

# 21. SEARCHING FOR FREIRE

**Friday.** We are at Penn Community Center for three days of talk about "Learning and Change." Freire is the chief drawing card, and about 60 invited guests are present. It is a motley group: young and old, male and female, black and white, urban and rural, establishment and antiestablishment. Most of them are southerners, and all are interested in education, whether as a livelihood, a means of salvation, or a subject of discontent.

John Egerton is a former contributing editor of *Saturday Review of Education.* Here, he reports the results of a workshop in which Freire was the focus of attention.
Source: John Egerton, "Searching for Friere," copyright 1973 by Saturday Review Co. First appeared in *Saturday Review,* March 10, 1973, pp. 32, 34–35. Used with permission.

Freire's reputation has preceded him. He is, says the literature, "one of the most controversial educational figures in contemporary Latin America," a man who "provides the educational means by which the revolutionary rank and file can be assembled," and a personal friend of Ivan Illich (they have had a profound influence on each other). The initiators of the conference have advised us that he "performs best and is happiest in small group discussions," that he "tires easily and should not be overscheduled," and that he dislikes speaking English for long periods and prefers using a "language facilitator"—a translator.

At the first session after dinner, Freire and his wife, Elza, are introduced but do not speak; the silence adds to the mysticism around him. "He is like a sponge," one of the National Council people tells a small group afterward. "He soaks up everything, learns from every experience, every encounter."

**Saturday.** We divide into four groups for daylong discussions of selected topics: institutional reform, community development, cultural development, and the education of children. Freire visits three of the groups, listening intently but saying little. Late in the day he joins the education group. The familiar questions have been asked: How can you combat an educational system that domesticates, indoctrinates, and acculturates children? How can children be given the freedom to grow and to learn? What should schools teach—values, skills, survival, political consciousness? Can the system be changed to serve the people? What are the alternatives to schools? How can people get the power to influence the educational process? These are questions with multiple answers, or perhaps they have no answers at all.

"Education is so bad; maybe we should just shut it down," says one woman. "But what's the alternative? There are not enough jobs and none at all for uneducated people. If we stop school now, we'll produce mass illiteracy and make people easier to manipulate by an oppressive dictatorship—look at Freire's Brazil."

"There is no realistic alternative to the public schools," a black man says. "All this talk about abandoning the system is just a middle-class copout by blacks and white alike. It's naive." And a young black woman responds: "I think it's just as naive and unrealistic to think the system will ever do what we want." The argument has come full circle. Freire listens but still says nothing. After dinner the entire group comes together again to hear summations of the four discussions. The sense of frustration so prevalent in the education group also is apparent in the other three. They, too, have trouble in defining terms and objectives. There has been talk of reform, evolution, radical change, revolution, but an air of restive disunity is in the room. When the last report is finished, it is finally Freire's turn to respond.

In spite of a full, gray beard and long hair curling over the collar of his coat, there is little in Freire's appearance that suggests mysticism. A short, slightly built man with an incipient middle-age spread, he wears glasses, slacks, ankle-high shoes, and a dark sweater under his jacket. His round face is accentuated by a receding hair-line, and he puffs deeply and frequently on filter-tip cigarettes as he speaks in English, gesturing for emphasis with his small hands.

The gist of Freire's remarks is that without a "global perspective" of oppression, people are apt to lose themselves "in the alienation of daily life." You can understand the effects of oppression, he says, without understanding the reasons for the oppression. "Maybe I am not right," he says. "You are Americans; you are dealing with the dough. But I think maybe you are too concerned with the rooms and not concerned enough with the whole house, the whole community, the world." He goes on about "the risk of losing the perception of totality," saying that people are too submerged in local problems, too fragmented. You can't deal with educational problems without having a clear political and ideological objective, he says. You have to organize, be clear who it is you are against, and know who the enemy is. It is the same the world over, he says.

Freire talks about television as a "tool of alienation," calling it "a beautiful instrument that transforms us into empty bodies that have to be filled with propaganda." It internalizes people, he says, forcing them to be silent and passive, "with the illusion that they can think critically, know what they want, have opinions." In reality, he says, "this is one of the most alienated of all countries. People know they are exploited and dominated, but they feel incapable of breaking down the dehumanizing wall."

What do we do about it? He answers his own question: We can accept the rules of the game, he says, and like everybody else, strive for success, spending our energies in pursuit of a house in the suburbs and a new car every year. Or we can try to escape by getting close to a few people and perhaps starting a commune, seeking to build an isolated little island of happiness.

But, he adds, we will probably fail if we join the rat race or try to escape from it or try to fight it in small, narrowly focused ways. What we must do is organize, get a broader view, not just of education but of the entire social, economic, political, and ideological superstructure: "You are concentrating on a crisis in education, when it is really the whole system that is dominating you. In my opinion, this is one of the faults of Illich." Illich, he implies, is a reformer, not a revolutionary. "Don't delude yourself into thinking you can overcome the dehumanizing reality which alienates you by attacking little problems," he says.

After 45 minutes Freire stops. There is a brief silence, and the chairman starts to adjourn the meeting. "Aren't we going to get to ask him any questions?" a voice asks from the circle. Freire nods assent. "You talk about the danger of being co-opted by the system," says the questioner, "but aren't you yourself living in the belly of the beast by working for the World Council of Churches?" Well, yes, Freire admits. "The World Council can't be the vanguard of the revolution. But I can't be in Brazil. I could be working for a university, but that's the establishment, too. We all have different roles to play. In three years in Geneva I have never felt restricted by the World Council in any way. I have no choice. Nevertheless, my contradiction continues to exist." When the meeting is over, the young man who had asked the question goes up to Freire and says, "From all the buildup you got, I thought you could walk on water." Freire laughs and says, "I appoint you to demythologize me."

**Sunday.** There were to have been caucuses, small groups formed around common interests, but they don't materialize. Everybody wants to talk to Freire, to get down to cases. So Freire talks again to the entire group, for just over an hour. He talks about the time of praxis, which he defines as reflection followed by action; he disdains "reformist tactics"; he speaks of Marxian analysis, of dialectic, of a liberating pedagogy. He makes several points repeatedly: Education is never neutral. Education is a shared process between teacher and students, a creative act in which all parties both teach and learn. Verbal revolutionaries who talk but never act are false prophets. Students are not empty containers to be filled by teachers. Education must be grounded in political and ideological choice.

There is a coffee break. "If education is a shared process, then why are we not sharing? Why is he lecturing to us?" a disgruntled man asks. After the break, four or five people engage Freire and his interpreter in a conversation away from the larger group. Part of the exchange goes like this:

**Q:** *You are known in this country as an educator, an exile, and a radical. How do you describe yourself?  Are you, first of all, an educator?*

**A:** I would not say that I am an educator, apart from a person who has a political identity. If I responded affirmatively and said I am an educator by profession, then I would be admitting a separation of my profession and my political identity. Perhaps the best way to respond would be to say that I am becoming an educator with a political identity.

**Q:** *Could it be that your reputation is based on your exile? If you were still in Brazil, still involved in teaching adult literacy, might you not be just one of many people trying to bring about radical change in education—another religious, middle-class reformer?*

**A:** If I were in Brazil today, I would be silenced. I would perhaps be surviving by selling bananas. I could not have written *Pedagogy* —and, very possibly, I would not have become known.

**Q:** *If you were an American and not a Brazilian, do you think you would have a reputation as a revolutionary?*

**A:** That's a difficult question to answer. If I were an American, I might have a different perception of the problems. But that doesn't mean I wouldn't have an advanced ideological position. A young American educator whom I consider to have one of the greatest perceptions of education today is Jonathan Kozol. His book *Free Schools* is a beautiful book. Kozol is becoming more and more of a radical in our sense, not just in the American sense. He is not a naive man—he knows that free schools cannot change reality here; they cannot become the avant-garde of revolution in this country. But he sees them as one of the ways to proceed in this society. I would like to establish a working relationship with this man.

**Q:** *What would you do about the masses of children who cannot be accommodated by free schools such as Kozol talks about?*

**A:** We have many different tasks, tools, areas to work in. What is important is to organize these different tasks. We have to take advantage of the opportunity to act in this country and develop a thorough study of political education. We have to have political organization and political leadership of national stature. The problem you have here is the same as the problem in Latin America—possibly it is even greater here. The ideological divergences between the various revolutionary groups are enormous, and even within these groups there are great differences. What has to be done in this country is to effect a relative unification among the various revolutionary groups to develop a strategy and tactic for the political education of the entire country. But what happens is that blacks, Chicanos, and Puerto Ricans try to organize by themselves. They are not, by themselves, a social class. Sooner or later these groups have to become conscious of class, or else the revolution doesn't happen. Ideological and political unity is essential.

**Q:** *Are you saying, then, that it is a hopeless thing?*

**A:** No, no. On the contrary, I am optimistic. But we fight among ourselves while the right wing is united. For example, in Latin America I am considered a reactionary by a lot of people. They classify me as a bourgeois. They are helping the establishment by doing that. We have to unify. But it is very difficult. The establishment has a fantastic ability to popularize rebellion—it begins now, and two months later it runs the risk of becoming a hobby.

The conversation has lasted for two hours. Although those who took part feel a start has been made toward finding Freire, most of the people at the conference have been excluded and are not happy about it. After lunch a young Brazilian in Freire's traveling party shows a two-reel film about the torture of Brazilian revolutionaries and follows it up with a talk. When he finishes, Freire is gone for a rest. The people drift back to their quarters, grumbling, and before supper about half of them organize caucuses.

The criticisms tumble out: It has become fashionable among romantic radicals in this country to read and talk about Illich and Freire. But Freire is no more radical than most of us. There is no originality in what he says—it's the same old rap. He has lectured us, criticized our narrow focus on small problems, but his alternative —the global perspective—is stale rhetoric. He's a political and ideological theoretician, not an educator. There is nothing concrete and specific in what he says. One participant sums it up: "I don't know how Paulo reacts as a person to anything."

There is an assembly after the evening meal, and caucus spokesmen read the grievances and suggestions. Freire, showing frustrations of his own by now, reacts somewhat testily in Portuguese.

"There is apparently a very profound difference between the way I see the objectives of the workshop and the way you see them," he begins. "To me, it is just a little moment in the total process of learning and not a factory for solutions to problems." He goes on to say the workshop schedule is too demanding—"it looks like the schedule for a presidential campaign"—and adds: "When I accepted this invitation, I never thought of myself as coming to the United States to teach Americans how to liberate themselves or to learn how to liberate myself. You have your own problem, and it can't be solved in three days. It took centuries to get in this mess. A workshop is not a pill you take to change attitudes. If I had the formulas for liberation, I'd have gone back to Brazil long ago. I've learned to assume a humble attitude in the face of such enormous problems. Liberation is not a question of technique. If it were, it would be easy —just learn the formulas and apply them. Liberation is a political question. It implies having power, taking power, changing the structures of power. If I had simply discussed the problems of schools, it would have gotten us nowhere. I have tried to respond globally. You are waiting for the guru, the professor, waiting for the last word. I came here not to teach—not to give you formulas but to share something with you. I came here as an unfinished human being and not as a god."

It is easily his best performance of the weekend. A white woman speaks up: "We have all been frustrated. But maybe our days here have been a very real sort of workshop, a laboratory of Paulo's process in action." Then a black woman: "We have invited this man here and crucified him. He said what we needed to hear, but we didn't listen. I'm ashamed of this group. Paulo doesn't have to apologize to anyone. This is a dishonest conference." Others are not as convinced. "He didn't walk on water," says one, "but he showed us the nail holes in his hands." And another: "I still think the criticisms are valid, and he didn't deal with them."

**Monday.** Freire meets with a small group at breakfast, listens to the members talk about their problems, offers a few general comments and suggestions. "I don't have too many hopes that within your local school system you will be able to do a great deal. But do what you can. And beyond that there are a great many things you can do outside."

There is one final session, at which Freire talks about the adult literacy program that he organized in Brazil. After an hour or so he stops. Without further questions from the floor, the meeting is dismissed; the weekend ends.

"I came here to get some help—some ideas, some inspiration," a young man says, "—and I got it. It's right here in my notebook. I'm satisfied."

"I didn't get much from Freire," says another, "but I met a lot of very interesting people, and I learned a lot from them. At least I know a lot of people are trying to do the same thing I am. Maybe we can help each other."

"It was an impossible situation for Paulo," says a third. "Our expectations were too high. We were expecting some kind of all-wise guru. He could never have satisfied everybody, no matter what he said or did. Personally, I found him warm and affable, with a sense of humor."

"The rhetoric of revolution turns me off," says someone else.

Freire and his traveling party leave for a weekend conference in Phoenix, with an intermediate stop in the Mississippi delta region. After that there is Seattle and Chicago and New York and finally the return to Geneva. It is Paulo's search for America. And the Americans at Penn Center, their search for Paulo having ended on a mixed note of disillusionment and discovery, go back to their community organizations, their classrooms, their alternative schools, their day care centers, their school boards, their church agencies, to resume the search for ways to make a difference.

# Discussion Questions and Activities

1. Once the oppressed perceive their condition and apprehend the world of oppression, what action would you expect them to take toward their oppressors?

2. Applying Freire's conception of oppression, what groups have you known that you consider oppressed?

3. Why should teacher and student roles not be so fixed that a person invariably is either a teacher or a student?

4. Why is the problem-posing method superior to the banking concept? What distinctive features, if any, do you find in the method?

5. What conception of man does Freire hold? Does it differ from your conception? Clarify any differences and explain why you still believe your conception to be better.

6. How does Freire utilize the student's view of the world in his problem-posing method?

7. What are the many reasons why teachers attend workshops? Were the reasons any different in this particular workshop?

8. Analyze the hopes and fears that the participants projected onto Freire.

9. Some were pleased, others left disappointed. What expectations of the participants toward Freire seemed unreasonable? Explain.

10. Did the workshop demonstrate that Freire is not an outstanding educator? What weaknesses did it show? Does his humanity shine through?

11. If you had been at the workshop, how would you have participated in order to gain the greatest educational value?

# Part Two

## INNOVATIONS AND ALTERNATIVES

## INTRODUCTION

*As pointed out in Part One, recent years have been marked by wide-spread dissatisfaction with public education and numerous attempts to find more successful approaches to educating the young. Our schools have frequently been the focal point of controversy and these controversies have been placed in bold relief by the mass media. It is true that public schools, by the very nature of the fact that they are public institutions, are subject to scrutiny. At present, there is no single set of aims or widespread agreement on the priorities for public education; therefore, one can expect numerous innovations and new alternatives to be espoused.*

*In light of the problems that education faces today, it is natural that educators would seek to provide innovations and alternatives. By innovations, we mean any new programs, organizational changes, or modifications in the teaching-learning process that marks a departure from existing practices. Among the prominent innovations which will be discussed in this section are: behavioral objectives, computer-assisted instruction, nongraded schools, accountability, and performance contracting. These are generally considered among the most important innovations in public education today.*

*By "alternatives," we mean those proposals and programs which represent options to the public schools. In other words, such proposals would entail providing new educational opportunities outside the public school system. The major alternatives today are the voucher system and the free school movement. In contrast to the past when there was little questioning of the fact that public schools could do the job with which they were entrusted, some reformers and parents today believe that the public schools have failed, that they exercise a monopoly, and that alternatives to the established system must be made available.*

*Why are some innovations widely adopted while others are not? Why do some innovations and alternatives succeed and others fail? When clear thinking leads those in charge of programs to understand what steps to take, success is certain. When ignorance or inalertness or doubts accompany decisions, failure is most likely to result. While it is impossible to give definitive cues, we can illuminate some of the factors which need to be carefully considered before final decisions are made regarding employment of certain innovations or alternatives.*

*An innovation may prove successful when there is positive involvement of those who are expected to implement the plan. Interested and informed teachers and staff count heavily. One reason the curriculum reforms of the 1950's and 1960's failed to bring about the great transformations that the supporters anticipated was that scholars who devised the new curricula seldom involved classroom teachers in the development process.*

*Some innovations, before they can be put into operation, demand considerable retraining. The Dalton and Winnetka plans, team teaching, and the core curriculum all demanded retraining to varying degree.*

*Obviously innovations will not succeed if they are inadequately financed, but we may wonder what constitutes adequate financial support. For instance, some educators claim that compulsory education, in spite of the large sums granted, needs many billions of dollars more to succeed. On the other hand, as under the Elementary and Secondary Act passed in 1965, much new equipment was provided the schools, but it was found that the equipment went unused in some cases because teachers were not trained to handle it.*

*Some programs are not accepted because they run counter to prevailing philosophies and beliefs. This is especially evident in the case of A. S. Neill's school, Summerhill, where his principles of education are disapproved of by most parents and many teachers. However, although Summerhill will not serve as a total model for other schools, a few of its practices can be borrowed.*

*Before innovations can achieve their intended results, they must be properly planned and organized before implementation. Some compensatory education programs did not receive sufficient attention in these areas before they were set up; hence a few observers claim that this weakness led to their falling short of their intended objectives.*

*While educators may be given a free hand in introducing new changes in organization, curriculum, or teaching, the public may well become aroused and intervene if the change seems to them too radical or they do not understand the reasoning behind it. A rather radical change was the passage of compulsory education laws. Some parents expected their children to work; other parents did not see the need for a high school education.*

*In some cases innovations are improperly utilized. With educational television we have a medium where the best teachers can use new approaches that fully exploit the medium's potential. Unfortunately, in a number of cases the same lecture format found in traditional classrooms is employed. While not everyone would agree with McLuhan that the medium is the message, one must know his medium well in order to exploit its potentials.*

*It is easier to add a completely new structure than greatly change the internal organization of the present one. The addition of the junior college was successful not only because a need for its establishment was convincingly conveyed to the public, but also because it did not entail retraining high school teachers or dramatically alter administrative policies. A great deal of tact and intelligence are required for introducing many innovations or for gaining support for a certain alternative.*

*The quality of the staff administering any program is always a key factor in the success of that program; an alert, dedicated staff is priceless.*

*Finally, what we have done is to look at the meaning of innovations and alternatives and at some of the more prominent reasons why some innovations and alternatives may gain widespread adoption and prove successful. In light of these ideas, coupled with your own reasoning and experience, it may prove valuable as you read about the different innovations and alternatives, their virtues and weaknesses, to determine whether a particular innovation or alternative should be adopted in your own school system or community.*

# XI.   Behavioral Objectives

*Proponents of behavioral objectives claim that the old, traditional way of stating objectives resulted in statements so vague and ambiguous that it was difficult to know to what extent students had achieved the objectives.   For instance, the objective, "to learn to appreciate science," could lead ten different teachers to prepare ten quite different lessons.   Behavioral objectives are designed to relieve the uncertainty for the student in his learning activities because he supposedly knows exactly what he is expected to do, has evidence when he has fulfilled the objective, and knows the extent to which he has done so.   Teachers are also supposed to know exactly where they stand and can plan and evaluate learning activities with greater precision.   They are also in a position to make more accurate reports of pupil progress to the principal and to parents.*

*While proponents of behavioral objectives viewed their widespread adoption as means by which the teaching-learning process could be greatly improved, a host of critics arose to challenge this conviction.   Their criticisms covered the entire gamut of possible weaknesses: faulty theoretical assumptions, needless restrictions and controls on teaching and learning, conceptual confusion, lack of feasibility, and untoward consequences from their use.   Most of the salient shortcomings are delineated in the selection by George F. Kneller.*

Robert M. Gagné

# 22. BEHAVIORAL OBJECTIVES? YES!

Few people who are professionally concerned with education in the United States are unacquainted with "behavioral objectives." Knowledge of this term and its meaning has become widespread. It is therefore timely to pose a question which inquires about the need for behavioral objectives, the possible uses they may have, and the educational functions that may be conceived for them.

## NATURE OF INSTRUCTIONAL OBJECTIVES

The statement of a behavioral objective is intended to communicate (to a specified recipient or group of recipients) the outcome of some unit of instruction. One assumes that the general purpose of instruction is learning on the part of the student. It is natural enough, therefore, that one should attempt to identify the outcome of learning as something the student is able to do following instruction which he was unable to do before instruction. When one is able to express

Robert M. Gagné, Professor of Educational Research and Testing at Florida State University, presents a case for using behavioral objectives. He has served as a consultant to the U.S. Office of Education and the American Psychological Association. His books include *Education, Learning, and Individual Differences, Learning Research and School Subjects* (co-editor), and *The Conditions of Learning.*
Source: Robert M. Gagné, "Behavioral Objectives? Yes!" *Educational Leadership*, vol. 29, no. 5 (February 1972), pp. 394–396. Reprinted with permission of the Association for Supervision and Curriculum Development and Robert M. Gagné. Copyright © 1972 by the Association for Supervision and Curriculum Development.

the effects of instruction in this way, by describing observable performances of the learner, the clarity of objective statements is at a maximum. As a consequence, the reliability of communication of instructional objectives also reaches its highest level.

To some teachers and educational scholars, it appears at least equally natural to try to identify the outcomes of learning in terms of what capability the learner has gained as a result of instruction, rather than in terms of the performance he is able to do. We therefore frequently encounter such terms as "knowledge," "understanding," "appreciation," and others of this sort which seem to have the purpose of identifying learned capabilities or dispositions. Mager (1962) and a number of other writers have pointed out the ambiguity of these terms, and the unreliability of communications in which they are used.

Actually, I am inclined to argue that a complete statement of an instructional objective, designed to serve all of its communicative purposes, needs to contain an identification of *both* the type of capability acquired as a result of learning, and also the specific performance by means of which this capability can be confirmed (cf. Gagné, 1971a). Examples can readily be given to show that perfectly good "behavioral" verbs (such as "types," as in "types a letter") are also subject to more than one interpretation. For example, has the individual learned to "copy" a letter, or to "compose" a letter? The fact that no one would disagree that these two activities are somehow different, even though both are describable by the behavior of "typing," clearly indicates the need for descriptions of what has been learned which include more than observable human actions. Complete instructional objectives need to identify the capability learned, as well as the performance which such a capability makes possible.

The implications of this view are not trivial. If in fact such terms as "knowledge" and "understanding" are ambiguous, then we must either redefine them, or propose some new terms to describe learned capabilities which can be more precisely defined. My suggestion has been to take the latter course, and I have proposed that the five major categories representing "what is learned" are motor skills, verbal information, intellectual skills, cognitive strategies, and attitudes (Gagné, 1971b). Completing the example used previously, the statement of the objective would be "Given a set of handwritten notes, *generates* (implies the intellectual skill which is to be learned) a letter *by typing* (identifies the specific action used)."

The alternatives to such "behavioral" statements have many defects, as Mager (1962) and other writers have emphasized. However they may be expanded or embellished, statements describing the *content* of instructional presentations invariably fail to provide the needed communications. The fact that a textbook, or a film, or a talk by a teacher, presents "the concept of the family" is an inadequate communication of the intended learning outcome, and cannot be made adequate simply by adding more detail. The critical missing elements in any such descriptions of instruction are the related ideas of (a) what the student will have learned from instruction, and (b) what class of performances he will then be able to exhibit.

## USES OF BEHAVIORAL OBJECTIVES BY SCHOOLS

Statements describing instructional objectives have the primary purpose of *communicating*. Assuming that education has the form of an organized system, communication of its intended and actual outcomes is necessary, among and between the designers of instructional materials, the planners of courses and programs, the teachers, the students, and the parents. In order for the process of education to serve the purpose of learning, communications of these various sorts must take place. When any of them is omitted, education becomes to a diminished degree a systematic enterprise having the purpose of accomplishing certain societal goals pertaining to "the educated adult." There may be those who would argue that education should not serve such goals. Obviously, I disagree, but cannot here devote space to my reasons.

Some of the most important ways in which the various communications about objectives may be used by schools are indicated by the following brief outlines:

1. *The instructional designer to the course planner.* This set of communications enables the person who is planning a course with predetermined goals to select materials which can accomplish the desired outcomes. For example, if a course in junior high science has the goal of "teaching students to think scientifically," the planner will be seeking a set of materials which emphasize the learning of intellectual skills and cognitive strategies, having objectives such as "generates and tests hypotheses relating plant growth to environmental variables."

In contrast, if the goals of such a course are "to convey a scientific view of the earth's ecology," the curriculum planner will likely seek materials devoted to the learning of organized information, exhibited by such objectives as "describes how the content of carbon dioxide in the air affects the supply of underground water."

2. *The designer or planner to the teacher.* Communications of objectives to the teacher enable the latter to choose appropriate ways of delivering instruction, and also ways of assessing its effectiveness. As an example, a teacher of foreign language who adopts the objective, "pronounces French words containing the uvular 'r,' " is able (or should be able) to select a form of instruction providing practice in pronunciation of French words containing "r," and to reject as inappropriate for this objective a lecture on "the use of the uvular 'r' in French words."

Additionally, this communication of an objective makes apparent to the teacher how the outcome of instruction must be assessed. In this case, the choice would need to be the observation of oral pronunciation of French words by the student, and could not be, for instance, a multiple-choice test containing questions such as "which of the following French words has a uvular 'r'?"

3. *The teacher to the student.* There are many instructional situations in which the learning outcome expected is quite apparent to the student, because of his experience with similar instruction. For example, if the course is mathematics, and the topic changes from the addition of fractions to the multiplication of fractions, it is highly likely that the naming of the topic will itself be sufficient to imply the objective.

However, there are also many situations in which the objective may not be at all apparent. A topic on "Ohm's Law," for example, may not make apparent by its title whether the student is expected to recognize Ohm's Law, to state it, to substitute values in it, or to apply it to some electric circuits. It is reasonable to suppose that a student who knows what the objective is will be able to approach the task of learning with an advantage over one who does not.

4. *The teacher or principal to the parent.* It is indeed somewhat surprising that parents have stood still for "grades" for such a long period of time, considering the deplorably small amount of information they convey. If the trend toward "accountability" continues, grades will have to go. Teachers cannot be held accountable for A's, B's, and C's—in fact, grades are inimical to any system of account-

ability. It seems likely, therefore, that the basis for accountability will be the instructional objective. Since this must express a learning outcome, it must presumably be expressed in behavioral terms. Several different forms of accountability systems appear to be feasible; objectives would seem to be necessary for any or all of them.

These appear to be the major communication functions which schools need to carry out if they are engaged in systematically promoting learning. Each of these instances of communication requires accurate and reliable statements of the *outcomes of learning*, if it is to be effective. Such outcomes may be described, accurately and reliably, by means of statements which identify a) the capability to be learned, and b) the class of performances by means of which the capability is exhibited. There appears to me to be no alternative to the use of "behavioral objectives," defined as in the previous sentence, to perform these essential functions of communication.

## REFERENCES

**R. M. Gagné.** "Defining Objectives for Six Varieties of Learning." Washington, D.C.: American Educational Research Association, 1971a. (Cassette tape.)

**R. M. Gagné.** "Instruction Based on Research in Learning." *Engineering Education* 61: 519–23; 1971b.

**R. F. Mager.** *Preparing Instructional Objectives.* Belmont, California: Fearon Publishers, Inc., 1962.

George F. Kneller

# 23. BEHAVIORAL OBJECTIVES?
# NO!

The use of behavioral objectives in instruction is characteristic of a culture which sets a high value on efficiency and productivity. Such a culture seeks to measure accomplishment in standard units. Theoretical justification for behavioral objectives comes from behavioral psychology (Kendler, 1959, p. 179). This type of psychology defines learning as behavior that is changed in conformity with predicted, measurable outcomes and with little or no measurable "waste."

Teacher education institutions that advocate the use of behavioral objectives transmit methods of instruction that are standardized, empirically tested, and aim at measurable results. Such methods work best in school systems that are highly sensitive to the economic and behavioral determinants of educational practice.

## ANALYSIS

This approach to instruction rests on assumptions about human behavior that are reductionist, deterministic, and physicalist. It is op-

George F. Kneller, Professor of Education at the University of California at Los Angeles, is an educational philosopher who has written on a wide range of subjects in the foundations of education. He was educated at Clark University, Yale University, and the University of London, and also served on the faculties of the latter two institutions. Holder of honorary degrees from Sheffield and Heidelberg Universities, his books include *Educational Philosophy of National Socialism, Education of the Mexican Nation, Higher Learning in Britain, Existentialism and Education, Educational Anthropology, The Art and Science of Creativity,* and *Logic and Language of Education.*
Source: George F. Kneller, "Behavioral Objectives? No!" *Educational Leadership,* vol. 29, no. 5 (February 1972), pp. 397–400. Reprinted with permission of the Association for Supervision and Curriculum Development and George F. Kneller. Copyright © 1972 by the Association for Supervision and Curriculum Development.

posed to the view that learning is self-directed, unstructured, and in large part unpredictable.

Advocates of the behavioral approach deny these two points (Popham, 1968; Block, 1971). Behavior, they say, covers a wide range of experience, including creativity, imagination, even serendipity. Nor need objectives be fixed; they can be modified, adjusted to individuals, even abandoned in favor of others (Baker, 1968; Block, 1971, p. 291). But if so, if the terms "behavior" and "objectives" can be made to mean many different things, what things could they not mean? If a term is to have a clear-cut meaning, we must at least be able to define its contradictory.[1]

Many advocates now speak of "instructional" rather than "behavioral" objectives (Mager, 1962). Nevertheless, one's notion of instruction depends on assumptions about the nature of the mind and of the persons involved in the instructional process (Noddings, 1971, p. 40). The new term may imply a more modest approach to instruction and force us to concentrate on matters more central to education. Yet learning still is conceived as a series of measurable responses to carefully prearranged stimuli (Steg, 1971). The sameness of individuals is judged to matter more than their differences; schooling is systems-oriented; adjustment to the curriculum is presupposed; replication is prized; and computer-assisted instruction is cordially welcomed (Broudy, 1970, p. 49; Dreyfus, 1967, pp. 13–33).

It is claimed that, using behavioral objectives, a teacher can teach an entire class and cater to individual differences as well (Block, 1971). He can do so, it is said, either by adapting predetermined objectives to individuals or by composing a special set of objectives for each member of the class. However, this proud claim entails that the teacher must a) handle a staggering number of objectives,[2] b) accept a scientific theory of human behavior which tends

---

[1] The meaning of "behavior" becomes more complicated still when, in relation to learning, it is stratified according to dispositions. Learning defined as changed behavior then includes changes in *dispositions* to behave. See: James E. McClellan. "B. F. Skinner's Philosophy of Human Nature." *Studies in Philosophy and Education* 4: 307–32; 1966; and L. B. Daniels. "Behavior Strata and Learning." *Educational Theory* 20 (4): 377–86; Fall 1970. A satisfactory theory of human behavior has yet to be proposed.

[2] Behavioral objectivists maintain that the number of objectives for a single course could run as high as two thousand, if the teacher sought to cover everything. If there were 30 students in a class, the number of individual objectives would amount to as many as sixty thousand. The high school teacher of 150 students would be handling millions of objectives—conceivably. Given the behaviorists' claim that behavior includes everything that can occur

to exclude individualized (idiosyncratic) learning, and c) act on the false assumption that learning, knowing, and behaving are the same process.

As regards c), not only are there many kinds of learning, pacing being only one of them, there are also many kinds of knowing and behaving. These processes, psychologically speaking, are separate and distinct. The subject is too complex to be argued here, but this much may be said: Learning leads to no particular behavior. It is impossible to coordinate learning or knowing with behaving, because there is no theory which interrelates these phenomena, and consequently there is no way of understanding how their putative instances might be brought into relation in actual practice (Deese, 1969, pp. 516–17). To use behavioral objectives in individualized instruction is to overlook the essential differences between individual learning, knowing, and behaving.

Behavioral objectivists are apt to be scornful of teachers who refuse to adopt clearly specified goals. This refusal, we are told, is partly responsible for the "present failure" of American education (Popham, 1968). I do not see how this could be shown to be the case. I am still less impressed by the claim that if we adopted behavioral objectives, we would solve most of our instructional problems.

All depends on what one considers good teaching and learning to be. Teachers might be held more "strictly" accountable, learning might be evaluated more "reliably," and parents might perceive their children's achievements more "accurately"—but only if teaching and learning are drastically circumscribed. Here is the heart of the matter. Undoubtedly, the process of education can be more tightly controlled, most simply by giving everyone less freedom of choice. This suits the behavioral objectivist, because his philosophy is one of control, but it does not suit educators of other persuasions.

## SPECULATION

Under what circumstances may schools be said to "need" behavioral objectives? For one thing, such objectives can be used to define and

---

in a learning situation, these figures are plausible enough. Block (1971, p. 292) correctly observes that the computer has a tremendous capacity to tailor-make programs. Item banks could be constructed and stored. Yet this of course would require that the teacher specify goals in appropriate computer terms.

measure accomplishment in those basic intellectual abilities that all students need if they are to pass successfully from one learning experience to another.   Failure by a student to acquire a basic skill may, if uncorrected, hinder all his future learning and so his whole attitude toward education.   The young man who desires to be a master mechanic must first acquire the skills of an apprentice, and then of a journeyman.   He cannot acquire them unless he can read, write, and compute.   A long history of painful, unsuccessful learning experiences can severely damage a student's self-concept, his personality development, and his entire life style (Block, 1971, pp. 297–98).

That many of our youth are damaged in this way, especially in the elementary school, is distressingly obvious.   The school has a clear responsibility to ensure that *all* students succeed in learning basic skills.   In order to meet this responsibility, the school must possess a schedule of clearly specified objectives for all students to achieve, together with adequate instruments for measuring what is achieved.   Every student must know concretely and specifically what he is accomplishing relative to a) what may reasonably be expected of him, and b) what his peers are achieving.

## "SPECIFIED" OBJECTIVES

The objectives I suggest are "specified" rather than "behavioral." They are chosen, or specified, by the school according to its own philosophy of education, and they are specified only for certain subject matter which the school considers basic.[3]   Certain specific content (or skills) could be required of all students at certain levels, and the students could be tested on how well they had acquired it.   It would be the sort of content on which it is fairly easy to test in accordance with minimum standards of achievement.

Yet at another level, a level at which standardization is difficult, impossible, or undesirable, the individual teacher should specify objectives, to be achieved by either the individual student or groups of students, in accordance with (a) a theory of knowledge and value

---

[3] I agree with Maccia (1962) and Steg (1971) that although some learning goals can be specified, we should give wide play to the discovery impulse in learning.   Much knowledge may be set out for the student to acquire.   Yet the teacher must also open the gates for students both to acquire knowledge that interests them personally and to inquire beyond the knowledge we now have.

adopted by the teacher himself, and (b) the talents and choices of the student. Take two subjects where rigorous evaluation is quite impossible, art and music. The teacher might perhaps stipulate that a certain number and kind of songs be learned, that at least one song be composed, and that a symphony be analyzed. He might also stipulate that a number of drawings be made, and that one essay be written on a painting and another on an art movement such as dadaism or impressionism. In teaching these and other subjects, the teacher should be guided by a defensible philosophy and psychology of learning and instruction.[4]

Ultimately, however, it is not the schools but the teachers who must decide what objectives should be specified, and they must do so as individuals, taking their students into consideration. They must therefore acquire the knowledge and skills that are needed to specify educational objectives and evaluate the results obtained. Behavioral objectivists can help by providing models to spur investigation. Yet if these models are adopted uncritically by the rank and file of teachers, education will decline into an inauthentic and spiritless conditioning.

For, properly conceived, education is a dialogue between persons in the community of the school, a dialogue in which the teacher encourages the student to enter into acts of learning that fulfill him personally. This is education at its finest, and the program of the behavioral objectivist has very little place in it.

## REFERENCES

**Eva Baker.** *Defining Content for Objectives.* Los Angeles: Vincet Associates, 1968.

**James H. Block.** "Criterion-Referenced Measurements: Potential." *School Review* 79 (2): 289–98; February 1971.

[4] On learning goals and knowledge considerations, see Maccia (1962) and Steg (1971). Maccia shows that knowledge is an open system, and Steg warns against using objectives as anything more than a means for focusing purposes: "They must never become the overriding concern of education." Although both writers deal primarily with teaching machines, they are concerned with means by which students can create knowledge (and values, for that matter) instead of simply absorbing it. Learning, says Steg, is "the possibility of *going outside* a frame of activity" (p. 49). "We must consider logical goodness," says Maccia, "in relation to [new] knowing as well as in relation to knowledge" (p. 238).

**Harry S. Broudy.** "Can Research Escape the Dogma of Behavioral Objectives?" *School Review* 79 (1): 43–56; November 1970.

**L. B. Daniels.** "Behavior Strata and Learning." *Educational Theory* 20 (4): 377–85; Fall 1970.

**James Deese.** "Behavior and Fact." *American Psychologist* 24 (5): 515–22; May 1969.

**H. I. Dreyfus.** "Why Computers Must Have Bodies To Be Intelligent." *Review of Metaphysics* 21 (1): 13–33; September 1967.

**Robert L. Ebel.** "Behavioral Objectives: A Close Look." *Phi Delta Kappan* 52 (3): 171–73; November 1970.

**E. W. Eisner.** "Educational Objectives: Help or Hindrance?" *School Review* 75 (3): 250–66; Autumn 1967.

**E. W. Eisner.** *Instructional and Expressive Objectives: Their Formulation and Use in Curriculum.* AERA Monograph Series. Chicago: Rand McNally & Company, 1969.

**Howard H. Kendler.** "Teaching Machines and Psychological Theory." In: Eugene Gallanter, editor. *Automated Teaching.* New York: John Wiley & Sons, Inc., 1959.

**Elizabeth S. Maccia.** "Epistemological Considerations in Relation to the Use of Teaching Machines." *Educational Theory* 12 (4): 234ff.; October 1962.

**Robert F. Mager.** *Preparing Instructional Objectives.* Belmont, California: Fearon Publishers, Inc., 1962.

**Nellie L. Noddings.** "Beyond Behavioral Objectives: Seeing the Whole Picture." *Focus on Learning* 1 (1): 35–41; Spring 1971.

**David Nyberg.** *Tough and Tender Learning.* Palo Alto, California: National Press Books, 1971. p. 68.

**W. James Popham.** "Probing the Validity of Arguments Against Behavioral Goals." Symposium presentation, AERA meeting, Chicago, February 1968.

**D. R. Steg.** "The Limitations of Learning Machines and Some Aspects of Learning." *Focus on Learning* 1 (1): 43–51; Spring 1971.

# Discussion Questions
## and Activities

1. What is a behavioral objective, as opposed to nonbehavioral, general statements of objectives?

2. Although some proponents of behavioral objectives limit the statement of their form to performances, Gagné also includes another outcome part of the statement. What is this type of outcome, and what changes must first be made before it can be stated behaviorally?

3. Why are behavioral objectives, according to Gagné, superior to other types of objectives? Can you support his stance?

4. Has Gagné conclusively established the importance and the need for all teachers to use behavioral objectives?

5. Obtain a list of behavioral objectives in your field and compare them to nonbehavioral, general statements of objectives.

6. Can you use behavioral objectives in your teaching? Give reasons for your answer.

7. Is it a loss for the teaching-learning process if behavioral objectives rest upon assumptions that are opposed to a view of learning as "self-directed, unstructured, and in large part unpredictable"?

8. Is the term "behavioral" lacking in needed precision? Would substituting the term "instructional" for "behavioral" objectives help overcome the problem?

9. Does the use of behavioral objectives presuppose that "the sameness of individuals is judged to matter more than their differences"?

10. Underlying the notion of behavioral objectives, according to Kneller, is the false assumption that "learning, knowing, and behaving are the same process." Write out what you understand Kneller to mean by this statement.

11. Support or reject the following: Proponents of behavioral objectives could demonstrate the charge that, because many teachers have failed to use behavioral objectives, their rejection of them is partly the cause of the "present failure" of American education.

12. Does the use of behavioral objectives restrict the teaching-learning process and place education under tighter control?

13. What is the difference between objectives which are "specified" and those that are "behavioral"? Which type, if either, would you use?

14. Review the latest curriculum materials in your field to determine whether behavioral objectives are used widely.

15. Imagine that you are teaching a class using a set of behavioral objectives as your guideline. You find that your class is very creative and acts in a completely different way than you had anticipated. You find that you are accomplishing a great deal with your students through following your own intuition. At this point, would you abandon your behavioral objectives? What would you do?

# XII. Computer-assisted Instruction

*Some educators believe that materials which can be designed for independent use by the pupil and can be adapted to individual differences relieve the teacher of drill, certain types of remedial work, and provide attention to individual learning difficulties which is not possible in large group instruction.*

*The first self-instructor device (later to be called a "teaching machine") was developed by the psychologist Sidney Pressey in the late 1920's. His invention, however, did not capture the interest of educators, and it was about twenty years before there was a revitalization of interest. Later psychologists realized that a mechanical device was not actually necessary once suitable programmed materials could be developed. There are several ideas behind programmed materials. They are designed to take into consideration individual differences by considering the readiness of pupils to learn certain types of material. The learner is expected to make frequent responses as he proceeds through the material. Emphasis is placed on immediate feedback which reinforces correct responses. Materials must be organized sequentially so that the pupil can proceed in small steps from simple to complex material and have a high assurance of success.*

*These and other principles underlie computer-assisted instruction. Programs now are stored in computers and offer the advantage of elaborate programs which allow the pupil to proceed through the sequence of instruction in a variety of ways. The uses and advantages of this type of instruction are discussed by Patrick Suppes.*

*Minor changes in education usually merit a minor degree of attention. But computer-assisted instruction (CAI) is not a minor change; it will appreciably alter classroom instruction, will entail retraining teachers, and will involve very large expenditures. Before a school system decides to adopt this form of instruction, a careful evaluation should first be made of its advantages and objectionable features. While there are a number of CAI enthusiasts who extol its potential, some educators have become cautious and even skeptical over the claims advanced in its behalf. Skepticism is evident and specific criticisms are presented by Richard S. Barrett.*

Patrick Suppes

# 24. THE TEACHER AND COMPUTER-ASSISTED INSTRUCTION

Educators have shown increasing interest in the use of computers for classroom teaching, especially during the last year or two, and they have raised a number of fundamental questions that need analysis and discussion. The purpose of this article is to acquaint the reader with some of the ways that computers can be used for instruction, and to answer, at least briefly, some of the questions that are frequently asked about computer-assisted teaching.

Some of the most important questions are: How can the computer help in individualizing instruction? How might it change the teacher's role? How will computer-assisted instruction change teacher-administrator relationships? Will it lead to impersonality and regimentation in the classroom? How can teachers play a part in planning and using computers for instructional purposes?

Let us begin by looking at a student seated at a console or station that is connected by a telephone line to a central computer. The console will usually contain a typewriter keyboard that the student can use to "talk to" the computer and a television screen that can display written messages as well as drawings, equations, and other graphic material. In many cases, the student will also have a "light pen," which he can use to select answers to the problems shown on

Patrick Suppes is one of the leading figures in the development of computer-assisted instruction. Professor Suppes, presently director of the Institute of Mathematical Studies in the Social Sciences at Stanford University, studied at the University of Chicago and Columbia University. He is the author of *First Course in Mathematical Logic* (co-author), *Experiments in Second-Language Learning*, and *Computer-Assisted Instruction.*
Source: Patrick Suppes, "The Teacher and Computer-Assisted Instruction," *Today's Education*, Journal of the National Education Association, vol. 56 (February 1967), pp. 15–17. Reprinted by permission.

the screen; he can even erase or change the images that appear. The computer talks to the student through a pair of earphones or a loud-speaker, thus providing him with the verbal communication necessary for effective learning, particularly when new concepts are being presented.

The central computer, which controls the presentation of information and evaluates the students' responses, need not be in the school but can be located at a central point in the school district. Because of its great operating speed, one large computer can serve many students, and a number of students can "time-share" the computer simultaneously.

Computer-assisted instruction is possible with only one console per classroom, which would be shared by many students during the school day. In a more expensive and elaborate arrangement, a classroom would have a large number of consoles, and each student could spend considerable time—as much as an hour and a half a day—at the console. It is important to emphasize, however, that in either arrangement the student would still be spending most of his time in the regular class setting, directly under teacher supervision.

Recent research indicates that students at all age levels come to feel at home with this sort of equipment and are quite willing to make its use a part of their daily school experience.

The student and the computer program may interact at three distinct levels, each of which comprises a particular system of instruction. (This use of the word *system* also corresponds to its use in the computer industry).

*Individualized Drill-and-Practice Systems.* This kind of interaction between the student and the computer program is meant to supplement the regular teaching process. After the teacher has introduced new concepts and ideas in the standard fashion, the computer provides regular review and practice of basic concepts and skills. In elementary school mathematics, for example, each student would receive 15 or 20 exercises a day. These would be automatically presented, evaluated, and scored by the computer program without any effort by the classroom teacher.

In addition, these exercises can be presented to the student on an individualized basis, with the brighter children receiving harder-than-average exercises, and the slower children receiving easier problems. One important aspect of this individualization shoud be emphasized: In the drill-and-practice computer system, a student need not be placed on a track at the start of school in the fall and held there the entire year. At the beginning of each new concept block—whether in mathematics or in language arts—a student can be "recalibrated" if the results indicate that he is now capable of handling more advanced material.

Drill-and-practice work is particularly suitable for the skill subjects that make up a good part of our curriculum. Elementary mathematics, reading, and aspects of the language arts, such as spelling, elementary science, and beginning work in a foreign language, benefit from standardized and regularly presented drill-and-practice exercises.

*Tutorial Systems.* In contrast to the individualized drill-and-practice systems, tutorial systems take over the main responsibility for helping the student to understand a concept and develop skill in using it. Basic concepts, such as addition or subtraction of numbers, can be introduced by the computer program in such systems. The aim is to approximate the interaction a patient tutor would have with an individual student.

In the tutorial programs in reading and elementary mathematics that we have been working with at Stanford University for the past three years, we have tried hard to avoid having slower children experience any initial failures. On the other hand, the program has enough flexibility to avoid boring the brighter children with too many repetitive exercises. As soon as the child shows that he has a clear understanding of a concept by successfully working a number of exercises, he is immediately introduced to a new concept and new exercises.

*Dialogue Systems.* Dialogue systems are computer programs and consoles that enable the student to conduct a genuine dialogue with the computer. It will be some years before we are able to implement dialogue systems in classrooms, because a number of technical problems remain unsolved. One problem is the difficulty of devising a computer that can "understand" oral communication, especially that of young children. We would like to have a computer that would respond to questions. To attain this interaction, the computer would have to recognize the speech of the student and to comprehend the meaning of the question. It will be some time before a computer is developed that will be able to do either of these with any efficiency and economy.

Dialogue systems have been mentioned here in order to give readers an idea of the depth of interaction we ultimately hope for.

Drill-and-practice systems and tutorial systems, on the other hand, are already in operation on an experimental basis and will no doubt find an increasing application throughout the country in the next few years.

Effective programs of computer-assisted instruction now exist for elementary school mathematics, parts of language arts programs (particularly reading and spelling), and various topics in mathematics and science at the secondary and university levels. The programs have been developed primarily at universities, the following of which are currently the main centers of activity: Stanford, Illinois, Michigan, Texas, Pennsylvania State, Pittsburgh, Florida State, and the Los Angeles campus and the Irvine campus of the University of California.

Let us now look at some of the most frequently asked questions about computer-assisted instruction:

*What role can computers play in individualizing instruction?* The theme of individualized instruction has been prominent in American education for over 50 years. Psychologists have shown that individuals differ in their abilities, their rates of learning, and often even in their general approaches to learning. Unfortunately, the cost of providing individualized instruction that adapts to these differences is prohibitive if it depends on the use of professional teachers. For example, consider what it would cost to reduce present classroom size to four or five students per teacher.

The computer offers perhaps the most practical hope of a program of individualized instruction under the supervision of a single teacher in a classroom of 25 to 35 students. The basis for this practical hope is the rapid operation of the computer, which enables it to deal on an individual basis with a number of students simultaneously and thus lowers the cost per student of the computer.

*How will the computer change the teacher's role?* Drill-and-practice systems will modify the teacher's role only slightly. What they will do is relieve teachers of some of the burden of preparing and correcting large numbers of individualized drill-and-practice exercises in basic concepts and skills and of recording grades.

The teacher will be more significantly affected by tutorial systems. Let us consider a concrete example: teaching addition and subtraction of fractions at the fourth-grade level. The computer will provide the basic ideas and the procedure of how to add and subtract the fractions. The program will probably be written so that if a student does not understand the basic concepts on first presentation he will receive a second and possibly even a third exposure to them.

The new role of the teacher will be to work individually with all students on whatever problems and questions they may have in assessing and handling the new concepts. Tutorial systems allow teachers greater opportunity for personal interaction with students.

*How will computer-assisted instruction affect teacher-administrator relationships?* Teachers and administrators should be able to develop even closer relations in a setting where computers are used to aid instruction. The information-gathering capacity of the computer enables administrators to have a much more detailed profile and up-to-date picture of the strengths and weaknesses of each area of curriculum. As they develop skill in interpreting and using the vast amount of information about students provided by the computer, administrators and teachers should be able to work together more effectively for improvements in curriculum.

*Is there a danger that the computer will impose a rigid and impersonal regime on the classroom and even replace teachers?* Contrary to popular opinion, the computer's most important potential is to make learning and teaching *more* an individual affair rather than *less* so. Students will be less subject to regimentation and moving in lockstep because computer programs will offer highly individualized instruction. In our own work at Stanford, for example, we estimate that the brightest student and the slowest student going through our tutorial program in fourth-grade mathematics have an overlap of not more than 25 per cent in actual curriculum.

The computer program is neither personal nor impersonal. The affect and feeling of the program will depend on the skill and perceptivity of those responsible for constructing it.

There seems to be little reason to think that computers will ever replace teachers or reduce the number of teachers needed. The thrust of computer-assisted instruction is to raise the quality of education in this country, not to reduce its cost. In any sort of computer-assisted instructional system used in classrooms in the near future, teachers will continue dealing with children on an individual basis and doing most of the things they are now doing during most of the school day with only slight changes.

Finally, we emphasize once again that no one expects that students will spend most of their school hours at consoles hooked up to computers. They will work at consoles no more than 20 to 30 per cent of the time. All teachers everywhere recognize the help that books give them in teaching students. The day is coming when computers will receive the same recognition. Teachers will look on computers as a new and powerful tool for helping them to teach their students more effectively.


Richard S. Barrett


# 25. THE COMPUTER MENTALITY


With the introduction of computers into education, there has come to sudden prominence a system of beliefs that may best be called "the computer mentality." It is found most often in the computer programmer, although members of other professions occasionally become fascinated by the magical box and adopt the way of thought that springs up around it.

There are two major sources of the computer mentality. The first is natural selection. Computer programming is an exacting profession, one that appeals to those who possess the capacity for meticulous attention to detail and a willingness to adapt to the rigid means of communication dictated by the computer. They are fascinated by its complex gadgetry and language. The second is environmental. Once involved with the computer, the computer mentality comes gradually to accept the idea that the whole world can be understood

Richard S. Barrett is a senior associate with the Chicago office of Case and Company, an international management consulting firm with headquarters in New York City. He works with public and private organizations in the application of the behavioral sciences to a variety of problems, including education, training, and organization.
Source: Richard S. Barrett, "The Computer Mentality," *Phi Delta Kappan* (April 1968), pp. 430–433. Reprinted by permission.

in the same terms as the computer. The computer mentality looks for and finds the pervasiveness of mathematics, the rule of logic and order, and a simplicity and predictability in the most complex psychological and social processes.

Here are some of its distinguishing beliefs:

**1. Everybody is fascinated by the computer.** To prove this point, the computer mentality cites evidence, much of which is drawn from studies of bright children in a university lab school, members of a mathematics club who volunteer to learn how to use the computer, and neophyte computer programmers who are learning their trade. Also cited is the common impression that visiting firemen enjoy the computer room where they can see the tape reels whirl, lights flash, typewriters type (seemingly of their own volition), and listen to equipment which is programmed to play "She'll Be Comin' 'Round the Mountain." Children, with an apparently innate love of gadgets, enjoy the demonstration in which they type messages to the computer and the computer types back.

Short demonstrations may be fascinating, but even for the high school dropout education is likely to run nearly 200 days a year for almost 10 years. For some of us it goes to 16 to 20 years. If the student operates the computer for about a half-hour a day, he can easily spend 1,500 hours working with it from kindergarten through college. Strange as it may seem to the computer mentality, there may be people who will find that exposure too much. Even more strange, there are people who go through life with no particular interest in the computer. The soul of the poet, the used car salesman, the mountain climber, and the Trappist monk may well find the computer and the way it teaches to be objectionable.

Even those who are sympathetic to the computer can be frustrated by it. Flaws in the original programming or simple mistakes by the student in typing the material to be entered into the machine can force him to repeat steps he already knows and can do perfectly. Despite the awesome speed at which the computer can process data, there can be substantial delays when a number of students are being served simultaneously by one computer, however large its capacity. The frustrations caused by the machine are neither trivial nor transient. Computers have suffered physical violence from dissatisfied users.

**2. Tell 'em once and you've told 'em.** No one has to tell the computer the same thing twice. Barring breakdowns, once an instruction is satisfactorily entered, it will be followed repeatedly and without fail. People, on the other hand, rarely absorb anything complex on one trial, requiring a variety of approaches, explanations, applications, and elaborations before they get the point. As soon as the material is learned, the student begins to forget it, and he requires review to make it stick in his mind.

The computer mentality sometimes recognizes the need for redundancy in exposition, but there is a tendency to introduce complex and specialized terms for use by the layman, describing them once and thereafter using them as if they were perfectly clear and completely understood. The greater problem is in review. In those cases where the student types his material on a standard typewriter keyboard and the computer types its responses, he can take a copy of his printout with him for later review. By the time the end of the term arrives, however, he may find it difficult to interpret the cryptic comments that he and the computer have made to each other. Reconstructing the exercise may be more trouble than it's worth. He is in even worse shape when the material is presented to him and his responses are made ephemerally on a television screen. Not only is the material unavailable for review later in the year, it is even destroyed during the course of the lesson so that he cannot go back to see what he did or to find his mistakes.

**3. Telling the student that he got the right answer is informative and rewarding.** To the computer mentality, it is obvious that if someone got the right answer, he must know the subject; and if he is told he got the right answer, he knows that he knows the subject, and he feels good. Students, as well as those who study the behavior of students, know that people can go mechanically through a step-by-step routine and get the right answer without understanding what they are doing. The alert student who has just been told that he has successfully solved a problem given to him by the computer may well wonder whether he could apply the information in a different context.

Computer programs vary widely in the ways in which they inform the student that he is right. Some simply acknowledge correct responses with a symbol, such as a plus sign, or a letter "R" for "right." Others spell out "good," or may even be more effusive in their praise. The student who has stumbled through many blind alleys or has been deliberately giving some wrong answers to see what the computer will do, can be counted on to look with a little cynicism on such feeble attempts to reward him. Besides, many people do not need to be rewarded every few seconds for their proper behavior, and they find the constant repetition of "good" or "well done" to be a bore, especially when they know they have not done particularly well.

**4. The computer is responsive.** To the computer mentality, a teacher with a class of 30 students cannot be responsive because there is so little time for individual interaction; but the computer, since it is used on an individual basis with each student, is truly responsive. If we take the first definition in Webster's International Dictionary, second edition, of *responsive* as being characteristic of something "that responds; answers; replies," the computer programmer mentality is indeed correct. The machine does respond, answer, and reply to the student. A little further reading in the same dictionary yields another definition, "ready or inclined to respond, or react; as a *responsive* child; always *responsive* to affection; his eloquence stirred a *responsive* chord in his listeners." That sounds more like a good teacher, even one with 30 students, than it does like a computer.

**5. The computer will individualize instruction.** Conceptually, the model for individualizing instruction is clear. The students at the beginning of instruction are given a long, thorough diagnostic test. Each student's performance is analyzed to determine the kind of instruction he needs to achieve the goals of the unit of instruction. The appropriate prescription is made for him to read materials, solve problems, watch films or video tapes, or get private tutoring or some other form of instruction. At various points throughout the sequence his progress is assessed, and a new prescription is given if necessary.

All of this sounds very neat and elegant, but there remains one unsolved problem—the nature of the tests that should be given and the kinds of prescriptions that are appropriate. Aside from the pervasive fact that smart people learn faster than dull people, we do not yet have a firm basis for diagnosing skills and making a prescription. The answer to this problem comes from the development of tests that meaningfully assess the student's achievement, and the adoption of techniques for making prescriptions that are better than the common-sense assignments of a reasonably capable teacher. Further research must be made into the allied processes of teaching and learning. Once the basic information is at hand, the computer may or may not be a useful and economic tool.

**6. Science is data.** According to the computer programmer mentality, simulation of the laboratory, particularly in physics and chemistry, will teach the student in a way that is impossible today, because the computer can simulate experiments that cannot be conducted in a typical laboratory of the school or college. The plan is that the student will be able to set up experimental conditions, and the computer, having been programmed in advance by someone who knows the mathematical principles involved, will give him the data that he would have read from his instruments in real life. Experiments that are dangerous, expensive, or impractical can be simulated in a way that gives the student an experience beyond that he would have by reading about the experiment or observing it on film. He could, for example, learn about the laws of ballistics by firing simulated guns with varying angles of elevation and muzzle velocity, or he could study physical phenomena in the inaccessible regions of outer space.

When the objection is raised about the unreality of it all, the computer mentality concedes that there must be enough laboratory work to give the student some real practice. Or, rather patronizingly, the point is made that once he has washed a few test tubes, looked through a few microscopes, and weighed a few samples on laboratory balances he has had enough hands-on experience. What he really needs, the computer mentality argues, is data.

This emphasis on data can lead to the false impression that numbers are the stuff of science, when actually science is a complex and disorderly process, beginning with some knowledge of the phenomenon being studied, from which hunches and, later, formal hypotheses may be derived. These are tested, the blind alleys are abandoned, and the more promising leads followed. New hunches and hypotheses develop, and are tested, until a meaningful conclusion can be reached. During this process the alert mind must be opened to accept and understand the unexpected and to capitalize on the happy accidents that occur.

Of course, much of the scientist's effort is directed to developing data collection procedures, particularly when he is exploring near the fringes of his science. But he does not blindly rely on the numbers that come out, since he knows they are no better than the techniques by which they have been collected. He can obtain some index of the reliability of his information by analyzing the numbers themselves, but the more important criteria are that the data collection procedures are relevant to his problem, that they do not leave out important information whose absence will distort his results. Viewed in this context, the actual numbers that appear on the machine take on limited significance.

**7. Computation serves no useful purpose in education.** The computer, it is further argued, can be used not only to generate the simulated data, but also to perform the calculations that are necessary to develop an understanding of the physical laws involved. More intricate problems requiring too much calculation for what they are worth could then be handled as broadening the scope of the student's learning.

Computation is tedious, and extended computations can kill the motivation of the student. Indeed, before the modern computers, many investigations were not undertaken because the results were seen as not being worth the computational labor involved.

Nevertheless, letting the computer do all the computation leaves something out of the learning process. There once was a psychologist who had only hand-operated calculators in his laboratory, explaining that the physical action of literally cranking numbers into the machines gave his students a feel for the data that they would not otherwise have. Perhaps this was a rationalization for his inability to get a more modern calculator, but most people have found that by doing problems, whether the course is arithmetic, physics, or statistics, they have learned something they did not get simply by reading the material or watching the teacher work out problems on the blackboard. We learn, to some extent, with our fingertips. Being handed the answers to all our mathematical problems by the infallible computer may breed a generation of students with basic deficiencies in understanding the data that they are dealing with.

Let us agree that there is some virtue to the proposition that, after the student has done enough calculations to get what psychologists in their technical jargon call a gut-level understanding of what his computations mean, there is still need for him to have access to computed results from raw data. Is the computer necessary? Can we not give him tables showing the data as if he collected it in an experiment and the correctly calculated results? Tables are much cheaper than computers. If tables won't work, can they use slide rules, calculators, or more limited but cheaper computers that are already available?

**8. The world is at its foundations mathematical.** The computer mentality, preoccupied as it is with numbers, tends to build instructional systems that emphasize the numerical aspects of the subject, and to deemphasize its qualitative feature. Much of physics, astronomy, and chemistry is best understood mathematically; but particularly insofar as the nonspecialist is concerned—and this includes the vast majority of those who never learn about these subjects—many of the most fascinating issues need not be presented mathematically. The political and moral issues that evolve from man's mastery of nuclear fusion, the questions of whether the universe started all at once with a big bang or is continually being created, and the economic and medical issues that stem from the widespread use of insecticides, can all be dealt with by intelligent citizens without the intimate knowledge of the data and the calculations essential for the specialists.

**9. Computers will bring about a revolution in education.** It is easy to understand how the computer mentality can expect a rapid revolution in education, because the computer has brought about such a great and dramatic revolution in handling information. In a scant 25 years, operations that were timed in thousandths of a second are now timed in billionths of a second. Slow-acting electromechanical relays gave way to vacuum tubes, which in turn were replaced by transistors that are now being supplanted by minute printed circuits. One might say that the physiology of computers has gone through several evolutionary cycles, changing in form, structure, function, size, and capability. In the same 25 years, the physiology of the student who is to learn on this computer has changed little, if at all. He carries on his shoulders his own portable computer, miniaturized beyond the dreams of the computer engineer, endowed with a remarkable memory and retrieval system, but slow in processing information, and subject to lapses in memory, to inattention, and to distraction. This is the equipment that the educator has to work on, and he cannot redesign it.

During the millions of years during which man has been evolving, he has always been concerned with teaching his young. He has told them directly what he knows, and he has tried to help them to discover it on their own; he has rewarded and punished; he has given instruction in concentrated doses and he has spread it out; he has applied the simplest forms of Pavlovian conditioning and the most intricate, complex learning theories; he has offered intrinsic and extrinsic motivation; he has wheedled, threatened, stimulated, and diverted; he has, in fact, tried just about everything he could think of. Certainly, he will develop new techniques that will be successful, but one can hardly say that there is a wide open field for the development of radically different and successful techniques.

There will be significant progress in education, but changes will take time. If, by exerting the massive efforts now being undertaken

with government support, we are able to improve the effectiveness of
education by 3 percent per year for 25 years, it will then be more
than twice as effective as it is today.  This would be a revolution indeed, and to expect a single electronic tool to have the revolutionary
impact predicted by the more enthusiastic supporters of the computer
is to invite disappointment with more modest but truly significant
improvements.

**10.  Computer-assisted instruction is economical.**  Computers have
won their place in business because they save clerical time and provide
information that is too expensive to collect in any other way.  A saving of 10 percent in the salary of the office force can be balanced
directly against the cost of the computer, and the competitive advantage of better information can be estimated even when it cannot be
directly calculated.  The situation is different in the schools because
students aren't paid, and it is difficult to estimate the value of what
they learn from the computer that they would not learn in more conventional instruction.  Emphasizing the savings that might accrue by
displacing instructional staff is obviously a poor selling point among
teachers.

Making an economic study of the computer in education is virtually impossible because no realistic figures are available.  Wild estimates that it will cost 25¢ per hour for each student are not backed
up by a sober analysis of the rental cost of the computer and the terminal at which the student works, the cost of tie-lines that must be
leased to connect the schools with centrally located equipment, the
number of student hours that can be realistically scheduled in
the school year, the extent to which costs can be defrayed by using the
computer for other purposes during off-hours, and the share of
the cost to be charged for developing equipment and materials.  However, it is safe to say that it will be a long time before computer-
assisted instruction can be profitably sold at $1.50 per student hour,
a rate at which the school could hire one teacher for every four or
five students and give them close personal attention.

**11.  Computer-assisted instruction will be so good that it will be ac-
cepted on the basis of its merit.**  Truth will prevail, but truth prevails only when it has won a long struggle to overcome the *status quo.*
Let us look briefly at some of the things that have to be accomplished
before the computer will take its rightful place in education.

Students will have to take time away from other activities to learn how to use the computer. The school operates on two budgets. In addition to the financial budget there is a time budget of the student, already burdened; in fact, there are many voices saying that we are demanding too much of our students and that we should reduce the load imposed on them. Somewhere in this time budget the school must find time to train students to use the computer, even though they may never see a computer again after they leave the school. No one yet knows how long it will take to train the typical student to use the computer with the same level of ease that the engineer uses his slide rule, but indications are that it is substantial.

Teachers will need to be trained to use the computer. Some of them must be trained to teach the students to use it, and all of them must be able to deal with malfunction and to recognize the need for maintenance. Not only that, they must learn how to teach with the computer at their elbow. The well-programmed computer is going to be more up to date and more knowledgeable than many teachers, who must either update their education or run the risk of looking foolish. Certainly all reasonable people are in favor of teachers having a broad and up-to-date store of knowledge, but not all teachers are reasonable and some of them will resist.

Teachers must learn to turn over much of their rights, duties, and responsibilities to an inanimate object over which they have little control and toward which at least some of them will have considerable hostility. It will take a long process of education and motivation to make sure that teachers accept the contributions that the computer can make.

With all its problems, the computer has tremendous potential for improving education. With careful study of the learning process, development of methods of instruction that have not been thought of yet because the unique capabilities of the computer have not been available, and long-term planning of the introduction of the computer into the classroom, it can become one of the most progressive forces in education. For this program I would like to add one assumption of my own:

*The use of the computer in education is too serious a business to be left to the computer mentality.*

# Discussion Questions
# and Activities

1. Describe the three levels at which the student and computer interact. What functions do each of these levels serve?

2. What are the problems that first must be overcome before dialogue systems can be made operational?

3. How will the use of computer-assisted instruction change the teacher's role? Or does it change the teacher's role?

4. Does Suppes adequately answer the charge that the use of the computer will tend to make learning more mechanical and impersonal?

5. Has Suppes failed to respond to other possible criticisms? If so, what are these criticisms?

6. Is there such a thing as a "computer mentality"? If so, what are its characteristics? Its dangers?

7. Why is the built-in reward system not effective for all students?

8. Is the fact that a computer cannot respond in the same manner as a teacher a fair criticism of computer-assisted instruction?

9. Do we now have conclusive evidence that suitable tests can be developed for diagnosing skills and making sound prescriptions?

10. Barrett contends that the computer's emphasis on data can lead to a faulty notion of science and scientific thinking. Evaluate this criticism.

11. Does the computer tend to overemphasize the numerical aspects of a subject at the expense of the qualitative side? What do you believe are the dangers in this overemphasis?

12. State your own conclusions as to the use of computer-assisted instruction. Especially focus on creativity related to computer-assisted instruction.

13. Invite a proponent of computer-assisted instruction to speak before your class. Raise questions and criticisms.

# XIII. Nongraded Programs

*American schools were ungraded until the latter half of the nineteenth century. It was at that time that American educators, impressed with the graded schools they had seen in Germany, sought to organize public education on this plan. They believed that knowledge could more meaningfully be organized on a graded basis, that public schools could better handle their growing enrollments and that teachers could more readily be trained if their training was concentrated on preparation to teach at certain grade levels.*

*Many criticisms have been directed against graded schools during the past one hundred years. These criticisms have finally mounted to a point where new alternatives have been devised and tested in many school systems. It would be a serious mistake to consider nongraded programs simply a return to the past. Nongraded plans, in contrast to many of the ungraded schools during the nineteenth century, are specifically designed to offer greater flexibility of vertical organization to provide for individual differences, remove rigid time standards of student achievement, and overcome the problems of promotion-nonpromotion. Greater flexibility in the use of staff, curriculum, and facilities is also expected to be a feature of such plans.*

*In their enthusiasm for nongraded schools, some of the proponents underestimated the difficulties of reorganizing schools to accommodate these programs. Some difficulties have become increasingly evident. Teachers need special preparation to operate in these programs, and the demands upon teachers are greater than in traditional graded plans.*

*Most curriculum materials are designed for graded schools and, therefore, teachers will have to rely on programmed materials and related self-instructional devices. Moreover, many schools that claimed to have made the transition to nongraded programs have actually not done so but merely substituted homogeneous grouping within the same grade and left vertical organization curriculum and teaching practices unchanged.*

*Many characteristics of the nongraded programs are discussed in the article by James F. Lindsey. David Lewin writes of some of the limitations of nongraded programs.*

James F. Lindsey

# 26. NON-GRADED PROGRAMS—
# WHICH ONE?

"What I don't like about the non-graded school is. . . ." These words
are often heard in school circles, and the complaints add up to a long
and conflicting list. Critics have found fault with homogeneous
grouping and with heterogeneous grouping, with the use of reading
levels and the lack of reading levels, with cross-age groupings and
with single-age groupings, with teacher cycling and with team teaching, with lack of standards and with overrigid standards, with competition and with lack of competition, with curriculum change and
with lack of curriculum change, with report cards and with lack of
report cards, with excessive attention to structure and with lack of
attention to structure, with overemphasis on each subject and with
underemphasis on each subject.

Each objection may be valid for a given program. But can one
generalize from a particular program that is non-graded in name
only—a program that may include many practices which are unre-
lated to vertical organization?

In theory, the graded school follows a definite pattern of organization. The children in a graded school are divided by age and at-
tainment. If possible, there is only one grade in each classroom. The
teacher teaches the class as a whole. The course of study is planned
in detail, and certain textbooks are used in each grade. In graded

James F. Lindsey is a graduate of San Francisco State College, Stanford University, and the University of California at Berkeley. He has served as a
curriculum consultant to NDEA English institutes and to a number of public
school systems. As Professor of Early Childhood Education and reading and
department chairman at Chico State College, his professional interests are non-
grading, reading, and early childhood education.
Source: James F. Lindsey, "Non-Graded Programs—Which One?" *Elementary
School Journal* 68 (November 1967), pp. 61–62. Copyright © 1967 by The
University of Chicago. Reprinted by permission.

schools, children are expected to make a uniform, set rate of progress. Children who do not meet grade standards are retained. Grade levels signify definite levels of achievement. Promotion policy is assumed to limit achievement range within a grade. Individual differences among children in each classroom are to be reduced as much as possible in order to make a homogeneous group.

Many "graded" schools make wide use of organizational and curriculum innovations that go far to meet the problems of individual differences. The innovations that are adopted often violate every component of graded school structure. Graded school organization does little to hinder provisions for individual differences precisely because none of the basic components of graded organization is in use. In these schools, a grade placement means nothing in terms of an individual child's achievement level in curriculum areas, nor does grade placement indicate physical, mental, or social maturity.

What purpose, then, does the "grade" serve? The grade may inhibit optimum pupil placement. Overplacement produces tension and failure. Underplacement limits learning opportunity for the more able. The grade serves to evaluate a child as "ahead" or "behind" in terms of grade standards rather than in terms of the pupil's capacities, needs, strengths, and interests. Does the "grade" really serve a useful purpose?

Non-grading is a vertical form of school organization that offers flexibility in providing for individual differences. The flexibility is accomplished by removing rigid time standards of pupil achievement. How the flexibility is used and how well it is used depend on the school, the staff, and the supporting policies of the school district. Ideally, the staff of the non-graded school develops flexibility in curriculum, staff utilization, materials, and organizational policy to meet the challenge of individual differences among its pupils. The nongraded program recognizes the goal of continuous progress for each pupil. In addition, effective non-graded programs are notable for their variety in details of practice. Each school is unique in its pupil population, its staff make-up, its leadership, its location, its resources, its physical features, its patrons, and its conception of acceptable flexibility at a given time. The best non-graded program is one that meets the needs in an individual school. An effective non-graded program gives first priority to providing for individual differences among children so there may be continuous progress over a span of years.

Too often a program that has been successful in one school is applied to an unlike situation in another school. The result is the same as wearing a pair of shoes that almost fit—there is discomfort and difficulty in running. Gains toward the goal of continuous progress come only through innovations that a school staff develops to meet pupils' needs as they are perceived in the light of a given school situation.

Graded structure inhibits flexibility in meeting individual differences. Non-grading, by removing some of the obstacles, encourages flexibility. Non-grading can be helpful when it is used to meet instructional needs. The successful non-graded school is always unique. Non-grading is an organizational principle applied to a specific school situation to realize educational objectives. Schools, like children, have individual differences and need non-graded programs that are conceived and operated to meet those differences.

What we do not like in any particular non-graded program we can do differently in our own non-graded program.

David Lewin

# 27. GO SLOW ON NON-GRADING

The idea of non-grading seems to be taking hold in the minds of many educators who are anxious to be in step with new trends. Since non-grading is a major departure from traditional organization in the elementary school, we should examine the implications of this approach with the greatest care before we make commitments.

Mr. David Lewin, who has written articles for a number of journals, is a teacher in the New York City public schools.
Source: David Lewin, "Go Slow on Non-Grading," *Elementary School Journal* 67 (December 1966), pp. 131–134. Copyright © by The University of Chicago. Reprinted by permission.

Those of us who have experimented with non-grading would do a service to the educational community if we pointed out the weaknesses of the approach, if and when they appear, as well as the strengths. It is much too facile—and not particularly helpful—to say that non-grading works or does not work. Non-grading, from my experience, can produce desirable results, but it is difficult to implement. We must be aware of the problems and the difficulties as well as the advantages.

The arguments for a non-graded organization are cogent. Here is how they are expressed by one of the foremost theoreticians of the movement:

> Organizationally, a nongraded school is one in which the grade levels and grade labels representing years of vertical progress are replaced by a plan of continuous upward progress. Conceptually, it is intended to eliminate the promotion-nonpromotion adjustment mechanism of graded schools; to raise the ceilings and lower the floors of attainment expectancies for learners, thus encompassing their individual differences; to encourage the utilization of content and materials in accordance with pupil individuality; and to force pedagogical attention to individual differences and the individual [1].

Non-grading offers advantages to all kinds of children—the slow, the disadvantaged, the bright, and the so-called average. For the slow child and the disadvantaged child, there can be no doubt that the stigma of failure can be avoided by non-grading. For disadvantaged children, particularly, it is inconsistent to say that we must minister to their needs while we subject many of them to psychological defeat.

For the bright child, non-grading lowers barriers to progress. It enables the child to move ahead as far and as fast as his abilities can take him.

For the average child, non-grading offers the advantage of liberation from a predetermined norm. In a non-graded program the average child can be judged in terms of his own rate of growth and his own needs.

## PROBLEMS FOR TEACHERS

Let's look at the problems that will be encountered in starting a non-graded system. The major areas of difficulty seem to be teacher-training and curriculum.

It is much more difficult to teach a non-graded class than a graded class. In a non-graded program the ability range of a class is so widened that a totally new approach is required. If the class is organized homogeneously to restrict the range, the purpose of the program is defeated; a new "box" is substituted for the old. If the range is not restricted, the average teacher will flounder. She can be effective only if she is exceptionally well prepared and sustained at every step.

The teaching must be better in a non-graded class than in a graded class because so much more is going on all the time. It is harder to teach three groups than two, and this is what may have to be done in some areas. Ideally, the teaching is done on as many levels as there are children.

Non-grading calls for superior teachers. To teach a non-graded class, one must be young in spirit, creative in devising new ways to meet new situations, and eager to meet challenges. Does this description fit the typical teacher on the average staff?

Even superior teachers who have had careful preparation may require extra help. Our experiment, which involved only part of the school, recognized that the non-graded teachers had to have assistance —either a student teacher or a school aide, as well as a resource teacher who devoted all her time to the needs of the five or six teachers in her cluster.

Extensive in-service training, before and during the program, was a necessity. Because of the specialized nature of the teaching, substitutes, when they were needed, were not able to do justice to the program. A lengthy absence or a permanent midyear change presented a critical situation.

## CURRICULUM TROUBLES

The problem of curriculum may be solved in many ways, depending on the school, but in some respects there is no completely satisfactory solution. Instruction should be individualized, but materials for individualized instruction do not exist in all areas.

A look at the major subject areas will clarify some of the problems of curriculum in a non-graded approach. In reading, gradedness is easily removed. Basal reading can be superseded by an individualized reading program supplemented by the use of reading laboratories and skill materials. In literature and other language arts, however, techniques for individualizing instruction have been inadequately developed. Mathematics materials, including modern mathematics programs, remain graded and, for the most part, geared to group instruction. To teach mathematics in a non-graded school, it may be necessary to resort to leveling between classes, that is, establishing homogeneous groups by interchanging pupils on the same levels. Social studies presents a problem for the non-graded school. Certainly, we must retain the developmental lesson, which is uniquely suited to the teaching of concepts, and the unit method, which is needed to organize the diverse body of material. To avoid repetition as children move from one non-graded class to another, it may be necessary to reorganize the social studies syllabus into three-year cycles for every two-year cluster. The area of science also presents a difficulty. The teaching of science, using graded textbooks and the demonstration method, is more strongly oriented to the needs of the group than the needs of the individual.

## QUESTIONS ON MATERIALS

Non-graded teaching depends on programming material. This fact raises important questions. I have already raised one: What do we do if there is no programmed material on the level and in the area needed? Then, what do we do if existing material is of dubious quality? Finally, we must ask ourselves a more profound question: Do we want to institute a system of instruction which relies heavily on programmed textbooks, teaching machines, self-teaching and self-checking devices, tape-recorded lessons, and laboratories? In materials and methodology, the traditional system of organization is more flexible than the non-graded system. The traditional system may make use of individualized materials as readily as it uses conventional textbooks, direct teaching, and group instruction.

## COSTS

A non-graded program, certainly in the introductory stage, is more expensive than a traditional program. The materials needed would seem to cost considerably more, even after the heavy outlay in the "retooling" phase. More personnel is required. The teacher of a non-graded class cannot be expected to plan, co-ordinate, and direct the activities of as many children as the teacher of a graded class.

Increased guidance service is called for in non-grading, since constant evaluation of pupil progress is a strong feature of this approach. Reports from non-graded programs in operation also indicate a greater use of specialists and clerical assistants.

Other problems are far less formidable, but I am including them here to make this presentation more comprehensive. Teachers have to be given time to meet to co-ordinate their activities, to have conferences with supervisors, guidance personnel, and curriculum specialists, and to prepare assignments for the individual needs of the children. A new system of reporting to parents should be developed. In the opinion of some observers, the complexities of record-keeping require electronic data processing. Since educational decisions will no longer be made by textbook publishers and by syllabus writers at "headquarters," each school will need an outstanding curriculum specialist. As we become more concerned with the individual achievement of children, the testing program will have to be revised. Diagnostic testing to aid us in assigning the correct unit of work for each child will assume great importance. Achievement tests yielding a grade equivalent will be replaced by tests that measure the children on the basis of their expectancy.

There remains the role of the administrator. With more teachers, more materials, more scheduling of activities, more guidance of teachers, more staff interaction, more explaining to the community, and more kinks to work out, the administrator must be prepared for hard work. Hopefully, the added burdens will apply only to the transitional period.

None of the problems I have described here is insuperable. If we find the advantages of a non-graded program sufficiently compelling, we can overcome the obstacles. If, in addition, we feel that non-grading is part of the shape of things to come and that the future is close at hand, we had better get started in this direction.

## IS NON-GRADING NECESSARY?

One final question deserves to be considered: Can schools get the advantages of non-grading through other means? Let's examine this possibility.

The chief purpose of non-grading is to individualize instruction. This goal is accomplished by removing the restrictiveness of gradedness with its norms, standards, and expectations, all of which apply to the general child rather than the specific child. We can, however, move toward a higher degree of individualization of instruction within the confines of the graded school. The newer materials designed for this purpose are available to the graded school as well as the nongraded school.

A proponent of non-grading, after listing the advantages, writes:

"Again, this is what any fine teacher does in a professional job of teaching. But in a graded group it is possible for many teachers to avoid their responsibility for providing appropriate learning opportunities. In a non-graded group teachers are forced to assume that responsibility" [2].

This argument, which has been expressed by other writers, frankly admits that non-grading is not the only way of meeting the individual needs of children. If the goal of greater individualization is achievable in graded classes, should we not carefully question the need to overhaul our present method of organization?

## REFERENCES

1. **John I. Goodlad.** "Cooperative Teaching in Educational Reform," *National Elementary Principal* 44 (January 1965), p. 10.
2. **Madeline Hunter.** "The Dimensions of Nongrading," *Elementary School Journal* 65 (October 1964), p. 21.

1. What are the advantages of nongraded programs? Are these advantages substantial?

2. What are some problems that could be encountered in starting a nongraded system? Imagine that you are a school principal in charge of opening a nongraded school. Think of steps you could take to eliminate problems.

3. Does a nongraded program require greater use of programmed materials, tape-recorded lessons, and other self-instructional devices? Or, are audiovisual aids and materials used dependent on a teacher's choice?

4. List and explain the problems and shortcomings found in nongraded programs. Suppose you are a teacher encountering these problems. How would you deal with them?

5. Can schools gain the benefits of nongrading through other means? If so, what changes should be made in graded schools to provide these advantages without resorting to nongraded plans?

6. There have been many criticisms of nongraded schools. List some of these criticisms and evaluate the validity of them.

7. Why is it that in some graded schools innovations for handling individual differences can be successfully introduced within this form of organization? Center your critique around school personnel.

8. Compare graded and nongraded schools. What are the distinctive features of the latter type of school organization?

9. Can one school borrow the plans for a nongraded program that was successful in another school, or must each school develop its own plans?

10. Organize a debate among classmates on graded vs. nongraded schools.

11. Visit a nongraded school and report to the class on your findings. What were the attitudes of the staff members you encountered? What signs did you see that student creativity was encouraged? Was there a prevailing atmosphere of fear in the school, or were warmth and freedom in evidence? What was distinctive about class scheduling in the school? Before you make your visit, devise a checklist of any features or traits that you plan to observe while in the school.

# XIV. Accountability

*Earlier we read the works of educational reformers and were apprised of the weaknesses they found in public education and their proposals for change. Some parents also are dissatisfied with their children's lack of progress in school; and citizens are frequently irate over increases in taxes, even though the additional revenue may be used for schools. Some people oppose school bond issues and resist the attempts of teachers to secure higher salaries and better working conditions until they can demonstrate more positive results for their efforts. The beginnings of a ground swell for accountability are manifest.*

*For many years the quality of schools was judged by certain "inputs"—per pupil expenditures, size of the school library, teacher salaries, value of the physical plant, and other measures. But a number of studies, beginning with the Coleman Report, have cast doubt on inputs alone for bringing about quality education. "Outputs" in terms of the performance of students on standardized achievement tests are still largely used today for determining quality even though they have come under increased criticism. Accountability is a demand to judge schools by their outputs, to demonstrate a positive relationship between expenditures and desired results obtained.*

*A program's performance objectives must first be specified—and this is where behavioral objectives tie in. It is thought that the program and instructional goals of a school system must be stated so they are susceptible to measurement. Only in this manner, some believe, can the outputs be appraised and the costs of programs be assessed.*

Some skeptics believe that the assumptions underlying accountability lead to a mentality alien to the educational process. The emphasis on measurement, efficiency, systems models, and competitiveness, it is argued, has no place in education. While some limited forms of accountability could be found in the past, the forms found in present-day designs, skeptics assert, is especially pernicious.

Leon M. Lessinger, a leader of the accountability movement, presents what he considers to be the positive features of the movement, Robert J. Nash and Russell M. Agne, the negative.

Leon M. Lessinger

# 28. ACCOUNTABILITY FOR RESULTS: A BASIC CHALLENGE FOR AMERICA'S SCHOOLS

Today, too many young Americans leave school without the tools of learning, an interest in learning, or any idea of the relationship of learning to jobs. It is a mocking challenge that so many of our children are not being reached today by the very institution charged with the primary responsibility for teaching them. A Committee for Economic Development report issued in the summer of 1968 summarizes the indictment: Many schools and school districts, handicapped by outmoded organization and a lack of research and development money, are not providing "the kind of education that produces rational, responsible, and effective citizens."

Now, the educational establishment—right down to the local level —is being asked ever more insistently to account for the results of its programs. This fast-generating nationwide demand for accountability promises a major and long overdue redevelopment of the management of the present educational system, including an overhaul of its cottage-industry form of organization. Many believe this can be accomplished by making use of modern techniques currently employed in business and industry, some of which are already being used in the educational enterprise.

Leon M. Lessinger served as superintendent of the San Mateo Union High District in California, Associate Commissioner of the Bureau of Elementary and Secondary Education in the U.S. Office of Education, and Professor of Education at the University of South Carolina. His book, *Every Kid A Winner*, is a full-length study of accountability.

Source: Leon M. Lessinger, "Accountability for Results: A Basic Challenge for America's Schools," *American Education* 5 (June-July 1969), pp. 2–4. Reprinted by permission.

Before America's schools can productively manage the massive amount of money entrusted to them—and the even greater amount they need—they must be armed with better management capability. If education is going to be able to manage its budget properly, it must devise measurable relationships between dollars spent and results obtained. Education, like industry, requires a system of quality assurance. Anything less will shortchange our youth.

Sputniks and satellite cities, computers and confrontation politics, television and the technology of laborsaving devices—all have placed new and overwhelming demands on our educational system. Americans could say with the angel Gabriel of *Green Pastures*, that "everything nailed down is coming loose." How can we provide the kind of education that would assure full participation for all in this new complex technological society? How to prepare people to respond creatively to rapid-fire change all their lives while maintaining a personal identity that would give them and their society purpose and direction? How to do this when the body of knowledge has so exploded that it no longer can be stored in a single mind? How to do this when cybernetics is changing man's function? How to do this when the cost of old-fashioned education soars higher every year with little significant improvement?

In 1965 the passage of the far-reaching Elementary and Secondary Education Act gave the public schools of America a clear new mandate and some of the funds to carry it out. It was a mandate not just for equality of educational opportunity but for equity in results as well. In place of the old screening, sorting, and reject system that put students somewhere on a bell shaped curve stretching from A to F, the schools were asked to bring educational benefits to every young person to prepare him for a productive life. Under the new mandate the schools were expected to give every pupil the basic competence he needed, regardless of his so-called ability, interest, background, home, or income. After all, said a concerned Nation, what's the purpose of grading a basic skill like reading with A, B, C, D, or F when you can't make it at all today if you can't read?

In essence, this meant that education would be expected to develop a "zero reject system" which would guarantee quality in skill acquisition just as a similar system now guarantees the quality of industrial production. Today's diplomas are often meaningless warranties. In the words of one insistent inner-city parent, "Many diplomas aren't worth the ink they're written in." We know, for ex- ·
ample, that there are some 30,000 functional illiterates—people with

less than fifth grade reading ability—in the country today who hold
diplomas.   And untold more are uncovered each day as manpower
training and job programs bring increasing numbers of hardcore
unemployed into the labor market.

Instead of certifying that a student has spent so much time in
school or taken so many courses, the schools should be certifying that
he is able to perform specific tasks.   Just as a warranty certifies the
quality performance of a car, a diploma should certify a youngster's
performance as a reader, a writer, a driver, and so on.

If, then, the new objective of education is to have zero rejects
through basic competence for all, how can the educational establishment retool to respond to this new challenge?   Developing a system
of quality assurance can help provide the way.

The first step toward such a system is to draw up an overall
educational redevelopment plan.   Such a plan must first translate the
general goal of competence for all students into a school district's
specific objectives.   These objectives must be formulated in terms of
programs, courses, buildings, curriculums, materials, hardware, personnel, and budgets.   The plan must incorporate a timetable of priorities for one year, for five years, 10 years, and perhaps even for 20
years.   Such a plan should be based on "market research," that is,
an investigation of the needs of the students in each particular school.
It should also be based on research and development to facilitate
constant updating of specifications to meet these needs.   Through
the plan the school district would be able to measure its own output
against the way its students actually perform.   It would be able to
see exactly what results flow from the dollars it has invested.

The purpose of the educational redevelopment plan, of course,
is to provide a systematic approach for making the changes in educational organization and practice necessitated by the new demands on
the education system.   To assure that the plan will provide quality,
it should use a mix of measurements that are relevant, reliable, objective, easily assessable, and that produce data in a form that can be
processed by modern-day technology.   As a further guarantee of
quality, teams of school administrators, teachers, and modern educational and technical specialists competent to interpret the results
should be available.   The plan should also spell out a clear relationship between results and goals, thus providing for accountability.

In reality, this educational plan is only a piece of paper—a set
of ideals and a set of step-by-step progressions which schools and
districts can approximate.   But it does provide a blueprint for the

educational managers of the district—the superintendent, teachers, principals, and school boards—who must provide the leadership and the understanding to carry out educational change.

To be effective and to assure that its specifications remain valid, an educational redevelopment plan must set aside dollars for research and development. The Committee for Economic Development in last summer's report revealed that less than one percent of our total national education investment goes into research and development. "No major industry," the report said, "would expect to progress satisfactorily unless it invested many times that amount in research and development." Many private companies plow as much as 15 percent of their own funds back into research and development.

If one percent of the yearly budget for education was set aside for research and development, we would have a national educational research and development fund of roughly $500 million. Such money could attract new services, new energies, new partnerships to education. And they would inspire competition that would spur rapid educational development. This research and development money could be used to buy technical assistance, drawing on the expertise of private industry, the nonprofit organizations, the universities, the professions, and the arts. The administrative functions of a school system—construction, purchasing, disbursement, personnel, payroll— also demand business and management skills.

Why not draw on business for technical assistance or actual management in these areas? Or for that matter, in formulating the educational redevelopment plan itself? The final step in setting up a quality assurance system is providing for acccountability of both the educational process and its products, the students. Do pupils meet the overall objectives and the performance specifications that the school considers essential? Can Johnny read, write, figure? Can he also reason? Can he figure out where to find a given piece of information not necessarily stored in his head? Does he understand enough about himself and our society to have pride in his culture, a sureness about his own personal goals and identity, as well as an understanding of his responsibilities to society? Does he have the various cognitive and social skills to enter a wide range of beginning jobs and advance in the job market?

The accountability of process, of classroom practice, is somewhat harder to get at. At the risk of mixing it up with ideas about educational hardware, we might call it the technology of teaching. To find out a little about it, we might start by asking whether things are being done differently today in a particular classroom than they were done in the past.

A host of disenchanted teachers and others—from Bel Kaufman in her *Up the Down Staircase* to Jonathan Kozol in *Death at an Early Age*—have been telling us over the past few years what has up to now been happening in many classrooms in America. In *The Way It Spozed To Be,* James Herndon, a California schoolteacher, describes one kind of advice he got from experienced teachers during his first year in an inner-city school: "This advice was a conglomeration of dodges, tricks, gimmicks to get the kids to do what they were spozed to do. . . . It really involved gerrymandering of the group—promises, favors, warnings, threats . . . A's, plusses, stars. . . . The purpose of all these methods was to get and keep an aspect of order . . . so that 'learning could take place. . . .' "

Today, teachers often try to teach order, responsibility, citizenship, punctuality, while believing that they are in fact teaching reading or French or gym. If Johnny forgets his pencil, for example, he actually may not be permitted to take the French quiz and might get an F—presumably for forgetfulness, certainly not for French, for the grade does not reflect Johnny's competence in French.

In one State's schools, girls' physical education regularly chalks up far more F's than any other course. A study of the reasons indicated that gym teachers actually were attempting to measure citizenship by tallying whether Jane kept a dirty locker or failed to take a shower. The grade hardly reflected her competence in physical education. Requirements such as punctuality, neatness, order, and time served, ought not to be used to reflect school subject mastery.

Despite considerable evidence to the contrary, many schools and teachers are still grouping youngsters as good or bad raw material. What can you do with bad raw material? some teachers ask, much as some doctors once asked about the mentally ill. What we are searching for in place of a "demonology" of teaching is sensitive and sensible classroom practice—a practice that treats every child as a person and uses a variety of pleasurable techniques to improve his performance in anticipated and replicable ways. We are not sure this will result in more learning—though we think it will—but we do know that sensitive and sensible classroom practice is good in itself. As such it will pay off in human ways, even if it doesn't pay off in learning.

As teachers' salaries rise and their demands for rights and benefits are rightfully met by the communities they serve, those communities can expect that teacher responsibility will also grow. In fact, they can insist on it. They can insist that better pay, more rights, and more status bring with them better standard practice in the schools and classrooms. They can insist that teachers become accountable for relating process and procedures to results. And pupil accomplishment, though it may reflect some new hardware and construction, by and large reflects teacher and administrator growth and development. This is the true meaning of a new technology of teaching.

Thus the changes that result when the redevelopment plan has been carried out must be demonstrably apparent in terms of both teacher and pupil progress. In order to measure how these actual results compare to the detailed objectives of the plan, it makes sense to call for an outside educational audit, much like the outside fiscal audit required of every school system today. The school system could request an audit either of its overall program or of specific parts of that program.

This new approach could conceivably lead to the establishment of a new category of certified educational auditors whose principal job would be to visit school districts, on invitation, to help determine the success of local program planning in achieving prestated goals. One expert suggests that an educational audit need take only 10 school days a year for a single school system. His idea is to send a completely equipped and staffed mobile educational audit van to visit about 20 school systems a year.

Educators should also be encouraged to describe and measure the behavior expected of each student upon completion of programs funded from Federal sources. To reinforce accountability for results, contracts for Federal funds might be written as performance agreements. Thus a proposal for funds to back a reading program might stipulate that 90 percent of the participating students would be able to satisfy criteria by demonstrating they had achieved a particular advance in grade level in the time proposed.

Furthermore, special financial incentives based on meeting performance criteria might be specified in these contracts. For example, a certain amount of dollars might be awarded to a school for each student who achieves a high school diploma (defined as a verification that 16 credits have been attained in specific subjects with a credit defined as 72 hours of successful classroom study). Or a school might be given monetary awards for each student who has been employed for a year after leaving the institution.

Lest the idea of performance contracts strike anyone as novel or bordering upon the impossible, it should be pointed out that they have been formulated and applied with great success by both industry and the armed services for years. The fact that many results of education are subjective and not subject to audit should not stop us from dealing precisely with those aspects that do lend themselves to definition and assessment.

Most directors of ESEA projects should have more training in how to manage large sums of money than they have had in the past. Anyone who knows business knows you don't run half-million and million-dollar programs without considerable expertise in management. Obviously, managers of these projects need technical assistance if they are to manage in the best and most modern sense. For example, there should be technical reviews of all successful programs, practices, and materials used in embryo experimental projects. Educational objectives should be translated into a clearer framework for the purposes of reporting, evaluation, and feedback. In most cases, schools would need outside technical assistance to carry out either of these tasks.

Greater educational management competence is also needed in an area that might be called "educational logistics." Many projects don't get off the ground because the equipment, personnel, and training they depend upon are not properly coordinated. The notion of staging, for example, to bring together all the elements that are necessary for a project to achieve performance, is very important. Virtually the only time you see this, in education in general as well as in ESEA projects, is in the school drama programs or on the athletic field.

Today formal education is the chief path to full citizenship. School credits and diplomas and licenses are milestones on that path. Schooling is literally the bridge—or the barrier—between a man and his ability to earn his bread. Without it a citizen is condemned to economic obsolescence almost before he begins to work.

If we accept competence for all as one of the major goals of education today, then we must devise a system of accountability that relates education's vast budget to results. It is a paradox that while our technologically oriented society is a masterful producer of the artifacts our civilization needs, it seems incapable of applying that technology to educating our young citizens.

We can change the way our educational system performs so that the desired result—a competently trained young citizenry—becomes the focus of the entire process. In the same way that planning, market studies, research and development, and performance warranties determine industrial production and its worth to consumers, so should we be able to engineer, organize, refine, and manage the educational system to prepare students to contribute to the most complex and exciting country on earth.

Robert J. Nash
Russell M. Agne

# 29. THE ETHOS OF ACCOUNTABILITY— A CRITIQUE

The accountability movement is generating an ethos among educators that must not go unchallenged. This ethos—whose governing principles are based on a technological-economic world-view—is distinguished by its frenzied insistence on the large-scale transportation of attitudes and practices from the world of business, engineering, and science to the world of education. One result of this slavish dependence on the beliefs and procedures of other fields has been to reduce the total educational endeavor to a tired litany of achievement, performance, and production characterized by the blank torpor of systems analysis, technological engineering, quality control, and rep-

Spearheading the struggle against the spread of the accountability movement as it presently is constituted are such persons as Robert J. Nash, Assistant Professor of Educational Anthropology and Philosophy and Russell M. Agne, Assistant Professor of Science Education, both of the University of Vermont. Source: Robert J. Nash and Russell M. Agne, "The Ethos of Accountability— A Critique," *Teachers College Record* 73 (February 1972), pp. 357–369. Reprinted by permission.

licability. The creeping extrusion into education of an ethos which defines the successful educational experience primarily in terms of systems engineering and measurable outputs signifies a tragic loss of larger vision and purpose among educators. The unsettling implication is that the nearer we come to the realization of accountability in our educational institutions—as accountability is presently being defined and huckstered—the greater will be the cleavage between our educational ideals and our actual practices; and the greater will be the consequent clamor for sweeping educational reform.

## THE CASE FOR ACCOUNTABILITY

Leon Lessinger has argued eloquently for accountability in education.[1] He has asserted that each child has an inalienable right to be taught what he needs to know in order to be a productive, contributing citizen. Furthermore, each citizen has a right to know what educational results are being produced by specific expenditures. Finally, the schools have a right to draw upon talent, enterprise, and technology from all sectors of society, instead of relying exclusively on the "overburdened" resources of professional educators.[2] From these basic premises Lessinger has concluded that educators must guarantee the acquisition of basic skills to all children, regardless of their background. He has compared the educational system to a malfunctioning machine and has emphasized the necessity of preparing "educational engineers" who can look for the precise causes of the malfunction, test the variables and the performance of each part of the machine to determine what has gone wrong, and then carefully define the performances which educators ought to isolate, and the changes which need to be made in order to bring about the desired learning of basic skills.[3] Lessinger believes that this type of accountability can lead to "a symbiosis of technology and humanism, wedding the skill of the one to the values of the other."[4]

Myron Lieberman has advanced another type of rationale for educational accountability.[5] His premise is that accountability ought to prevail in the schools. He warns that if public schools fail to de-

[1] Leon Lessinger, *Every Kid a Winner: Accountability in Education* (New York: Simon and Schuster, 1970).

[2] Ibid., pp. 4–5.

[3] Ibid., p. 33.

[4] Ibid., p. 37.

[5] Myron Lieberman, "An Overview of Accountability," *Phi Delta Kappan*, vol. 52, no. 4 (December 1970), pp. 194–195.

velop acceptable criteria and procedures for accountability, they will provoke the emergence of accountability through alternative school systems. Lieberman contends that unless school systems do a better job of relating school costs to educational outcomes, they will continue to be battered by the persistent demands of disgruntled parents, critics, and youth for alternative schools. Both Lessinger and Lieberman reason that the most convincing kind of accountability to patrons which educators can produce is to deliver in tangible, demonstrable ways on the promises they have made to teach all children the basic reading, writing, communicative, and computational skills they will need to live in a demanding technological society. Kenneth B. Clark, in a similar vein, has gone even further than Lieberman and Lessinger to propose that teachers in the inner city be held accountable to the extent that they be paid solely on the basis of their abilities to teach children the fundamental reading and computational skills.[6]

And, finally, Fred M. Hechinger, the education editor for the *New York Times*, has summarized the negative rationale for accountability. He maintains that if we hold educators accountable in objective ways, we can effectively counter three impending educational trends: a widespread dissatisfaction with the public schools; an alarming frequency of performance contracting with the educational establishment and its attendant ethically questionable practices of "teaching to the test"; and the introduction of voucher plans which might result in the demise of public education in this country.[7]

## HISTORICAL BACKGROUND

As a guiding ideal for professional behavior, accountability is imbedded deeply in the American tradition. An anthropologist, Francis L.K. Hsu, has observed that for three hundred years Americans have remained suspicious of most overt forms of authority. In order to prevent their institutions (such as the government) from becoming unresponsive to the individual citizen, Americans have watched their "government and check[ed] it when it misbehaves or fails to deliver the goods."[8]

[6] Fred M. Hechinger, "A Program to Upgrade Schools for the Deprived," *New York Times*, July 26, 1970, p. 56.
[7] Fred M. Hechinger, "Accountability: A Way to Measure the Job Done by Schools," *New York Times*, February 14, 1971, p. 7.
[8] Francis L.K. Hsu, *The Study of Literate Civilizations* (New York: Holt, Rinehart and Winston, 1969), p. 82.

Historically, white middle-class Americans have demanded that schools be held accountable to the extent that they enable students to master the basic skills which allow them to share in the rising standard of living. Richard Hofstadter documented the American tendency toward anti-intellectualism due to the traditional expectancy that schools "be practical and pay dividends." He observed that progressive education always has capitulated to the demands of its clientele for accountability in those areas of learning which are exclusively utilitarian, rather than in those areas which stress knowledge for its own sake.[9] Merle Curti, in tracing the response of the American educational establishment to the demands of its constituency to be accountable in life-adjustment programs, homemaking, vocational preparation, intergroup relations, and technical training, has shown, by inference, that accountability has existed, at least as an implicit educational principle, in this country for three hundred years.[10]

In spite of the historical warrant for accountability, we believe that the new accountability cult in public school education must be challenged. Amidst the paroxysms of testimony from performance contractors and educational technologists that accountability will be the soothing alembic which will purify our beliefs and procedures, there persists the unmistakable reality that we are trivializing the aims of education at a time when we ought to be examining our basic purposes and expanding our vision. In our reluctance to challenge the necessity of being held accountable for failing to teach our clients to read, write, and compute, we have failed to understand that the ethos which professional educators are generating is itself a numbing critique of the limited ends we are striving to realize.

In the sections that follow, we will be examining three tendencies in American education which have been generated by the ethos of accountability. First, we will examine what is happening as a result of the technological imperative to adopt the procedures of educational engineering, performance criteria, behavioral objectives, and assessment techniques, at a time when we ought to be raising questions about the proximate, intermediate, and long-range ends of our educational procedures. Second, we will show how we are reinforcing a technocratic value system, based on a pseudoscientific *Weltanschauung*, at a time when educators ought to be challenging the very valid-

---

[9] Richard Hofstadter, *Anti-Intellectualism in American Life* (New York: Vintage, 1963).

[10] Merle Curti, *The Social Ideas of American Educators* (New Jersey: Littlefield, Adams and Company, 1965).

ity of the contemporary technocratic-scientific ethos which controls so much of our lives.  And third, we will demonstrate that we are perpetuating an economic and political status quo, at a time when we ought to be probing to the roots the valuational and ideological base upon which the whole system rests.

## MEANS AND ENDS

The myopic fixation on the means of accountability, to the systematic exclusion of any serious concern with ends, is amply demonstrated by recent writing on the subject.  Leon Lessinger, in his pioneering work on accountability, has stipulatively defined education as the mastery of a set of skills.[11]  From this definition, he constructs a model of the teacher as an "educational engineer" who must help schools to obtain a "workable technology of instruction."  According to Lessinger, the educational engineer must be able to convince school officials to adopt "certain managerial procedures that both stimulate the demand for performance and help [officials] to provide it."[12]  Also the educational engineer must be able to report with "tables and text" how much it will cost a community to frame performance criteria for a program, obtain an independent educational audit to measure the actual performance against these criteria, and provide for an auditor to report publicly his findings.[13]  Nowhere in Lessinger's analysis of accountability, vis-à-vis the new educational engineering, is there even the slightest concern with any purpose of the educational process beyond the teacher's transmission of a basic set of skills to students.

In another context, Leo Tolstoy once observed that the fundamental and inescapable preoccupation of any human being is "What should I do?" and "How should I live?"  Tolstoy concluded that since these are questions of ultimate ends, and not means, and since science cannot answer them, it follows that science is useless.[14]  Lessinger and many other spokesmen for accountability[15] are guilty of a

[11] Lessinger, op. cit., p. 133.

[12] Ibid., p. 32.

[13] Ibid.

[14] See F. William Howton, *Functionaries* (Chicago: Quadrangle Books, 1969), p. 39.

[15] See theme issue, "Accountability in Education," *Educational Technology*, vol. 11, no. 1 (January 1971).

reverse kind of syllogistic overstatement. They are saying that the fundamental concern of any educator ought to be "What can I accomplish that I can measure?" "How can I translate these objectives into performance criteria?" and "How can I effectively assess what I have tried to accomplish?" Since these are questions of means, and not purpose, it follows that other kinds of educational concerns are useless (or, if not useless, of no value since they cannot be objectively assessed).

There can be no denial of the need to identify the means by which educators strive to realize their ends. There is also an equally compelling need for educators to state more sharply and carefully the kinds of learning outcomes they hope to induce in their students. However, the danger in specifying an educational end in the language and belief system of educational engineering is that the desirable end will be subordinated to, and distorted by, that language and those beliefs. Charles Silberman, writing about the failure of educational reforms in this country, criticizes the tendency of educational engineers to model their curricula on production and computer processes.[16] Silberman warns that no engineering model is value-free. The technology we use to frame and specify a curriculum dictates its own values, and in many cases transforms desired ends. According to Silberman, The Individually Prescribed Instruction Program, based on a programmed sequence of instruction, requires such a high degree of precision and specificity of goals that students are often forced into passive learning roles. Students have no voice in specifying their own goals and they are limited to the preordained answers of the program. The weakness of the I.P.I. Program, and other programs which have been contrived by the new educational engineers, is to make their users so dependent on the technological system which specifies and dispenses what must be learned that there is very little opportunity for an individual to realize intermediate educational ends. Silberman has shown that those educational ends which are most significant (autonomous choice-making; independent, critical judgment; the specification of one's own goals) simply cannot be— nor should they be—defined in precise behavioral terms.[17]

Proponents of accountability fail to realize that every educational program has at least *three* kinds of ends or purposes. The proximate

---

[16] Charles Silberman, *Crisis in the Classroom: The Remaking of American Education* (New York: Random House, 1970), p. 201.
[17] Ibid.

ends include the learning of basic skills, and Lessinger deals with accountability preponderantly on this level. But there are two other kinds of purposes which are the *sine qua non* of the educational endeavor, and they obdurately resist being specified in the rigorous language of educational engineering. The intermediate ends include those educational objectives toward which the basic skills ought to be directed, and for which the basic skills should be applied. These are the ends which initially may have attracted people into teaching and they are best expressed in the emotive language of "appreciation," "understanding," "enthusiasm," "discrimination," "judgments," and "enjoyment." These ends continue to thwart precise behavioral classification, but they are no less important because they do so. And, finally, there are long-range ends which galvanize the first two levels and bestow ultimate meaning on the total educational experience. These are the sociopolitical ends which guide all educational activity serving as a constant reminder that the ultimate objective of any learning experience is to help the private person communicate with, evaluate, and reform the public world.[18]

When the procedures of accountability result in educational programs which fixate on proximate ends, or which reduce the other two kinds of ends to the proximate, there then occurs a deadly distortion of educational purpose. The New York City examination for teachers of high school English is a wrenchingly lucid example of distorted, short-range ends. The Board of Examiners, in an effort to be accountable to the New York taxpayers, have devised an objective, mechanical, machine-marked test that purports to measure the competency of prospective English teachers. The questions on the most recent test were based exclusively on the candidate's ability to recall instantly a fact such as the month in which Chaucer's pilgrims started for Canterbury, or to remember an obscure line or word in a poem. There were no questions which required any demonstration that the teacher understood or appreciated literature, or was able to relate a poem or short story to contemporary events. Because such goals were too subjective, and resistant to rigorous test specification, the examiners were content to measure only those dimensions of the English teacher's performance which they considered testable. Unfortunately, according to a teacher who took the test, the unintended

---

[18] See the latest writing of the social reconstructionist, Theodore Brameld, *Patterns of Educational Philosophy: Divergence and Convergence in Culturological Perspective* (New York: Holt, Rinehart and Winston), 1971.

testable outcomes became skill in instant factual recall, guessing ability, and test-taking endurance.[19]

We close this section on means and ends with a passage by Ann Cook and Herbert Mack, two former public school teachers who have raised radical questions concerning the aims of education. They maintain:

> It isn't because children can't read that our country is torn by internal conflict. It isn't because our children can't add that we elect politicians who campaign on personality, not program, that the country is embroiled in a divisive war, that consumers purchase defective merchandise, that television is a wasteland and our environment polluted. These conditions are not due to deficiencies in reading and math. It is rather that our population is not being educated in critical areas: how to judge, to ask questions, to seek information, to analyze, and to evaluate.
>
> It is not sufficient to concentrate on reading and math skills. We must look beyond the "decoding" procedures that most programs are designed to teach. What is the purpose of learning such skills? Does teaching a child to discern between the *a* in cat and the *a* in fate mean automatically that the child will want to read, make meaningful sense of his knowledge, broaden his vision or satisfy his curiosity? Learning to read is really a lifetime activity based fundamentally on one's attitudes about books and is generated by curiosity and by an eagerness to explore and find enjoyment. It is critically important that children learn to question their world, to deal with the ambiguity in their environment, and to realize that not every issue has a "correct" answer.[20]

## TECHNOCRACY AND SCIENCE

According to Theodore Roszak, a technocracy is a social form in which an industrial society reaches the peak of its organizational integration.[21] The technocratic ethos can be identified as follows: a

[19] See Flasterstein, "A Test for Teachers?" *Boston Sunday Globe*, April 4, 1971, p. B-43.

[20] Ann Cook and Herbert Mack, "Business in Education: The Discovery Center Hustle," *Social Policy*, vol. 1, no. 3 (September-October 1970), p. 10.

[21] Theodore Roszak, *The Making of a Counter Culture: Reflections on the Technocratic Society and Its Youthful Opposition* (New York: Anchor Books, 1969), p. 5.

relentless pursuit of efficiency and productivity; an extensive rational control over every human endeavor; an organizational logic which stresses integration, modernization, and extreme systemization; an emphasis on technique, omnicompetency, and expertise; a passionate concern with objective data and predictability; and a conscious effort to transmute the beliefs and procedures of all fields to the scientific world-view.

Roszak has fulminated against the technocratic ethos on the grounds that it has become a "mechanistic imperative" which exerts an all-consuming pressure on people to conform to the prevailing value orientation of bureaucrats, managers, operation analysts, and social engineers. He maintains that modern man is becoming indistinguishable from the cybernated systems he is assisting. Modern man is cold, precise, logical, indifferent, efficient, dispassionate, and objective. He is every inch a "professional" who spends his time observing, classifying, measuring, and quantifying, and he communicates these findings through the mediation of bloodless models, mechanical gadgets, abstract schemas, and chilly jargons. The stark outcome of technocratic professionalism is the creation of a hollow, contemporary expert who has relinquished forever any kind of awesome, tender, and spontaneous engagement with the world.[22]

In spite of Roszak's caricature of the modern technocrat, one only has to look at the field of education to see how the exaggeration has become reality. The cult of accountability has given birth to a new category of educational technocrat, the systems engineeer. What follows is a systems description of the school as an educational technocrat sees it:

> Any given school, or school district, can readily be seen as a system for several reasons. It has incoming energies (inputs), is organized into a structure of processes and controls (functioning subsystems), and yields energies to the larger, or, suprasystem (outputs). Further, it is bounded spatially by other institutions which are non-schools, or, not primarily educational in nature. And, it is encased in the limitation of time. For, all systems have a tendency towards entropy. Such entropy may be described generally as the result of minimizing the energy exchange with the environment, or with other systems, thus "closing" the system. A long-term resistance toward the system results in a "death-state."[23]

[22] Ibid., pp. 1–41.

[23] Francis J. Pilecki, "The Systems Perspective and Leadership in the Educa-

When the systems engineer describes the school in the nomenclature of "inputs," "outputs," "entropy," "suprasystem," "subsystem," and "death-state" (the imagery of organizational management and physics), he illustrates an all-encompassing faith in the basic tenets of the technocratic ethos. In his controlled euphoria over predictability, accuracy, reliability, integration, and organizational tautness, he expresses a commitment to the ideals of efficiency engineering for the effective organization of men and machines.

The fallacy of the systems model resides in the assumption that a physics-management prototype can be used to explain adequately the polymorphous intricacy of an institution like the school. A corollary fallacy is that people can be considered as simple, mechanomorphic units within a structure of interactions as unique and as diverse as the educational experience. W. Ross Ashby, a cyberneticist, has pointed out the central illusion in systems engineering—the myth of *ceteribus paribus* (other things being equal).[24] Complex systems resist the wholesale application of simpler systems models. Organizations such as the school are so unique, dynamic, and unpredictable, that crude analogies to business or engineering models must ignore the special complexity of an institution whose overarching function is to facilitate purposeful, educational transactions among developing human beings. And, finally, the danger of a facile systems application to the field of education is that often a so-called "subsystem" can be successful in one context, but when it is absorbed by a larger system, its success is mitigated. The educational reformer, the experimental school district, the innovative teacher, and the administrative dissident all have in common the possible enervation and dissolution of their programs once they are coopted into a larger system whose objective may be more survival than reformation.[25]

Perhaps the major misuse of the systems model is the implicit faith that a systems approach will guarantee predictability, objectivity, and efficiency in the educational enterprise.[26] Lessinger has

---

tional Organization," *Journal of Education*, vol. 153, no. 1 (October 1970), p. 50.

[24] W. Ross Ashby, *An Introduction to Cybernetics* (New York: John Wiley & Sons, 1956), p. 5.

[25] See P. Michael Timpane, "Educational Experimentation in National Social Policy," *Harvard Educational Review*, vol. 40, no. 4 (November 1970), pp. 547–566.

[26] See Frederick D. Erickson and Eliezer Krumbein, "A Systems Approach to Reforming Schools," in James W. Guthrie and Edward Wynne, eds., *New Models for American Education* (New Jersey: Prentice-Hall, 1971), pp. 116–132.

written that the new educational engineer will be a "manager" who will function to construct a management system and support group. Together, they will develop programs, design requests for proposals based on *objective* and *predictable* performance specifications, assist in evaluating proposals, and provide *efficient* management services to performance contractors.[27] Herein lies the ultimate *reductio ad absurdum*. Simply stated, educators have failed to understand that in an enterprise like education, where human beings are always ontologically prior to the system they constitute, the technocratic values of predictability, objectivity, and efficiency are either undesirable or unattainable.

Many scientists have realized this, and have become properly chary of transgressing the natural limits of science. They avoid casting their discipline in the mold of "scientism" (the belief that the techniques of science can be applied in all areas of human investigation).[28] Human behavior is subject to so many variables that many scientists are skeptical of the accuracy of measurement. The Heisenberg uncertainty principle has led scientists to the conclusion that they can never accurately predict or measure the velocity of subatomic particles let alone the behavior of human beings. When any kind of data are collected in a dynamic system, the data can never represent the current situation. Hence predictability is almost impossible with human beings.[29]

So too, while scientists stress the methodology of objectivity in their laboratory, the wiser of them willingly suspend the methodology when they enter the world of values. The scientist is unable to deal directly with human values, and consequently he can never prove objectively what ought to be good or desirable. He refuses to extend predictability and objectivity to the world of human feeling because he cannot claim certainty here. While the scientist is aware of his investigative limits, the educational engineer has yet to define his own boundaries.[30]

Efficiency is a value which has not been of much concern to the natural scientist. And yet the educational engineer has reasoned that if educators are "scientifically" efficient, then they will be accountable. Raymond E. Callahan has traced the history of "the cult of

---

[27] Lessinger, op. cit., p. 65.

[28] Garvin McCain and Erwin M. Segal, *The Game of Science* (Belmont, California: Brooks-Cole Publishing Company, 1969), pp. 164–171.

[29] Ibid., pp. 151–163.

[30] See a typical overstatement, Felix M. Lopez, "Accountability in Education," *Phi Delta Kappan*, vol. 52, no. 4 (December 1970), pp. 231–235.

efficiency" and the tragic misapplication of business and industrial values to education during the last fifty years.[31] He concludes his study with the admonition that in the future the quest for efficiency in education must always be secondary to the pursuit of quality learning experiences—even if these are inefficiently administered and costly. The scientist has learned what the educational engineer has not—that a concern with efficiency (maximizing output while minimizing input) is a technocratic value which has produced effective guillotines, bombs, and assembly lines, but has never created an audacious experimental insight, or major scientific breakthrough. Efficiency is a normative term which tends to impede rather than facilitate the creative endeavor.

Much of the current literature on accountability is filled with the metaphor of the school as a malfunctioning machine that systems engineers can repair with massive infusions of predictability, objectivity, and efficiency.[32] What is so often ignored in these proposals is the root question which must guide the total educational experience: what kind of human beings do we want our students to become? If we reconstruct the profession of education in the image of technocracy, then we are going to produce a society of technocrats. If we convert the school to a systems model, then we run the risk of unconsciously establishing as our primary educational objective the maintenance of an inert, airtight system, devoid of the unpredictable sparkle which dynamic human beings must provide if an organization is to be self-renewing.

We close this section with a warning and a question. George W. Morgan, a philosopher, has identified the pathetic—but inevitable—human outcome of an ethos which compares human beings to machines, and apotheosizes the quantitative properties of timing, dimension, speed, output, and efficiency. He calls this creation, "the prosaic mentality," and he describes it as follows:

> . . . the prosaic man is forever incapable of considering issues in depth. He stays at the surface; he remains with things that permit readily specifiable action. He entertains no questions with respect to life, man, or society that do not obviously lead to specific things to do. Everything else, it seems to him,

---

[31] Raymond E. Callahan, *Education and the Cult of Efficiency* (Chicago: The University of Chicago Press, 1962).

[32] Lessinger, op. cit., pp. 3–19. See also William A. Deterline, "Applied Accountability," *Educational Technology*, vol. 11, no. 1 (January 1971), pp. 15–20.

is mere words—idealistic, not realistic; sentimental, not practical. Confronted with a difficulty, the prosaic man gets busy:
he works at one thing and works at another; he changes,
modifies, and manipulates; he institutes projects and programs; . . . holds meetings, collects data . . . develops techniques. And he does all this without ever asking a single
fundamental question, without ever attending to such basic
things as the aims, underlying assumptions, values, or justification of what he is dealing with and what he is doing.
Therefore, all his busyness—restless, nerve-racking, and exhausting—is at bottom only tinkering with and an accelerating
of what already exists.[33]

We ask to what extent will the emphasis on accountability in education prevent the "prosaic man" from becoming a flesh-and-blood
reality in the world of the future? Ultimately, this will be the most
crucial test, regarding the contribution of accountability to the plight
of modern man.

## MAINTENANCE OF THE STATUS QUO

The current emphasis in accountability is on micro-concerns. There
is no attention being given to the sociocultural norms which govern
these preoccupations. Instead, as one spokesman for accountability
has stated: "There is no escaping the fact that accountability is not a
neutral device—it encapsulates a view of the educational function in
which basic cognitive and mathematical skills are primary." He goes
on to argue that "cultural, artistic, or political" learnings might still
receive attention "but they would not be dominant."[34]

Throughout the literature on accountability there is a gaping
absence of any recognition of the educational experience as encom-
passing such concerns as political reform or social reconstruction.
Leon Lessinger continues to stress the necessity of educators being
responsible to the "legitimate demands" of their constituents. However, there is never any doubt that for Lessinger these "legitimate
demands" must always be for the "special skills" which will enable

[33] George W. Morgan, *The Human Predicament: Dissolution and Wholeness*
(New York: Delta, 1970), pp. 89–90.
[34] Aaron Wildavsky, "A Program of Accountability for Elementary Schools,"
*Phi Delta Kappan*, vol. 52, no. 4 (December 1970), p. 216.

citizens to become literate, insatiable consumers.[35]   Lessinger and other spokesmen[36] limit their rationale for accountability to such educational factors as cost analysis, system governance, educational management, instructional feedback, performance incentive, and data assessment.   Rarely do these writers consider the possibility of expanding the parameters of accountability to include the political dimensions of the educational undertaking.   At times it would seem that the reason why these writers have not speculated on the "outer limits" of accountability is that they are too busy using the school to maintain and strengthen the status quo.

But what if the existing system is in need of sweeping reform? What if accountability is stretched to include the educator's responsibility to analyze, discredit, disassemble, and reconstruct his profession so that it is more directly responsive to the cries of human beings who suffer from the iniquitous defects of the social order?   Where in the present efflux of literature exhorting us to adopt accountability techniques is there a voice, like Paulo Freire's, which goads educators to be accountable to the oppressed peoples of the world?   Where are we being urged to apply Freire's concept of "praxis," which directs us to help our students to reflect upon the social, political, and economic contradictions in the culture and to take systematic political action against the oppressive power blocs?[37]   Who among the spokesmen for accountability would ask us to be accountable for helping students to come to the deepest possible understanding of themselves and their relationship to society?   Where is the accountability advocate who speaks out against a concept of education which has been desiccated into programmatic forms and paralyzed by a dead-end preoccupation with careerism?

What is evident in much of the apologia for educational accountability is a shocking blindness to the political structure upon which the theory and practice of American education are based.   The school and the society cohere in a sociopolitical unity.   Whether educators know it or not, education is a ruthlessly political process.   Frequently when educators are cautioned to act as "professionals," they are

---

[35] Lessinger, op. cit., pp. 123–137.

[36] See Roger A. Kaufman, "Accountability, A System Approach and the Quantitative Improvement of Education—An Attempted Integration," *Educational Technology*, vol. 11, no. 1 (January 1971), pp. 21–26.

[37] Paulo Freire, *Pedagogy of the Oppressed* (New York: Herder and Herder, 1970).

being reminded that their principal and exclusive function must continue to be to integrate the younger generation into the unquestioned logic of the present sociopolitical system. The more effortlessly this can be accomplished, the better. But to restrict the function of education to the mechanical fitting of young people to the economic demands of a social system is to use the schools to maintain social realities as they are.

For example, the Dorsett Educational Systems, Inc., (the performance contractor for the Texarkana schools) is basing its entire program on motivational techniques which are insidiously competitive.[38] In using token rewards such as transistor radios to motivate students toward achievement, the Texarkana schools are transmitting a value constellation necessary for the survival of the socioeconomic system. The sociologist, Philip Slater, has shown that competition for marketable skills in the schools is based on a false assumption of scarcity. We have grounded our motivational practices in the larger cultural belief that the society does not contain the resources to satisfy the needs of all its inhabitants. We insist that students compete with each other to develop the skills which will enable them to win scarce resources. Those who learn the most skills are told that they will grab the largest share of the resources, and consequently the economic system manages to perpetuate itself through the schools. Slater goes on to demonstrate that the key flaw in the scarcity assumption is that the important human needs can be easily satisfied and the resources for doing so are plentiful. Competition is unnecessary and the primary danger to human beings is not the mythical scarcity of resources, but the aggression which is unleashed when human beings are forced to compete with themselves and each other for spurious, system-serving skills and goods.[39]

Ten years ago Jules Henry, an anthropologist, charged the schools with fueling the free enterprise drives of achievement, competition, profit, mobility, performance, skills competency, and expansiveness. He warned that unless the schools stopped serving the narrow interests of the economic system, and began to stress the values of love, kindness, quietness, honesty, simplicity, compassion, cooperation, critical judgment, and autonomy, then the United States

[38] Lessinger, op. cit., "Excerpts from Texarkana's Formal Project Application to the U.S. Office of Education," pp. 155–171.
[39] Philip Slater, *The Pursuit of Loneliness: American Culture at the Breaking Point* (Boston: Beacon Press, 1970), pp. 96–118.

would become a "culture of death."[40]   Today Bertram M. Gross, an expert on urban affairs, has described the American society in terms which make Henry's "culture of death" a prophetic reality.   Gross claims that the United States can best be epitomized as follows:

> A managed society ruled by a faceless and widely dispersed complex of warfare-welfare-industrial-communications-police bureaucracies caught up in devoting a new style empire based on a technocratic ideology, a culture of alienation, multiple scapegoats and competing control networks.[41]

What is so often ignored in the literature on accountability is the realization that educators are as responsible for learning outcomes which are moral and political as they are for outcomes which are skills-centered.   It makes little sense to speak of accountability to our students solely because we are teaching them to read, write, and compute, if, as an unintended outcome, we are also preparing them to fit—painlessly and interchangeably—into Gross' nightmarish vision of American society.   To the extent that we produce citizens who are one-dimensional in their thinking, compulsively rigid in their value orientations, and excessively competitive in their interpersonal relationships, we have produced human selves who are fractured, and for this we are accountable.

Whenever we root our philosophy of education in a belief in "stable democracy," excluding from the learning experience the possibilities of "participatory politics," we are responsible in an indirect way for maintaining a political system which is hierarchical and self-serving.   Until we begin to perceive our technological society as emergent and capable of resolving its deepest dilemmas only through an alliance of all races and social classes, then we are merely perpetuating an inequitable social order which cries out for root reform.   And finally, until we realize that education has been used to strengthen a class system in the Western world, and to prop up military-industrial bureaucracies which desperately need dismantling, we will continue to be responsible for adventurist wars which our government may choose to wage in the future.

Accountability in education will have meaning only when we

---

[40] Jules Henry, *Culture Against Man* (New York: Vintage Books, 1965), pp. 13–15.

[41] Bertram M. Gross, "Can It Happen Here?" *New York Times,* January 4, 1971, p. 31.

begin to hold ourselves responsible for causing students to accept the myths of scarcity, competitiveness, American supremacy, productivity, and acquisitiveness. We must examine carefully the possibility that the technology of accountability is much more than a set of techniques and machines to attain certain objective learning outcomes. We must consider the possibility that accountability is fundamentally an ideological appeal to the means of power that enables one group to dominate another group.[42] How this power is used will determine the future direction of education in this country.

In order to make the ideal of educational accountability itself a more responsible one, we suggest that educators begin to raise certain questions. The first step in legitimizing any ideal is to ask political and moral questions about its underlying assumptions and its desired ends. We propose to take this first step by framing a set of questions which are meant to provoke controversy.

Who are the people most forcefully imploring educators to be accountable? Who has the most to gain, politically and economically, from a large-scale adoption of accountability in public education? Who is making the decisions regarding the ends toward which accountability will be applied? How will we insure that teachers, parents, and administrators will be heard and treated fairly? At this point, why have the students been silent? Will they really have the most to gain when educators are held accountable? What procedures will allow all the participants in the educational experience to be heard? And finally, who will be making the final decisions concerning accountability?

Unless educators and their clientele can challenge and reform the current ethos which is being generated by the case for accountability, the disparity which exists between our most visionary educational and social ideals and the actuality we are now living will become even more striking.

---

[42] William M. Birenbaum has advanced a similar argument in relation to the American university. See *Overlive: Power, Poverty, and the University* (New York: Dell Publishing Company, 1969).

1. Explain the essential features of the "educational redevelopment plan."

2. Lessinger introduces a concept of accountability for both the educational process and its product. What does he mean by accountability, and how does it relate to the plan?

3. How does accountability relate to the technology of teaching?

4. Why should each school district have an "educational audit"?

5. How does Lessinger suggest that federal contracts can ensure accountability? How do you suggest that accountability can be assured? Think in terms of quality of the teachers you employ.

6. Lessinger in several places offers analogies between industry and education. Are the analogies sound?

7. What are some advantages and disadvantages of accountability?

8. The ideas of different proponents of accountability are discussed. What is distinctive about Kenneth B. Clark's position? Why does Fred M. Hechinger fear the demise of public education if accountability is not introduced?

9. Why do Nash and Agne object to the fact that Lessinger concentrates on developing a basic set of skills? Is their objection valid?

10. Is there actually a danger of specifying educational ends in terms of the language and belief system of educational engineering?

11. Nash and Agne state that every educational program has three kinds of purposes. Are they correct in their judgment? Are they able to show the weaknesses of the educational engineers by their statement of purposes?

12. What is the "fallacy of the systems model"? Do the strengths of the systems approach sufficiently compensate for its shortcomings so that it can be used in education with desirable results?

13. Is predictability "almost impossible with human beings"? Is this an overstatement? If their claim is true, does

it nullify many things that we are presently doing in education?

14. What are the dangers of basing motivation on competition? What is the connection between accountability and competition?

15. Suppose you visit two school systems in the same state with approximately the same enrollment. One school system is using accountability procedures similar to those outlined in the Lessinger article and the other is not. Could you recognize significant differences between the two systems?

16. Looking at yourself as a student in one of your current courses, as an employee on any job you have, or as a friend, draw up your own "accountability contract." At the end of one week, audit it. How do you feel about operating under such a system?

17. "What kind of human being do we want our students to become?" Is this the root question which must guide educational experiences? Are your educational experiences helping you to live in a more meaningful manner? Are you becoming more alert? More apathetic?

18. Organize a panel to discuss the strengths and weaknesses of accountability.

19. Visit a school system that has instituted accountability, interview the principal and raise some of the above, and other, questions. Report your findings to class.

# XV. Performance Contracting

*The widespread dissatisfaction with public schools, both on the part of reformers and the public alike, has led to innovations within the schools and a search for alternatives to present organizational patterns and arrangements. The growing sophistication of educational technology has made possible new types of learning environments. Nevertheless, some schools are not equipped or adequately staffed to take full advantage of these developments. The very fact that the achievement levels of many students have failed to measure up to expectations has led to a search for alternatives to traditional operating procedures. Performance contracting has emerged in recent years as an attempt to fill these needs. Private learning corporations contract with public schools to teach one or more subjects, or to operate the entire school program by assuming responsibility for providing qualified teachers and the needed equipment and educational materials. The corporations would be paid at the end of the contracted period on the basis of the stipulated achievement scores registered by each student on standardized tests. Utilizing the latest knowledge from educational technology, coupled with the use of behavioral objectives, behavioristic learning theory, and individualized instruction, performance contracting furnished a number of new ideas for schools.*

*The Office of Economic Opportunity considered performance contracting sufficiently important to allocate $5–6 million for eighteen experimental programs in order to determine their effectiveness and whether additional programs merited funding.*

*The findings of their study, together with comments on these findings by certain educators, indicate that the programs did not live up to expectations.*

*In the following selection, James C. Gillis, Jr., explains three contracted plans, their rationale, operational procedures, and the advantages they are likely to offer.*

James C. Gillis, Jr.

# 30. PERFORMANCE CONTRACTING
# FOR PUBLIC SCHOOLS

It is generally accepted that American public education is less successful than it could be. Its future directions also are uncertain, due to pressures and influences such as:

- great increases in knowledge, especially in scientific and technical areas, in the last few decades;
- continuing population increases, placing more children in schools—and for longer periods of time;
- increasing pressure from minority groups to have a voice in the administration of the schools;
- student demands for greater relevancy of courses and study material;
- dissatisfied teachers using collective bargaining techniques to make their demands known.

Local school boards and school administrators are searching for solutions to this rash of problems. Unfortunately, only a few school boards and superintendents have seriously explored alternatives to the existing organizational structure. The public school system is over a hundred years old, and it is unrealistic to expect it to operate well in today's new environment.

Enormous strides have been made in management techniques

James C. Gillis, Jr., is president of Quality Educational Development, Inc., in Washington. He is a graduate of Boston and Harvard Universities. Formerly a high school teacher and department chairman, he also served in administrative capacities in the Job Corps and the U.S. Office of Education.
Source: James C. Gillis, Jr., "Performance Contracting for Public Schools," *Educational Technology* (May 1969), pp. 17–20. Reprinted by permission.

and educational technology within the past two decades. I estimate that 75 percent of the knowledge required to build and operate a modern learning system exists today. However, very few schools employ any of the components of such a system, and virtually no one has synthesized a fully functioning system that takes advantage of all the components.

One is compelled to ask why. Usually the answer is a complicated one that places blame obliquely on everyone and squarely on no one. Furthermore, despite the fact that quality educational opportunities are not available to large segments of our population, there has not been an appropriate response from the citizenry—a demand to fully utilize the existing technological resources to provide the best learning opportunities for each student.

Few alternatives to current patterns of schooling have been presented for the student or his parents to consider. In a country that has risen to world leadership based largely upon open competition and technological advances, it seems strange that one of the most profound institutions, the school, should remain a direct *operational* responsibility of the government—whether local, county, state or federal. With the exception of a few private schools, some form of government exercises a monopoly over formal schooling below the college or university.

Most educators believe that learning is a linear process that takes place in a specified sequence over a predetermined period of time— at least the present system behaves this way.

Most of today's teachers and administrators were not trained in educational technology (it is not an option at most colleges), and are simply not aware of its potential. It is difficult if not impossible for them to envision a computer mediated instructional system with learning modules creating a mosaic pattern based upon student performance and interest option, rather than as an instructional system based upon a linear pattern and elapsed time.

## ALTERNATE MODELS

Let us consider a few alternate approaches to the operation of a school system. Though the public agencies should continue to have the best interest of the individual and community as their primary concern, better procedures than are now in widespread use may be available for discharging this responsibility. Let us briefly examine three models.

## Model I—Limited Sub-contracting

The school system remains under local jurisdiction; it receives state and federal financial assistance and is operated by superintendents and their personnel, like most school systems today. The innovation of Model I, however, is the provision of certain courses or functional areas by another organization, either profit or non-profit, on a contractual basis.

For example, a request for proposals (RFP) might be sent out by the school system to corporations qualified and interested in providing learning experiences to students in, say, welding. The RFP would include the school system's criteria defining the kind and quality of student performance to be demonstrated at the end of the instructional block. The corporations would then submit a technical proposal and dollar bid, and the school system would select the one best able to meet the school's defined needs, at the best price. Depending upon the proposal, the corporation might send staff and equipment into the school, or transport students to a more appropriate facility in order to learn about welding.

The procedure of limited sub-contracting may be equally well applied to history, English, chemistry and other academic subjects and at any level. It would be possible to have a number of concurrent contracts with different organizations, depending upon the needs of the system.

In Model I, it is probable that vocational education would be one of the early candidates for contractual arrangements. This, along with music and certain of the arts, has long been done on a private basis. Aside from cultural values and the development of special talents, one of the reasons for such private contracting is that relatively clear-cut behavioral outcomes can be defined. Thus, the student's progress can be easily measured by observing his performance, and the contractor's performance can be inferred accordingly.

Although it is more difficult to measure abstract or verbal learning than skill acquisition, performance criteria in these areas can also be defined, and programs developed to meet them. Performance criteria can also be linked with payment, such that payment to a contractor for his services becomes contingent upon successfully meeting agreed-upon criteria related to student learning.

Proceeding still further, performance criteria may be linked to profit-sharing between the contractor, the teacher and the student, with profit-sharing becoming a reward system for attaining specific behavioral objectives. Obviously, the system could have many options. Money is not the only "profit" than can be "shared," nor is it necessarily the best. One could think of the contractor subcontracting with the teacher, and the teacher sub-sub-contracting with the student. In each agreement, the criteria and the reward can be clearly defined.

## *Model II—Total Prime Contracting*

Model II, an extension of Model I, is to contract for the operation of the *entire school system* through one or more contractual arrangements. This model places the school board in the position of having to hire a very limited number of specialized staff to monitor the contracts and evaluate the contractors' performance. The responsibility for actual operation would be the contractor's, and pay would be on the basis of services received (learning by students), not on the basis of elapsed time. Each contract would be reviewed at the end of a two- or three-year period of operation, and put up for bid again.

In this model, the learning system might be characterized by the following:

- a large number of learning packages, each dealing with a few closely related concepts;
- modular learning packages that can either stand alone or relate to other learning packages within a given discipline or course;
- materials that are designed to provide constant feedback to the student regarding his progress;
- an instructional management system that constantly keeps track of each student, and presents alternatives for each on the basis of individual performance;
- a data bank that will allow researchers, curriculum developers and teachers to analyze individual performance, group performance, specific instructional items and tests;
- opportunities for teachers to earn additional money contingent upon levels of student behavior change (learning).

In short, the goal of Total Prime Contracting would be the production of a learning system using modern management techniques which are self-corrective and cost/effective.  The system would require: 1) a well-defined instructional management system (IMS) utilizing the latest in hardware and software; 2) properly trained personnel capable of using the IMS and acting as guides and counselors to individual students; 3) physical facilities that enhance the program, and aid its proper functioning, and 4) learning materials that are self-paced, with many options to select variations in content and media format.

## Model III—Individual Contracting

Maintaining the integrity of the concept of performance contracting, but drastically changing the organizational format, one could conceive of at least one more model: a severe modification of the "GI Bill," where each person shops for his own education.  The government would provide free education to all citizens of all ages.  Let each individual decide when he wishes to learn, what he is interested in learning, and where.

Sufficient educational technology exists today to offer learning opportunities in the home, at work, or at "play."  Television, radio, telephone, portable cartridge tapes and visuals, plus the usual array of printed material are all available for instructional purposes.  In addition, learning centers, run on a private or public basis, could compete for customers.

Learning centers might work according to the following plan.  First, an organization (either profit or non-profit, private or public) would submit its operation to a public agency for examination and general accreditation.  The learning center could be a single entity or part of a nationwide chain; it could offer comprehensive courses in all areas at all age (or competency) levels, or it could specialize in one subject area.  Each learning module or course it offered would be approved for reliability of content and would meet minimum pedagogical standards.

Students of any age could then shop and choose what they wanted to study, where, and with whom.  If they were not learning well enough with one school, they could go to another.  The learning centers would receive money from the government, depending on two criteria: a) "X" dollars for each student who is physically present, or taking the module or course, and b) "Y" dollars based upon the performance level at the completion of the study.

Certain variations would have to occur in patterns of course offerings, dependent upon the general ability levels of students, the difficulty of materials, areas of national concern, etc. A supply and demand relationship would evolve between the government and the learning centers, with an incentive system to provide certain courses.

## IMPLEMENTATION

Any one, all three, or some combination of the above models could be implemented within two to five years by communities and corporations. It is probable that many communities and several corporations would work together to achieve performance contracting.

Educational technology and a low labor-intensive posture must be the key to contractor-operated learning centers, or to involvement in schools as they are presently conceived. Many must be self-paced and capable of direct student interaction. Individualized instruction —provided through the full use of hardware and individualized software, and managed by an instructional management system—must be the mode of instruction, if performance contracting is to succeed.

Individualized instruction on a large scale demands both the instructional management system which keeps track of learning experiences for each student *and* sufficient quantities of curricular materials for all abilities and styles of student learning. The curricular materials should be developed through an empirical process of test and revision until they produce in students the specified behaviors they are designed to produce—and do so with a predetermined degree of consistency. They should be presented in multi-media formats for necessary redundancy as alternate ways to achieve certain ends; more important, media format should be selected to best convey the particular information that is being presented to the student.

Many groups have independently devised and are currently following an empirical curriculum development process with these goals. The process borrows heavily from behavioral psychology, defining criterion tests in behavioral terms, and individualizing the instruction through pacing and through branching techniques. The student often has options, and can begin to feel that he is a responsible agent in his own education.

The recent development of educational technology—both techniques and hardware—has made such individualization possible. Unfortunately, educational technology is only beginning to be used effectively; given the state of the *possible* in education, the *actual* does not come very close. Only the rare school or college uses educational technology to any reasonable degree. Many organizations with greater technological capability are in a position of "outsider," and are only allowed to perform on a limited basis within the school setting, although they could be very helpful to the schools, used properly.

It costs money to upgrade any system. The research and development effort is expensive, and the actual installation of new procedures and materials, including training of staff, is considerably more expensive than maintaining the status quo. Once a new system is installed and operational, however, it is probably more cost/effective than the one it replaces; in other words, more student learning will be in evidence per dollar spent. Few school systems, least of all urban ones, can afford to install and maintain new technology without considerable help from other sources. A large portion of the work accomplished to date has been done as a result of funds provided under Title III and Title IV of the Elementary-Secondary Education Act of 1965 (P.L. 89-10). However, it might be possible to take advantage of existing technology by proceeding differently, and reallocating a system's available funds to contract out for specific services, paying according to student performance.

In this way, performance contracting would provide more relevant learning to more students at less overall cost to the taxpayer. Because there is a profit incentive for the contractor, he will constantly update his procedures and materials, thereby placing the latest research findings into practice within a year or two, rather than having the 30- to 50-year gap that has been traditional in education. American business has usually found ways to reduce cost and to provide the consumer with the quantity, quality and diversity for which he is willing to pay. There is no reason to believe that business cannot do the same in education.

In the past, textbook publishers and furniture manufacturers were the major businesses in the education sector. In the past five years, more companies, especially electronic firms, have begun to move seriously into the education market—and not just to sell hardware. They have begun to know the "market," and soon they will realize that they must provide the leadership and direction for the wise use of the new educational technology.

It can be expected that the various levels of government will continue to provide funds, guidelines and monitoring function for efforts to advance the state of the art.  At the same time, it is equally predictable that industry's entry into the educational market will become an extended stay.

Performance contracting holds considerable promise for optimizing the relationship between these groups.  It is a means by which the requirements of the school and the needs of the student can shape the application of sophisticated technological talent, so that all people, of any age or background, may have full educational opportunity.

*Phi Delta Kappan*

# 31. OEO, EDUCATORS DEBATE VALUE OF PERFORMANCE CONTRACTING

"Back to the drawing board."

That's how Philip V. Sanchez, director of the Office of Economic Opportunity, reacted when he heard the results of OEO's 18 experiments in performance contracting for schools.  At the cost of $5–6 million we have learned that performance contracting for schools does not work, Sanchez said.

OEO officials said they will continue to experiment with alternatives to traditional systems—including the controversial voucher plan.  But they added quickly that they are through with performance contracting as a useful tool to improve learning in schools.

OEO's eagerness to "write off" performance contracting is being

This report, from *Phi Delta Kappan*, is the follow-up for the Gillis article.
Source: "OEO, Educators Debate Value of Performance Contracting," *Phi Delta Kappan* (March 1972), pp. 451–452.  Reprinted by permission.

challenged by many sources.  School officials and companies involved
in performance contracting charge OEO with trying to bury the concept with limited evidence.  Edward D. Trice, superintendent of the
Texarkana (Arkansas) School District, says OEO's assertion that
performance contracting has been found valueless to schools is "as
far wrong as can be."  Trice, who developed the nation's pioneer
performance contracting program three years ago, says his experience
shows that the idea "has a great deal of merit."  He offered this evidence: "The record of our performance contract anti-dropout program
speaks for itself—only eight out of 800 potential dropouts have left
school during the past two years.  The normal dropout rate for this
group," he said, "is 25%—or 200 students."

Despite charges that the findings were hasty and incomplete,
OEO officials are convinced that performance contracting was given
a fair test—and failed.  They also said only one of the 18 districts
involved in the experiment was continuing the innovations introduced
last year by the performance contractor.  A check with the participating districts, however, shows a different story: five—not one—
of the districts have picked up the contractors' programs and are
paying for their continuance out of their own funds.

The results brought "I told you so" comments from the presidents of the two leading teacher organizations.  David Selden, president of the American Federation of Teachers, said, "It just bears
out what we have been saying—that OEO should get out of the education business."  Donald E. Morrison, president of the National Education Association, said the results show that "simple and cheap
solutions" do not work.

A much more tolerant view was expressed by the leader of the
nation's school superintendents.  Paul B. Salmon, executive secretary
of the American Association of School Administrators, released this
statement: "Though the initial results have sometimes been disappointing, performance contracting should be retained as a useful
alternative for those who wish to use it.  Abandoning the idea at
this point would be shortsighted."

OEO summed up the test results at the end of the year-long experiments with these comments: "Not only did both groups (experimental and control) do equally poorly in terms of overall averages,
but also these averages are very nearly the same in each grade, in each
subject, for the best and worst students in the sample, and, with few
exceptions, in each site."

Thomas K. Glennan, OEO's acting assistant director for planning, research, and evaluation, said the wide variety of learning systems used in the experiments gave no clues as to which technique works better than others. "They all did badly," he said. He admitted, however, that a five-year span for the experiment may have come up with different results. Continuing his pessimistic view of performance contracting, Glennan discloses that four of the six companies involved in the experiment have given up performance contracting. All but one battled OEO over their payment.

Glennan said the companies, according to the procedure of performance contracting, promised to raise the achievement test scores of students a minimum amount. The companies were then paid on a sliding scale, depending on how much they exceeded the minimum guarantee. But they could also lose money if the results were poor. The major dispute over payments between OEO and the contractors centered on problems that were not anticipated at the time the study started. The companies claimed they didn't have the full 180 hours of teaching time promised. As a result, OEO negotiated changes in payments to reflect curtailments resulting from school assemblies, fire drills, and other interferences.

Glennan said pupils in second-grade performance contract reading programs gained, on an average, .4 of a grade level while those in the traditional program gained .5; for the third grade it was .3 for performance contract reading versus .2; seventh grade—.4 versus .3; eighth grade—.9 versus 1.0; ninth grade—.8 versus .8. In math, the second grade gained .5 in the performance contract program versus .5 in the regular program; the third grade—.4 versus .4; seventh grade —.6 versus .6; eighth grade—.8 versus 1.0; ninth grade—.8 versus .8.

Almost as an afterthought, Glennan also released preliminary results from two experiments with bonuses to teachers whose pupils achieved beyond certain levels. Neither effort—in Stockton, California, and Mesa, Arizona—resulted in any improved pupil gains, he said.

The OEO projects in the 18 school districts involved 13,000 pupils in the experimental program. They were selected from the "most academically deficient" student bodies. They were compared with 10,000 "control" pupils, who were selected because they received "next lowest" scores in reading and math.

Participating school districts were New York City; Philadelphia; Seattle; Dallas; Anchorage; Fresno; Hartford; Jacksonville; Las

Vegas; Grand Rapids, Michigan; Hammond, Indiana; McComb, Mississippi; Rockland, Maine; Selmer, Tennessee; Taft, Texas; Athens, Georgia; Wichita, Kansas; and Portland, Maine.

The six participating companies, each of which operated three programs, were: Alpha Learning Systems, Singer/Graflex, Westinghouse Learning Corporation, Quality Education Development, Learning Foundations, and Plan Education Centers.

The OEO experiment did not end performance contracting in education. About 100 contracts are now in effect in various forms—69 in Michigan alone.

# Discussion Questions and Activities

1. Is it true that "few alternatives to current patterns of schooling" have been presented for the student or his parents to consider? Make a survey of your own school district.

2. What is the difference between a linear and a mosaic pattern for arranging a learning environment? Do most public schools use linear patterns?

3. Describe and evaluate the "limited subcontracting" model.

4. Compare the "total prime contracting" model with the limited subcontracting plan.

5. While the "individual contracting" model, in comparison to the previous models, offers the widest range of options, it may also pose problems of equal access and segregation. Does the author show how these problems can be avoided?

6. How would Nash and Agne's criticisms (in the previous selection) apply to the instructional devices and learning environments created by performance contractors? Are their criticisms valid?

7. How do we reconcile the conclusions of the Office of Economic Opportunity's study of eighteen experiments in performance contracting with the report of the superintendent of Texarkana (Arkansas) school district on the dropout rate?

8. The presidents of the NEA and AFT were opposed to performance contracting. What could be some of the reasons for their opposition?

9. The executive secretary of AASA suggests that performance contracting "should be retained as a useful alternative for those who wish to use it." In light of the OEO's findings, why should it be retained? Give specific reasons.

10. Will the paying of bonuses to teachers whose pupils achieve beyond certain levels produce better results than by using the more traditional procedures of rewarding teachers? Is it right to pay a bonus to one for doing what he was hired for in the first place? Can this practice encourage manipulation?

11. Examine recent experiments with performance contracting to determine whether more positive results were achieved.

12. Visit a school that has introduced performance contracting and interview the sponsors of the program. Try to determine their basic purposes and motives.

13. Role-play being a salesman for one of the contracting models presenting his pitch to a group of teachers in their school lunch room. Others in the class should role-play the teachers.

# XVI.  Education Vouchers

*The many failures of the public schools which have been brought to public attention in recent years have led some educators to abandon the conviction that innovation within the system will bring about the desired changes. Instead, they have actively sought alternatives to the present system. One alternative that has been discussed and debated is the use of a voucher plan. Such a plan, its proponents contend, would break the monopoly of the public schools and open genuine alternatives by making it possible for parents to use their voucher to enable their child to attend the school of their choice. It would, for the first time, provide an open market for education so that each child could attend the school best suited for his educational development. It would also place the public schools in more direct and intensive competition with private schools, and some schools, which fail to provide the type of education parents want, might go out of business.*

*A number of groups are less than enthusiastic about the voucher plan. Many public school teachers and teacher associations are skeptical, while a number of citizens who fear the violation of a separation of church and state have made their opposition known. Would the voucher plan eventually lead to the dissolution of the public schools? Do we presently have enough private schools that are clearly superior to public schools? If not, this fact becomes self-defeating for the voucher plan. Could private schools participating in the plan discriminate on racial or religious grounds in hiring teachers? And would parochial schools have to give up sectarian religious courses to receive vouchers?*

*These and other significant questions are raised by George R. LaNoue following a presentation by Christopher Jencks of the ideas behind the voucher plan that he developed at the Center for the Study of Public Policy in conjunction with the Office of Economic Opportunity.*

Christopher Jencks

# 32. EDUCATION VOUCHERS

OEO announced in May that it hopes to fund an experiment which would provide parents with vouchers to cover the cost of educating their children at the school of their choice. This news has provoked considerable liberal opposition, including charges that the experiment is unconstitutional, that it is part of a Nixon plot to perpetuate segregation, and that it would "destroy the public school system." What, then, does OEO really have in mind?

If state and local cooperation is forthcoming, the first step will be the establishment of an Educational Voucher Agency (EVA) in some community. This EVA will resemble a traditional board of education in that it will be locally controlled and will receive federal, state, and local funds for financing the education of all local children. But it will differ from a traditional board in that it will not operate any schools of its own. That responsibility will remain with existing school boards, both public and private. The EVA will simply issue vouchers to all parents of elementary school children in its area. The parents will take these vouchers to a school in which they want to enroll their child. This may either be an existing public school, a new school opened by the public school board to attract families who would otherwise withdraw their children from the public system, an existing private school, or a new private school opened especially to cater to children with vouchers. If the school meets the basic eligibility requirements laid down by the EVA, it will be able to convert its vouchers into cash, which will cover both its operating expenses

Christopher Jencks is a former editor of *The New Republic* and a faculty member in the Harvard Graduate School of Education. He is co-author of *The Academic Revolution* and *Inequality*.
Source: Christopher Jencks, "Education Vouchers," *The New Republic* 163 (July 4, 1970), pp. 19–21. Reprinted by permission of *The New Republic*, © 1970, Harrison-Blaine of New Jersey, Inc.

and the amortization of capital costs. Such a system would enable anyone starting a school to get public subsidies, so long as he followed the basic rules laid down by the EVA and could persuade enough parents to enroll their children in his school. It would also give low-income parents the same choice about where they sent their children that upper-income parents now have. This would include all the public and private schools participating in the system.

The effect of these changes on the quality of education would depend on how effectively the EVA regulated the newly created marketplace, and especially on the rules it laid down for determining which schools could cash vouchers and which schools could not. Since the EVA would presumably be controlled by the same political forces that now dominate local school boards, some prophets anticipate that it would soon develop a regulatory system as complex and detailed as that now governing the public schools. If this happened, both publicly and privately managed voucher schools would soon be entangled in the usual bureaucratic and political jungle, in which everything is either required or forbidden. They would probably end up undistinguishable from existing public schools. Nothing would have changed, either for better or for worse.

This vision may, however, be unnecessarily gloomy. Today's public school has a captive clientele. As a result, it in turn becomes the captive of a political process designed to protect the interests of its clientele. The state, the local board, and the school administration establish regulations to ensure that no school will do anything to offend anyone of political consequence. By trying to please everyone, however, the schools often end up pleasing no one. The voucher system seeks to free schools from these managerial constraints by eliminating their monopolistic privileges. Under a voucher system, parents who do not like what a school is doing can simply send their children elsewhere. Schools which attract no applicants go out of business. But those which survive have a greater claim to run their own affairs in their own way.

Most opponents of the voucher system worry more about the possibility that the EVA would establish too few regulations than about the possibility that it would establish too many. They particularly fear the development of a system in which schools would compete with one another in terms of social and/or academic exclusiveness, much as colleges now do. Left to their own devices, many schools would restrict admission to the brightest and most easily educated youngsters, leaving the more difficult children to somebody else. Many would also try to increase their operating budgets by charging supplemental tuition. This would have the not-always-accidental effect of limiting the number of low-income children in the more expensive schools.

An unregulated system of this kind would have all the drawbacks of other unregulated markets. It would produce even more racial and economic segregation than the existing neighborhood school system. It would also widen the expenditure gap between rich and poor children, giving the children of the middle-classes an even larger share of the nation's educational resources than they now get, while reducing the relative share going to the children of the poor.

Fortunately, OEO has shown no signs of funding a completely unregulated voucher system. Rather, OEO is contemplating an experiment in which extremely stringent controls are placed on participating schools' admissions policies, and also on their tuition charges. At the same time, it is hoping for an experiment which places minimal restraint on schools' staffing practices and programs.

In order to cash vouchers, a school would have to offer every applicant a roughly equal chance of admission. To ensure this, the school would have to declare each spring how many children it could take the following year. Parents would apply to schools each spring, and unless a school had more applicants than places, it would have to take everyone who had applied. If there were more applicants than places, the school would have to fill at least half its places by a lottery among applicants. It would also have to show that it had accepted at least as high a proportion of minority group students as had applied. Thus no school would be able to cream off the most easily educated children or dump all the problem children elsewhere.

The redemption value of a middle- or upper-income family's voucher would approximate what the local public schools are currently spending on upper-income children. Vouchers for children from low-income families would have a somewhat higher redemption value. This reflects the fact that schools with high concentrations of low-income children also tend to have more than their share of educational problems. It should also help discourage schools from trying to attract exclusively middle-class applicants. Participating schools would have to accept every child's voucher as full payment for his education, regardless of its value. Otherwise, parents who could afford to supplement their children's vouchers would inevitably have a better chance of getting their children into high cost schools than parents who could not supplement the voucher.

These regulations would not result in as much racial or economic integration as massive compulsory busing. But that is hardly a likely alternative. The real alternative is the continuation of the neighborhood school, whose racial and economic composition inevitably and deliberately reflects the racial and economic exclusiveness of the private housing market. Under a voucher system, no child could be excluded from any participating school simply because his family was not rich enough or white enough to buy a house near the school. Furthermore, the EVA would pay transportation costs, so that every family would have genuinely equal access to every participating school. Most families, both black and white, would doubtless continue to prefer schools near their homes. But at least no family would be legally or financially required to choose such a school if they thought it was educationally inadequate. Those black parents who wanted their children to attend integrated schools would be in an excellent position to ensure that they did so.

If all goes according to plan, the OEO experiment would be far more permissive with regard to schools' staffing and curricular policies than with regard to admissions. Schools would have to conform to existing state and local regulations governing private schools, but these are relatively lenient in most states. Experience suggests that while such leniency results in some abuses, the results over the long run seem to be better than the results of detailed legal and administrative regulations of the kind that shape the public schools. While these regulations often seem rational on their face (as in the case of teacher certification requirements), they generally create more problems than they solve. Teaching and learning are subtle processes, and they seem to resist all attempts at improvement by formal regulation. Rule books are seldom subtle enough to prevent the bad things that can happen in schools, and are seldom flexible enough to allow the best things.

So instead of telling schools whom to hire, what to teach, or how to teach it, the EVA will confine itself to collecting and disseminating information about what each school is doing. Every family will be given extensive information about every participating school. This should ensure that families are aware of all the choices open to them. It should also help discourage misleading advertising, or at least partially offset the effects of such advertising.

One common objection to a voucher system of this kind is that many parents are too ignorant to make intelligent choices among schools. Giving parents a choice will, according to this argument, simply set in motion an educational equivalent of Gresham's Law, in which hucksterism and mediocre schooling drive out high quality institutions. This argument seems especially plausible to those who envisage the entry of large numbers of profit-oriented firms into the educational marketplace. The argument is not, however, supported by much evidence. Existing private schools are sometimes mere diploma mills, but on the average their claims about themselves seem no more misleading, and the quality of the services they offer no lower, than in the public schools. And while some private schools are run for little but profit, this is the exception rather than the rule. There is no obvious reason to suppose that vouchers would change all this.

A second common objection to vouchers is that they would "destroy the public schools." Again, this seems farfetched. If you look at the educational choices made by wealthy parents who can already afford whatever schooling they want for their children, you find that many still prefer their local public schools if these are at all adequate. Furthermore, most of those who now leave the public system do so in order to attend high-cost, exclusive private schools. While some parents would doubtless continue to patronize such schools, they would receive no subsidy under the proposed OEO system.

Nonetheless, if you are willing to call every school "public" that is ultimately responsible to a public board of education, then there is little doubt that a voucher system would result in some shrinkage of the "public" sector and some growth of the "private" sector. If, on the other hand, you confine the label "public" to schools which are really equally open to everyone within commuting distance, you discover that the so-called public sector includes relatively few public schools. Instead, racially exclusive suburbs and economically exclusive neighborhoods serve to ration access to good "public" schools in precisely the same way that admissions committees and tuition charges ration access to good "private" schools. If you begin to look at the distinction between public and private schooling in these terms, emphasizing accessibility rather than control, you are likely to conclude that a voucher system, far from destroying the public sector, would greatly expand it, since it would force a large number of schools, public and private, to open their doors to outsiders.

A third objection to vouchers is that they would be available to children attending Catholic schools. This is not, of course, a necessary feature of a voucher system. An EVA could perfectly easily restrict participation to non-sectarian schools. Indeed, some state constitutions clearly require that this be done. The federal Constitution may also require such a restriction, but neither the language of the First Amendment nor the legal precedents is clear on this issue. The First Amendment's prohibition against an "establishment of religion" can be construed as barring payments to church schools, but the "free exercise of religion" clause can also be construed as requiring the state to treat church schools in precisely the same way as other private schools. The Supreme Court has never ruled on a case of this type (e.g., GI Bill payments to Catholic colleges or Medicare payments to Catholic hospitals). Until it does, the issue ought to be resolved on policy grounds. And since the available evidence indicates that Catholic schools have served their children no worse than public schools, and perhaps slightly better, there seems no compelling reason to deny them the same financial support as other schools.

The most common and most worrisome objection to a voucher system, in my view, is that its results depend on the EVA's willingness to regulate the marketplace vigorously. If vouchers were used on a large scale, state and local regulatory efforts might be uneven or even nonexistent. The regulations designed to prevent racial and economic segregation seem especially likely to get watered down at the state and local level, or else to remain unenforced. This argument applies, however, to *any* educational reform, and it also applies to the existing system. If you assume any given EVA will be controlled by overt or covert segregationists, you must also assume that this will be true of the local board of education. A board of education that wants to keep racist parents happy hardly needs vouchers to do so. It only needs to maintain the neighborhood school system. White parents who want their children to attend white schools will then find it quite simple to move to a white neighborhood where their children will be suitably segregated. Except perhaps in the South, neither the federal government, the state government, nor the judiciary is likely to prevent this traditional practice.

If, on the other hand, you assume a board which is anxious to eliminate segregation, either for legal, financial, or political reasons, you must also assume that the EVA would be subject to the same pressures.  And if an EVA is anxious to eliminate segregation, it will have no difficulty devising regulations to achieve this end.  Furthermore, the legal precedents to date suggest that the federal courts will be more stringent in applying the Fourteenth Amendment to voucher systems than to neighborhood school systems.  The courts have repeatedly thrown out voucher systems designed to maintain segregation, whereas they have shown no such general willingness to ban the neighborhood school.  Outside the South, then, those who believe in integration may actually have an easier time achieving this goal than they will with the existing public school system.

George R. LaNoue

# 33. VOUCHERS: THE END OF PUBLIC EDUCATION?

In his essay in the tenth anniversary issue of the *Saturday Review's* educational supplement, Peter Schrag formulates a question that has been lurking on the edges of much of the contemporary debate about schools.  Have we, he asks, reached the "end of the impossible dream" of public education?[1]

George R. LaNoue studied at Hanover College and Yale University.  Presently, he is a professor at the University of Maryland, Baltimore campus.  He is a contributor to the *Encyclopedia of Education,* has written numerous articles on the politics of education and church-state relations, and is editor of *Educational Vouchers: Concepts and Controversies.*

Source: George R. LaNoue, "Vouchers: The End of Public Education?" *Teachers College Record* 73 (December 1971), pp. 304–319.  Reprinted by permission.

[1] Peter Schrag, "End of the Impossible Dream," *Saturday Review* (September 19, 1970), p. 68.

Schrag thinks we have. The time has come, he argues, to admit that the educational reforms of the sixties have been of little consequence and the public school system itself has failed. How do we know public schools have failed? For Schrag, like other educational romantics, the question need not be taken seriously in quantitative terms. He writes:

> Evidence? Is it necessary again to cite statistics, dropout rates, figures on black and white children who go to college (or finish high school), comparisons of academic success between rich and poor kids, college attendance figures for slums and suburbs?[2]

Actually, of course, the statistics are not that one-sided. For example, college board scores show that the public schools in the sixties did accomplish their post-Sputnik mandate of producing students with higher mathematical, scientific, and technological skills. Progress has been made with the more intractable problem of racial equality of opportunity. In 1960, the median school year completed by nonwhites in the United States was 10.8; by whites, 12.3. By 1968 the gap had narrowed to 12.2 for nonwhites and 12.6 for whites.[3] Furthermore, the number of black students in colleges doubled between 1964 and 1969, and black youngsters are now more likely to be enrolled in preschool programs than are whites.[4]

It is currently fashionable to dismiss these gains as too slow or even irrelevant. None of the very real problems that exist in public schools should be minimized. But if we become so cavalier in our criticism that we do not notice the achievements that have been made, the probability of successful diagnosis for further reform is diminished. Nevertheless, after a decade of intense concern about schools on the part of social scientists, it is still almost impossible to document the patterns of strength and weakness in school systems in terms that are policy-relevant. We have neither the data nor the conceptual models that would permit conclusions about relative achievement of school systems. If one takes into account their various socioeconomic

---

[2] Ibid.

[3] U.S. Department of Labor and U.S. Department of Commerce, "Recent Trends in Social and Economic Conditions of Negroes in the United States," Current Population Series, p. 23, No. 26, BCS Report No. 347, July, 1968.

[4] "Blacks in School at a Higher Rate," *New York Times*, October 11, 1970; Robert L. Jacobson, "Education Gains by Poor Called Revolutionary," *The Chronicle of Higher Education*, vol. III, no. 13 (March 10, 1969), p. 1.

and political contexts, who can say that the New York public school system is better or worse than those in Chicago, Los Angeles, or Atlanta.

A part of the problem is poor information. The public school establishment has been enormously successful in resisting pressures to gather and distribute data that could be used to challenge it. On the other hand, the educational research establishment, with its built-in incentive to discover failure which justifies ever more research, has not done much to develop comparative models which could add objectivity to the evaluation. Consequently, the debate has been dominated by the educational romantics whose rhetoric fits the current intellectual mood of condemning all American institutions, the Presidency, the Congress, the judiciary, state and local governments, the military, medicine, business, unions, universities, etc., etc., as failures. Such an undiscriminating mood may be personally cathartic, and many of us indulge in it at times, but no rational public policy can be based on it. Both the achievements and the problems of public education should be recognized. Any realistic strategy for educational reform must be prepared to deal with both.

There is also a more subtle problem. Schrag argues that our culture is changing so rapidly that Americans may no longer be able to define educational success. In losing our consensus about educational goals, we also inevitably undermine the basis of a public school system. Schrag believes that the problem with public schools is not, as others have suggested, that they are politically unaccountable, but that, to the contrary, they do "precisely what most Americans expect." He insists:

> Any single, universal public institution—and especially one as sensitive as the public school—is the product of a social quotient verdict. It elevates the lowest common denominator of desires, pressures, and demands into the highest public virtue. It cannot afford to offend any sizeable community group, be it the American Legion, the B'nai B'rith, or the NAACP. Nor can it become a subversive enterprise that is designed to encourage children to ask real questions about race or sex or social justice or the emptiness and joys of life.[5]

Accepting the currently fashionable definition of pluralism that borders on advocating cultural segregation as ideal, Schrag concludes that public education is no longer possible or desirable.

[5] Schrag, op. cit., p. 70.

The solution Schrag proposes is a dismantling of the public
school system by adopting a voucher system. The fundamental question in the politics of education today, then, is not curricular reform
or community control, but whether the public school system itself
should be abandoned or modified in favor of some new kind of relationship between parent, government, and school. Schrag would substitute consumer accountability between parents and schools for the
existing political accountability. He writes: "Separate schools, accountable not to public vote and citizen support but only to their
clients, may be immune to such [conformist] pressures; they will
have to make their way on the basis of performance." The implications of such a change for public schools are enormous. As Christopher Jencks expressed it in his early writing on vouchers, before he
became a more cautious political manager of the concept:

> Either tuition grants or management contracts to private
> organizations would, of course, "destroy the public school sys-
> tem as we know it." When one thinks of the remarkable
> past achievements of public education in America, this may
> seem a foolish step. But we must not allow the memory of
> past achievements to blind us to present failures. Nor should
> we allow the rhetoric of public school men to obscure the
> issue. It is natural for public servants to complain about
> private competition. But if the terms of the competition are
> reasonable, there is every reason to suppose that it is healthy.
> Without it, both public and private enterprises have a way of
> ossifying. And if, as some fear, the public schools could not
> survive in open competition with private ones, then perhaps
> they *should* not survive.[6]

## THE CONCEPT OF PUBLIC AND PRIVATE

Like most other voucher writers,[7] Schrag does not define the difference between public and private schools very precisely. The imagery

---

[6] Christopher Jencks, "Is the Public School Obsolete?" *The Public Interest*
(Winter 1965), p. 27.

[7] Jencks reconceptualizes the terms public and private to mean that public
schools must be open to all (they may not even have geographical or academic
requirements), must not charge tuition or "refuse to give anyone information
about what they are doing, how well they are doing it, and whether children
are getting what their parents want." *Education Vouchers* (Cambridge, Mass.:
Center for the Study of Public Policy, December 1970), p. 13. This definition

is clear, however. Public schools are monolithic, while private schools are more flexible and innovative. Establishing definitions and the facts of the matter are critical elements in the policy decision.

To consider private schools first, about 5,600,000 children, or about 11 percent of the total elementary and secondary population, attend schools traditionally classified as private. Almost 90 percent of these children are in Catholic schools; another 5 percent are in Protestant and Jewish schools; while the remaining 5 percent attend secular private or prep schools. Although it may be difficult for a Bostonian or New Yorker to believe, most nonpublic schools are conventional parochial or prep schools. The kind of "flexible, innovative" private school they envision is only a tiny minority, quite insignificant statistically (about 1 percent) in terms of national school enrollment. Given these facts, whether private schools when compared school for school with public schools are more flexible and innovative remains to be proven.

The public school "monolith" turns out to be divided into more than 16,000 local governing districts. Although public schools reflect a generally similar curriculum (most of the state laws establishing curricular requirements cover private schools too), it is difficult to think of other generalizations that can be made on a national level. The governing and taxing patterns of public schools, their size, constituencies, employment practices, quality, and innovativeness vary as much as the character of American life itself.

Indeed, there is only one common bond between the public schools of Jackson, Michigan, and Jackson, Mississippi, of Portland, Oregon, and Portland, Maine. Public schools are all bound by judicial interpretations of the federal Constitution, while private schools are exempt. While public schools may generally be larger, more bureaucratic, and more unionized than private schools, none of these characteristics is inherent or even uniform. The legal obligation to obey the freedom of religion, speech, petition, and assembly clauses of the First Amendment and the due process and equal protection clauses of the Fourteenth Amendment, however, is now universally binding.

Before the 1940s, the legal distinction between public and private schools made little functional difference. The Supreme Court studiously avoided becoming involved in what were considered local

may be useful to advance a normative argument, but it has no legal or historic validity. There are probably no existing schools that would meet all of the tests to be called public.

educational matters. But in 1943, in a dramatic reversal of an earlier opinion, the Court decided that public school authorities could not force children of Jehovah's Witnesses to salute the flag.[8] The modern era of judicial educational policy making had begun.

Five years later, Edward Corwin, then the dean of American constitutional scholars, wrote a satirical essay, "The Supreme Court as a National School Board," to express his distaste for this trend.[9] The Court itself has shown some hesitation about its new role, but it has acted nevertheless. While striking down a state prohibition against teaching evolution, the Court declared:

> Judicial interposition in the operation of the public school systems of the Nation raises problems requiring care and restraint. Our courts, however, have not failed to apply the First Amendment's mandate in our educational system where essential to safeguard the fundamental values of freedom of speech and inquiry and of belief. By and large, public education in our Nation is committed to the control of state and local authorities. Courts do not and cannot intervene in the resolution of conflicts which arise in the daily operation of school systems and which do not directly and sharply implicate basic constitutional values. On the other hand, "The vigilant protection of constitutional values is nowhere more vital than in the community of the American Schools."[10]

Professor Corwin's title has turned out to be prophetic. In case after case in the last thirty years, the federal courts have established themselves as a major determiner of public school policy. Today all public schools are bound by four principles which the courts have extracted from the First and Fourteenth Amendments: nondiscrimination, academic freedom, equality of opportunity, and public accountability. The courts are still developing their interpretations of these doctrines and some have met with widespread resistance, but these principles may be regarded as the constitutional framework within which all public schools will eventually have to operate.

Although the full impact of judicial intervention has yet to be felt, the principles already established are of considerable consequence. In 1954, the Court struck down the doctrine of racially sep-

---

[8] *West Virginia State Board of Education v. Barnette*, 319 U.S. 624 (1943).
[9] *Law and Contemporary Problems*, Vol. XIV, (Winter 1949), p. 3.
[10] *Epperson v. State of Arkansas*, 393 U.S. 97 (1969).

Nondiscrimination

Political
Accountability

Academic
Freedom

Equality of Opportunity

arate-but-equal schools that was the controlling public policy for over
40 percent of the nation's school children in seventeen states and the
District of Columbia.[11]   Enforcement of that decision has been slow
and painful, but de jure segregation is now dead and the courts are
whittling away at the boundaries of de facto segregation.  In addition,
the courts have challenged sexual discrimination and stand as guard-
ians against religious discrimination.

In the area of academic freedom the courts have moved to protect
teachers from invidious loyalty oaths[12] and have given them the right
to criticize official school policy without retaliation.[13]   They have
prohibited public schools from engaging in overt indoctrination[14]
and have defined them as neither the "partisan (n) or the enemy of
any class, creed, party or faction."[15]   Most dramatic has been the
judicial expansion of student rights.   Only a few years ago, *in loco
parentis*, a doctrine which permitted public schools to act as arbitrary
as families in dealing with children, was the acknowledged rule.
Today the courts are establishing a whole new set of procedural due
process rights for students in disciplinary cases.[16]   In decisions like
*Tinker v. Des Moines*,[17] which ruled that public school students had
the right to wear armbands protesting war if they did not otherwise

[11] *Brown v. Board of Education*, 347 U.S. 483 (1954).

[12] For a discussion of recent cases, see E. Edmund Reutter, Jr. and Robert R.
Hamilton, *The Law of Public Education* (Mineola, New York: The Foundation
Press, 1970).

[13] *Pickering v. Board of Education*, 391 U.S. 563 (1968).

[14] In addition to *West Virginia State Board of Education v. Barnette* and *Epperson v. Arkansas, Engel v. Vitale*, 370 U.S. 421, 82 S. Ct. 1261 (1962), and
*School District of Abington Township, Pa. v. Schempp*, 374 U.S. 203 (1963)
stand for this principle.

[15] *West Virginia State Board of Education v. Barnette*, op. cit.

[16] There has developed a substantial literature on this subject.   One of the
best pieces is C. Michael Abbott, "Demonstrations, Dismissals, Due Process and
the High School: An Overview," *The School Review* (June, 1969), pp. 128–142.

[17] *Tinker v. Des Moines Independent Community School District*, 393 U.S. 503
(1969).

disrupt the school, the Supreme Court has altered the concept of the right of student expression all over the country. One consequence in New York is the Board of Education's new student handbook which, if enforced, will give public school students more rights than most private college students now enjoy.

Protecting equality of educational opportunity has proved more difficult for the Court. This has been caused, not by a lack of constitutional justification or judicial commitment, but rather by the difficulty of creating a workable and enforceable definition of the concept.[18] So far the Supreme Court has avoided the simplistic and rigid interpretation that the equal protection clause requires equal spending per student,[19] but in *Hobson v. Hansen*,[20] a federal court has ordered the Washington, D.C. school board to shuffle its resources to improve the facilities available to poor children. The recent decision by a federal court of appeals requiring the town of Shaw, Mississippi, to provide equal public services to each section of the town surely has implications for education.[21]

Judicial articulation of political accountability is the least developed of the four principles. The courts have, however, applied the one-man-one-vote rule to school board elections and have intervened to see that rules of community consultation and adequate disclosure be followed.[22] Particularly as urban schools develop new decentralized or federalized patterns of government, we can expect to see courts intervene to protect public access and information.

This brief summary is barely adequate to describe the scope and import of judicial intervention into educational policy, but it does serve to indicate the constitutional framework within which public schools must legally operate. Public schools are bound by this framework through the Fourteenth Amendment which declares that no state "shall make or enforce any law which shall abridge the privileges or immunities of citizens of the United States; nor shall any State deprive any person of life, liberty, or property, without due process of law; nor deny to any person within its jurisdiction the equal pro-

---

[18] See, for example, the discussions in Charles U. Daly, ed., *The Quality of Inequality* (Chicago: The University of Chicago Press, 1968).

[19] *McInnis v. Ogilvie*, 394 U.S. 322 (1969).

[20] *Hobson v. Hansen*, 269 F. Supp. 401 (1967).

[21] *New York Times*, February 2, 1971, p. 1.

[22] For a discussion of the impact of judicial decisions on school board operating procedure, see Reutter and Hamilton, op. cit.

tection of the laws." Public schools are considered to be extensions of state governments or to involve "state action," and are therefore affected by the Fourteenth Amendment. Private institutions, if they are really private, are not considered to involve "state action" and are legally exempt from constitutional restrictions. For example, a church need not follow one-man-one-vote in electing its leaders or due process in disciplining its members. However, determining the legal definition of a private constitutionally-exempt institution is quite complicated.

When the Southern states began to devise legal maneuvers to confirm "private" status on previously public institutions, or began to channel public functions through traditionally private institutions, the federal courts expanded the concept of "state action" to prohibit further discrimination. Whether a particular private institution may involve state action is still subject to case-by-case litigation. But, in general, a "private" institution may involve state action, and thus be subject to constitutional sanctions, if it is substantially regulated by the state; if it accepts substantial amounts of state funds; or if it serves a public function. In addition, a "private" institution that significantly affects interstate commerce may be subject to legislation based on that constitutional clause.

These legalities raised a complicated problem for voucher advocates. Are schools that participate in tax-supported voucher plans involved in "state action"? If so, wouldn't that mean that parochial schools would have to give up sectarian courses in religion (*McCollum v. Illinois*)[23] and prayer and Bible-reading (*Abington Township v. Schempp*)[24] as public schools have had to do? Would a military academy be bound by the *Tinker v. Des Moines*[25] armband rule? Would private schools be involved in rulings like *Hobson v. Hansen*[26] against racial imbalance and expenditure inequalities?

If the answer to these questions is yes, then most private schools would refuse to participate in a voucher plan. If the answer is no, then substantial numbers of parents might use vouchers to buy education outside the constitutional framework. The questions are critical in understanding the effect vouchers might have on American education. The answers turn on the type of voucher being considered.

[23] *Illinois ex. rel. McCollum v. Board of Education,* 333 U.S. 203 (1948).
[24] *School District of Abington Township, Pa. v. Schempp,* op. cit.
[25] *Tinker v. Des Moines Independent Community School District,* op. cit.
[26] *Hobson v. Hansen,* op. cit.

# TYPES OF VOUCHERS

There is no one voucher plan. Vouchers have been proposed in about as many sizes and shapes as there are educational ideologies. The first of the modern voucher concepts was created by Father Virgil C. Blum, a Jesuit political scientist at Marquette University. In his book *Freedom of Choice in Education*,[27] he used the traditional Catholic social philosophy of subsidiarity to develop the concept that values in a school's curriculum and culture should be totally determined by parents. To promote this doctrine, Blum had earlier founded Citizens for Educational Freedom, a predominantly lay Catholic organization which has attracted adherents from other conservative religious groups.

CEF has consistently supported vouchers as the device that would provide the most tax funds for parochial schools with the least amount of public controls. It was Father Blum who first developed the analogy, still used by voucher proponents, between education vouchers and the GI Bill and social security payments. The analogy is not completely accurate, since, unlike most government programs, the beneficiaries in these programs have established their individual claim by prior service (GI Bill) or by prepayment of insurance premiums (Social Security). The money thus "belongs" to them and they can spend it without constitutional restriction. Veterans, for example, used GI payments to attend seminaries; nobody knows how social security payments are spent. Even if the sources and rationale of these two government programs are not analogous, CEF has found them to be a convenient model for the kind of educational voucher it advocates. The CEF voucher is unregulated—the recipient school need meet no additional statutory or constitutional standards—and noncompensatory—a parent's income would not affect the size of the voucher.

CEF has operated as a pressure group in the United States for about fifteen years. It has not had much success in obtaining vouchers, although some textbook and bus transportation battles have been won. Ironically, its greatest victory, a purchase-of-services law obtained through a coalition with the White Citizens' Councils in Louisiana, was its most short-lived. The Louisiana State Supreme Court struck down the law before it could be implemented on the grounds

[27] Virgil C. Blum, *Freedom of Choice in Education* (New York: Macmillan, 1958).

that that kind of aid to private schools violated separation of church and state.[28]

Another contribution to the development of vouchers was made by Milton Friedman, the University of Chicago economist, in his book *Capitalism and Freedom*.[29] In that general exposition of the virtues of marketplace competition as a device for creating choice and diversity, education is treated as merely one of the public services (hospitals, libraries, parks, etc.) that might be better rendered by private enterprise. Later, in magazine articles, Professor Friedman focused on the idea of an educational voucher, but his original commitment to the unregulated "free enterprise" voucher remained.

In contrast, the most recent proponents of vouchers, Christopher Jencks and his colleagues at the Harvard Center for the Study of Public Policy, and John B. Coons, William H. Clune II, and Stephen D. Sugarman in their book *Private Wealth and Public Education*[30] advocate only regulated vouchers. Indeed, Jencks concedes that "an unregulated voucher system could be the most serious setback for the education of disadvantaged children in the history of the United States."[31]

The Coons et al. proposal is a sophisticated and sensitive attempt to give families a choice, not only about the style of education they prefer, but also about the amount of family resources they wish to commit to education. Schools charging different levels of tuition would be established. The amount of the voucher would depend on the family income and the cost of the school. A high income family choosing a high cost school would receive a relatively much smaller voucher than a poor family choosing a low cost school.

The most publicized proposal, however, comes from the Harvard Center's report that was the result of an Office of Economic Opportunity grant of $193,000 to study vouchers. Since Christopher Jencks, the principal author, had already committed himself in print to vouchers, the final report might have seemed anti-climactic. However, the Jencks volume performs a very useful purpose in outlining alternative voucher models (some eleven versions are discussed). It confronts in a candid manner the possible inequalitarian and anti-

---

[28] *Seegers v. Parker*, 256 La. 1039 (1970).

[29] Milton Friedman, *Capitalism and Freedom* (Chicago: The University of Chicago Press, 1962).

[30] John B. Coons, William H. Clune II, Stephen D. Sugarman, *Private Wealth and Public Education* (Cambridge, Mass.: Harvard University Press, 1970).

[31] *Education Vouchers*, Center for the Study of Public Policy, op. cit., p. 17.

civil libertarian results of vouchers. Jencks and company clearly reject the concept of unregulated vouchers and develop instead a highly sophisticated set of regulations which recipient schools would have to follow. The major restrictions on a voucher school would be that it:

1. Accept a voucher as full payment of tuition.
2. Accept any applicant so long as it had vacant places.
3. If it had more applicants than places, fill at least half these places by picking applicants randomly and fill the other half in such a way as not to discriminate against ethnic minorities.
4. Accept uniform standards established by the educational Voucher Agency regarding suspension and expulsion of students.
5. Agree to make a wide variety of information about its facilities, teachers, program, and students available to the EVA and to the public.
6. Maintain accounts of money received and disbursed in a form that would allow both parents and the EVA to determine whether a school operated by a board of education was getting the resources to which it was entitled on the basis of its vouchers, whether a school operated by a church was being used to subsidize other church activities, and whether a school operated by a profit-making corporation was siphoning off excessive amounts to the parent corporation.
7. Meet existing state requirements for private schools regarding curriculum, staffing, and the like.[32]

The Office of Economic Opportunity, in its competition with the Office of Education for educational influence, has responded favorably to the Jencks report and has announced its intention to fund several five-to-eight year experiments. The effort has not gone well. Although federal money is usually a desirable commodity, school systems have been turning OEO down at an unprecedented rate. Indeed, the difficulty of fitting vouchers into local and state laws plus the size of the political opposition may mean that widespread experiments will prove impossible.[33]

On the intellectual circuit, however, vouchers are the hottest item

[32] Ibid., p. 15.

[33] Ironically, the major political consequence of the speculation about vouchers has been to reestablish the pre-ESEA, antiprivate school aid coalition of public schools, Protestant, Jewish, and civil liberties agencies.

going, and the idea must be taken seriously. Much of the debate has been dominated by considerations of ideology and vested interest, but there is the beginning of a careful critique of the plan on its own terms, with attention being focused on the adequacy of specific regulations on voucher schools. For example, neither the Jencks nor the Coons plan prohibits voucher schools from discrimination in the hiring of teachers. Not only is this a practical problem in the coming era of teacher surplus, but it is obvious that if a school discriminates rigorously enough in selecting its staff, it can discourage "undesirable" students from even applying. Under those circumstances, the careful lottery and dismissal procedures are meaningless. Nor is either plan specific about the use of academic qualifications or dress codes (an expensive school uniform, for example) to restrict enrollment. The alternatives available to a private school that wanted to restrict its enrollment are almost limitless, and perhaps no voucher system can fully cope with them.

## THE REGULATION OF VOUCHERS

Assuming for the moment the adequacy and good faith of the Jencks regulations, can they be enforced? For most of the voucher writers, the marketplace's ability to regulate competition and to produce consumer sovereignty is axiomatic. Adam Smith, not Ralph Nader, is their prophet, and their faith in the virtues of the market is in today's terms almost singular. But which of the great American industries would be a suitable model for the educational marketplace? The "free enterprise" transportation industry? Lockheed or Penn Central? How about the medical industry, now financed in part by Medicare vouchers, which do not seem to have done much to improve the overall health of Americans or even the fiscal solvency of hospitals, though some doctors are doing very well? Or perhaps that sector of education most based on free enterprise—correspondence and trade schools—is the model?

The point is that marketplace analogies, do not fit well to the educational world. In the first place, public schools are not a noncompetitive monopoly like the postal service. They are highly decentralized and they do compete, both with private schools, which enroll 15 to 35 percent of the students, and with each other. (There is, incidentally, no research which shows that public schools are "better" in cities where the greatest competition with private schools exists.

Because of the "drainoff" of the middle class in these cities, I suspect the reverse is more likely true.) City schools compete against suburban schools and with each other for appropriations, teachers, special projects, and status as well as in extra-curricular activities.

Competition in the private school sector does not correspond to market theory either. With the possible exception of the housing industry, most profit-making firms will sell their products to anyone with cash or credit regardless of his race, religion, social background, manners, intelligence, or skills. Private schools, however, generally prefer to be exclusive based on one or more of the above factors. They do not view increasing their share of the market in the same way corporations do. This severely limits the possibility of consumer accountability. Although there is no research on the matter, the most plausible generalization is that the more desirable the private school, the less the parental accountability.

The Harvard study is aware of the limitations of the market as regulator, however, and it proposes several devices to skew the market in liberal directions. First, the preferred voucher would be compensatory, providing perhaps twice as many dollars for disadvantaged children. One can make a case that it costs more to educate these children, and since OEO will control the experiments, one can imagine that the vouchers will actually be compensatory. But eventually vouchers will have to be funded by state and local legislatures. Nothing in their history (certainly not their distribution of Title I Elementary and Secondary Education Act money) warrants optimism about their compensatory proclivities. Almost all of the voucher schemes that have been taken seriously by the states thus far have been only mildly compensatory at best.

Secondly, voucher schools would be forbidden to charge amounts in addition to the voucher aid and, if oversubscribed, would have to choose at least half of their students through lottery. These rules reflect a genuine attempt to overcome the impulse toward selectivity in private schools that might discriminate against disadvantaged students. Furthermore, the eligible schools would have to disclose enough information about themselves to permit informed consumer choices. The difficulty of forcing schools, even public schools, to release this kind of information in the past does not lead to optimism about its future efficacy. There are more than 100,000 different schools in the United States, and the voucher system could be expected to increase that number. At the very least, the interpretation and enforcement of the voucher rules will create some enormously difficult problems.[34]

The key to the regulated voucher obviously is the regulatory mechanism. The Harvard study offers alternatives but is not very precise about the problem. The report states:

> An Educational Voucher Agency (EVA) would be established to administer the vouchers. Its governing board might be elected or appointed, but in either case it should be structured so as to represent minority as well as majority interests. The EVA might be an existing local board of education, or it might be a new agency with a larger or smaller geographic jurisdiction. The EVA would receive all federal, state and local education funds for which children in the area were eligible. It would pay this money to schools only in return for vouchers.[35]

Later, the report spells out alternatives for establishing the EVA in demonstration projects:

1. The existing public school board could set itself up as the EVA.
2. The public school board could appoint a separate board as the EVA.
3. An entirely independent board including representatives of parents and staff of the participating schools could be set up.[36]

Elected or appointed, public or consortiums of participating schools, local, state, or regional? If the difference between regulated and unregulated vouchers is social justice or social disaster, then decisions about the structure of the EVA are of paramount importance.

In the demonstration projects, the principal regulator will obviously be OEO itself, but what will happen if vouchers are adopted independently by states and localities? Which of the various regula-

---

[34] This provision does not mean, of course, that all schools will have the same amount of money to spend. Public schools presumably could not receive additional tax funds, but private schools could supplement their income through endowment or the support of a private organization, like a church.

[35] *Education Vouchers,* Center for the Study of Public Policy, op. cit., p. 14.

[36] Ibid., p. 214.

tory models—the federal agencies, state departments of education, private accrediting associations, or local school boards—leads to a reasonable belief that they could monitor this development? Which of the regulations would or could be enforced? Which would be dropped altogether? Pinning the reform of American schools on a series of ad hoc regulations to be enforced by a yet-to-be-defined EVA seems to be an enormous risk.

In reply, Jencks would insist that the current system of regulations doesn't work very well either, and EVA's wouldn't be any worse. But they might very well be worse. As I described earlier, the federal courts have become one of the principal regulators of social justice in public education. They have accomplished this by applying the First and Fourteenth Amendments to public schools. Would voucher schools involve state action and be subject to the constitutional rules the courts have established for public schools? If the answer is yes, then the ad hoc nature of Jencks' regulations and the fuzzy nature of the EVA become less dangerous, since the federal courts would continue to act as regulators. On the other hand, the concept of state action could substantially reduce the autonomy of traditionally private schools.

On this critical question the Harvard report appears to be of two minds. The two legal sections in the study are devoted primarily to discussions of the eligibility of racially segregated and parochial schools in voucher programs.[37] The authors conclude that the federal courts would prohibit the participation of any school that clearly discriminated racially, but that the participation of parochial schools awaits further court decisions. This seems to be a fair appraisal of the current state of the law. However, the report is less perceptive about the effect of state action on participating voucher schools.

In addition to being a complicated problem of law, the issue presents a tricky political situation for voucher advocates. Ninety-five percent of all private school enrollment is in parochial schools. Obviously, the support of that constituency is necessary if vouchers are to become a serious national option. Consequently, the report resuscitates the GI Bill and social security analogy to plead hopefully for the eligibility of parochial schools. But that analogy was made with unregulated vouchers and it provides a legal rationale that voucher schools do not involve state action and are thus free from constitu-

[37] Ibid., pp. 221–273.

tional restraints.[38] To concretize the issue, could a voucher school avoid judicial standards of academic freedom or discriminate religiously in the hiring of teachers? None of the regulated voucher proposals is clear on this matter.

While not every past or future federal court decision on civil liberties and education may be the most appropriate policy for every one of the 16,000 school districts in the United States, a system of financing that runs the risk of undermining all constitutional rules in education in favor of ad hoc regulations seems to me to be too great a price to pay. Neither is it fair to private schools to be ambiguous about this point. Courts can declare that past behavior on the part of an institution requires that it meet constitutional standards from then on. In the long run, it seems doubtful that the courts would regard schools funded by tax-supported vouchers and intensively regulated by public or quasi-public EVA's as free from state action. Far better to decide that question now and to give private schools a choice. Certainly, a declaration by the responsible legislative and administrative agencies that they intended voucher schools to involve state action would constitute a proper warning and would assist courts in deciding the matter. Such a declaration would not necessarily eliminate all private schools whose current practices did not meet constitutional tests. Just as some formerly sectarian universities in New York (Fordham, for example) have altered some of their religious practices in order to receive state funds, so private schools could change to meet constitutional tests as well as ad hoc rules to become eligible for vouchers.

## VOUCHERS AS A REFORM MECHANISM

Even if the questions about the constitutional obligation of voucher schools were clarified, other important reservations about vouchers

---

[38] Professor McCann and Miss Areens have suggested that, as long as a child chooses to attend a voucher-aided parochial school, no constitutional restrictions on the religious activity of the school would be required. Walter McCann and Judith Areens, "Vouchers and the Citizen—Some Legal Questions," *Teachers College Record* (February 1971), p. 401. This is not a persuasive argument for two reasons. First, the Supreme Court's decision regarding religion in public schools is not based on compulsory attendance laws, but on illegal state sponsorship of religious activity. Voucher-aided schools and their practices would be state sponsored under the Jencks model. Second, under a voucher system, attendance at all schools would be free and voluntary, so under their argument public schools might begin religious observations again.

remain. Still, shouldn't the voucher scheme be subject to experimentation? It is difficult for any scholar or educational reformer to object to an experiment, but one may be very skeptical about whether what OEO is proposing will constitute a real experiment. In the first place, Southern cities were ruled out, although a voucher system must be workable in Columbus, Georgia, as well as Columbus, Ohio. Secondly, the experiments will take place in such a few places (only three cities, Seattle, Washington, Gary, Indiana, and Alum Rock, California, have applied for planning grants) that the amount of official and media attention given to these programs will eliminate the abuses vouchers might create in less scrutinized circumstances. Finally, OEO has announced that the experiments will run five-to-eight years, but the uncertainty of program funding may cause many of the corporations and agencies otherwise interested in the educational market to hold back.

Probably a quicker, cheaper, and more accurate method of evaluating vouchers would be to test the idea through surveys. Marketing agencies do this kind of research all the time. By presenting the various voucher models to properly selected samples, reasonable forecasts could be made about what different groups of parents would do if they had vouchers. In addition, private school leaders and others who might be interested in starting schools could be surveyed to see which kind of vouchers would be acceptable to them and what kinds of new schools would be stimulated.

I suspect two findings would emerge from such a survey. First, only a tiny percentage of the traditional private or parochial schools would be willing to participate in the regulated voucher approach Jencks is proposing. Some schools would find the lottery admission feature acceptable. Entrepreneurs with the kind of organization and capital needed to offer new private educational alternatives would not find the Jencks regulations very attractive either. Some liberal, equalitarian, integration-minded parents would support the Jencks voucher model, but I suspect a much larger number of parents would opt for an unregulated, noncompensatory voucher that was free from constitutional restraints.

Those who advocate ideal or model vouchers don't seem to fully recognize the true nature of the voucher constituency. There is a latent coalition prepared to support vouchers, and it won't be led by the gentlemen scholars from Cambridge and Berkeley. The coalition is the one Kevin Phillips proposed in *The Emerging Republican Ma-*

*jority.*[39] It is composed mainly of Southern Protestant nativists and
Northern Catholic ethnics—plus, I would add, a touch of the far right
and the far left. Aid to private schools was one of the ways Phillips
suggested that coalitions might be brought together. The danger is,
then, that while the intellectual debate focuses on ideal vouchers, the
true voucher coalition will rise up to take command of the idea. Once
united, that coalition might be able to bring about the kind of unregulated, noncompensatory, constitution-free vouchers that would lead
to the social disaster Jencks himself warns about.

The preceding discussion may have sounded like a plea for the
status quo, but that was not its intention. Instead, I merely want to
assert that the prescription for educational reform should relate more
carefully to the diagnosis of the problem than do voucher proposals
and that their unintended consequences may be quite damaging. As
a vehicle for reform, vouchers are a very inefficient device. They
would prove costly by adding to existing state and local budgets the
expense of 1) all private school tuitions, 2) the EVA administrative
bureaucracy, 3) new buildings and inefficient use of existing structures, 4) inefficient use of existing tenured personnel, and 5) greatly
increased transportation costs. Since nonparents would be partially
disenfranchised from school politics by vouchers, they might be less
inclined to support educational budgets, so the total financial pie
would be reduced. Furthermore, to wait five to eight years for the
results of the voucher experiments and then to wait until new schools
are built which can provide choices is an inordinate delay of necessary educational reform. Depending on the goals chosen, there are
more effective and less dangerous reform models.

If the problem is diagnosed as fundamentally one of the quality
of public schools, then the experiments with performance contracting
and teacher accountability should be given a chance. Each of these
concepts raises difficult problems of implementation, but contains
fewer risks than do vouchers. Furthermore, we might experiment
with developing for the academic activities of public schools the kind
of competition and rewards that already exist for extra-curricular
activities.

If the problem is diagnosed as basically a problem of ideological
conformity, then the spread of dual enrollment (shared time) and

[39] Kevin Phillips. *The Emerging Republican Majority.* Garden City, New
York: Doubleday, 1970.

decentralization offer alternatives.  Dual enrollment permits a student
to select his curriculum from two or more learning centers.  In addition to giving individuals more choice, it allows groups which have
particular religious or ideological concerns to focus on those areas
rather than undertaking comprehensive schooling.  Many groups can
find private funding for selected courses, while managing a whole
school leads to public funding and public controls.  Dual enrollment
in some form currently exists in almost every state, and consideration
should be given to the type of law recently passed in Vermont which
permits the dual enrollment option in every community.

The trend toward decentralizing our large city school systems is
also growing.  Again, a lot of problems exist, but eventually urban
public schools can be expected to offer more curricular alternatives
and to be more responsive to parents than before.

We can go further.  In a pamphlet called "The Reform of the
Urban Schools," Mario Fantini suggests a concept called "public
schools of choice."[40]  Fantini and his colleagues are currently writing
a book on the subject and so the concept has not been fully spelled
out.  Essentially, however, the thesis is that we can have a lot more
choices of school culture and style in urban public schools if we
want them.  Rather than turning to vouchers, individual choice could
be promoted by developing the petition rights of parents and students.
For example, a state legislature and/or local school board could establish that whenever a certain percentage of parents wanted a particular school style (British infant model, for example) or a percentage
of students wanted a particular curriculum alternative, public school
authorities would be required by law to provide for it.  If the school
were set up on a house plan, as is Richard C. Lee High School in
New Haven, the alternatives would exist within the same school.  The
only limitations would be constitutional and, in some cases, financial.
Furthermore, within constitutional boundaries, there is a lot of room
for experimentation with alternatives to the traditional school board
as a management system.

Although these concepts are new enough to require much development, I believe they will eventually contribute more toward solving
our educational problems than will vouchers.  Substituting consumer
accountability for political accountability is not in the long run a good
bargain for either parents or society.  Majority rule should be tem-

---

[40] Mario Fantini, *The Reform of the Public Schools* (Washington, D.C.: NEA,
1970).

pered with a respect for minority differences, and public education should offer many alternatives, but deciding educational policy forces a society to confront ultimate questions about its future. Such decisions are better made through the democratic process than the marketplace.

# Discussion Questions and Activities

1. Jencks claims that the voucher plan would give low-income parents the same choice as upper-income parents now have as to the choice of school. Would the plan actually provide a choice of this type?

2. Would the voucher system force the public schools to give parents what they want or go out of business? If so, evaluate the consequences of such an outcome.

3. How will the voucher system avoid racial and economic segregation?

4. In terms of racial integration, the real alternative to the voucher system, according to the author, is the neighborhood school. Is his statement correct?

5. Can parents make wise choices as to the best school for their children in light of the fact that they lack expertise?

6. The voucher system, Jencks claims, would expand accessibility rather than control, thereby enlarging the "public" sector. Evaluate this claim.

7. Are sound arguments advanced for making vouchers available to children attending Catholic schools?

8. Look into those systems which have used the voucher plan to see the extent to which they deviated from the Jencks's plan and the degree of success they had.

9. Have some reformers overlooked or summarily dismissed the genuine achievements of the public schools cited by LaNoue?

10. Since the voucher plan is based on the assumption that the use of the voucher to attend a private school may constitute an improvement over the public schools, what evidence do we have that private schools are more flexible and innovative than public schools?

11. What four principles must public schools observe, and what is the constitutional source of these principles?

12. What conclusions does LaNoue reach as to whether parochial schools which accept vouchers would have to give up sectarian courses in religion? Would private schools be involved in rulings against expenditure inequalities and racial imbalances?

13. Why is the analogy between the voucher and the GI Bill and social security payments not completely accurate?

14. Among the many voucher programs discussed, which one is strongest? Give reasons for your choice. For a class project, construct your own voucher plan.

15. Explain and evaluate the basis for LaNoue's statement that "the alternatives available to a private school that wanted to restrict its enrollment are almost limitless, and perhaps no voucher system can cope fully with them."

16. Advocates of vouchers use a free marketplace model. What are the shortcomings of this model?

17. Is there conclusive evidence that the public schools are as noncompetitive as voucher advocates claim?

18. LaNoue claims that vouchers would eventually have to be funded at the state and local level and history fails to show that these levels (as opposed to the federal) would provide sufficient compensatory funding for the disadvantaged. Is LaNoue's belief correct? Support your answer.

19. Why are decisions about the Educational Voucher Agency (EVA) of paramount importance?

20. Could private schools participating in the voucher plan discriminate on religious grounds in hiring teachers or avoid judicial standards of academic freedom?

21. LaNoue states that "as a vehicle for reform, vouchers are a very inefficient device." Evaluate the reasons he offers.

# XVII. The Free School Movement

*Interested parents and teachers in many sections of the country are organizing their own "free schools." These schools differ considerably in their enrollment, staffing, and programs, but all of them seem to be interested in providing a humanizing experience and an atmosphere of greater freedom for learning. Free schools try to keep the tuition low so that their doors will be open to all children who want to enroll. At the same time, however, many of these schools are faced with serious financial difficulties, casting a pall over the future of the free school movement.*

*Bonnie Barrett Stretch takes us inside these schools, gives us a feel for what they are like, and shares with us their diversity and their problems. Jonathan Kozol writes realistically about the problems free schools face. He notes the imprecision surrounding the meaning of free schools and that the forms free schools take are exceedingly diverse and disparate. A tendency can be found to build models more on the basis of reacting to undesirable practices in the established system rather than thinking through one's position as a basis for creating coherent and supportable models. The future of the free schools is also threatened, according to Kozol, by the types of persons attracted to them and the way participants use power.*

Bonnie  Barrett  Stretch

# 34. THE RISE OF THE "FREE SCHOOL"

For the past five years, critics have been telling parents and teachers what is wrong with the public schools. Such writers as John Holt, Herbert Kohl, Jonathan Kozol, George Dennison, and Paul Goodman have described the authoritarianism that structures many classrooms, the stress on grades and discipline at the expense of learning, and the suppression of the natural curiosity and instincts of the young. Many parents and teachers have begun to see for themselves the boredom, fear, and grievous lack of learning that too often accompany schooling—not only for the poor and the black, but for suburban white youngsters as well—and they have begun to ask what can be done about it.

The revolt is no longer against outdated curriculums or ineffective teaching methods—the concerns of the late Fifties and early Sixties. The revolt today is against the institution itself, against the implicit assumption that learning must be imposed on children by adults, that learning is not something one does by and for oneself, but something designated by a teacher. Schools operating on this assumption tend to hold children in a prolonged state of dependency, to keep them from discovering their own capacities for learning, and to encourage a sense of impotence and lack of worth. The search is for alternatives to this kind of institution.

In the past two years, increasing numbers of parents and teachers have struck out on their own to develop a new kind of school that

Bonnie Barrett Stretch has contributed articles on education to *Saturday Review* and other journals.

Source: Bonnie Barrett Stretch, "The Rise of the 'Free School,'" *Saturday Review* (June 20, 1970), pp. 76–79, 90–93. Copyright 1970 by Saturday Review, Inc. Reprinted by permission.

will allow a new kind of education, that will create independent, courageous people able to face and deal with the shifting complexities of
the modern world. The new schools, or free schools, or community
schools—they go by all these names—have sprung up by the hundreds
across the country. Through a continuous exchange of school brochures and newsletters, and through various conferences, the founders
of these schools have developed a degree of self-awareness, a sense of
community that has come to be called "the new schools movement."

The new schools charge little or no tuition, are frequently held
together by spit and string, and run mainly on the energy and excitement of people who have set out to do their own thing. Their variety
seems limitless. No two are alike. They range from inner-city black
to suburban and rural white. Some seem to be pastoral escapes from
the grit of modern conflict, while others are deliberate experiments
in integrated multicultural, multilingual education. They turn up
anywhere—in city storefronts, old barns, former barracks, abandoned
church buildings, and parents' or teachers' homes. They have crazy
names like Someday School, Viewpoint Non-School, A Peck of Gold,
The New Community, or New Directions—names that for all their
diversity reflect the two things most of these schools have in common:
the idea of freedom for youngsters and a humane education.

As the Community School of Santa Barbara (California) states
in its brochure: "The idea is that freedom is a supreme good; that
people, including young people, have a right to freedom, and that
people who are free will in general be more open, more humane,
more intelligent than people who are directed, manipulated, ordered
about. . . ."

The Santa Barbara Community School is located in a converted
barracks on a hill above the town. The fifty or so children (ages
three to fourteen) almost invariably come from wealthy, white, fairly
progressive families who want to give their children "the nicest education possible," as one teacher put it. Inside the building are a large
meeting room; some smaller rooms for seminars, discussions, and
tutorials; a wood and metal shop; classrooms for the younger children; and a small library. Classes for the younger children are based
on the Leicestershire model. Rooms are organized by activity centers
—a math corner here, a reading corner there. Parents' money has
helped provide a remarkable amount of creative learning materials.
Children are free to move from one thing to another as their interest
shifts, and children of all ages frequently work and play together.
For the older kids, the method is largely tutorial: one, two, or three

youngsters working with a teacher. Although there is a "core curriculum" of literature, science, and social studies, the classes follow
the interests and preferences of the students.

Outside and behind the building is enough space for a large playground, a pile of wood and lumber, a large pile of scrap metal including bicycle and car parts, and an old car, whose motor the older children are dismantling as a lesson in mechanics or physics (depending
on whom you talk to). Children of all ages use the wood and metal
to carve or weld into sculpture, as well as to fix bikes and build toys.
"It's important for kids to learn about tools," explained a teacher.
"Most kids don't know how things work. You really have to see a
six-year-old in goggles with a welding torch to appreciate what it
means."

The parents like the school, although they sometimes worry about
how much the children are learning. By "learning" they mean the
three Rs, social studies, etc. Parent pressure has led the Community
School to place more emphasis on traditional subject matter than
many free schools do. Teachers, on the other hand, are more concerned about another kind of learning. They would like to help these
white middle-class youngsters develop a better sense of the world, to
expose them to styles of life and work besides those of their families.
There are frequent trips to ranches, factories, local businesses, and
other schools. But these experiences, being interludes, remain essentially artificial to children. What are real are the comforts and concerns that inform their daily lives and that are shared with their
friends.

In contrast to this isolation is the Children's Community Workshop School in New York City. Situated in an economically and
racially integrated neighborhood, the school makes a conscious effort
to keep its enrollment one-third white, one-third black, and one-third
Puerto Rican. Because it is intended specifically as an alternative
to the public schools, the Community Workshop charges no tuition.
It is supported primarily by foundation grants and private donations,
but the scramble for money is a continuous one that taxes a great
deal of the energy of the school's director, Anita Moses.

Like the Santa Barbara Community School, the Community
Workshop bases it structure on the Leicestershire method. And,
again like Santa Barbara, it does not hold strictly to that method.
There is a great deal of emphasis on the children's own interests, and
new directions and materials are being tried all the time. A visitor
to the school may find one group of children at a table struggling to

build arches out of sugar cubes; another two or three children may be working with an erector set, others with tape recorders and a typewriter. In the midst of all this independent activity may be found one teacher helping one child learn to write his name.

Except for the use of Leicestershire techniques, there is little similarity between the Children's Community Workshop and the school in Santa Barbara. The heterogeneity of the student body makes the educational and human problems far more complex. Where achievement levels and cultural backgrounds vary widely, there is a great deal of accommodation necessary on the part of teachers and parents. At the same time, there can be no question that the children are learning more than the traditional three Rs.

Both the Community Workshop and the Santa Barbara Community School, however, have more structure than many free schools. The tendency in these schools is not to stress conventional intellectual training, to offer it if and when the children want it, and in general to let the youngsters discover and pursue their own interests. The new schools agree fully with Piaget's statement that "play is the serious business of childhood," and a child may as easily spend whole days in the sandbox as in the reading center. The lack of structure, however, leads to a lot of noise and running around, and all this activity may seem like chaos to a visitor. Often that's exactly what it is. It is a difficult skill to attune oneself to individual children, and to build on their individual needs and concerns, and few teachers have mastered it. Often, too, older youngsters, suddenly released from the constraints of public school, will run wild for the first few weeks, or even months, of freedom. But gradually, as they work the pent-up energy out of their system, and as they learn that the adults really will allow this freedom, they begin to discover their own real interests and to turn their energy to constructive tasks.

"The longer they've been in public school, and the worse their experience there is, the longer it takes for them to settle down, but eventually they all do," says Bill Kenney, who has taught at Pinel School in Martinez, California, for ten years. Pinel is an essentially Summerhillian school where classes in subjects such as reading and arithmetic are offered, but the children are not compelled to attend. Based on his experience at Pinel, Mr. Kenney believes that in a school that is solidly middle-class it can be expected that any happy, healthy child will eventually learn to read, write, and do basic arithmetic, whether or not he is formally taught. The experience of other middle-class free schools tends to corroborate this assumption.

The appeal of this philosophy is enormous, judging from the

number of students and teachers applying to the new schools—all
these schools report more applicants than they can handle—and from
the constant flow of visitors who come to watch, ask questions, and
sometimes get in the way. A few schools have had to set up specific
visiting days in an effort to stem the tide. Three major conferences
on "alternatives in education" took place this spring—in Cuernavaca,
Mexico; in Santa Barbara, California; and in Toronto, Canada—and
people flocked to them by the hundreds to talk to such "heroes" as
John Holt and George Dennison, and to talk to one another and learn
who's doing what and how. Representatives from foundations, universities, and the U.S. Office of Education also came, eager to know
whether the critics' ideas can be given life.

Through the conferences and through correspondence and ex-
changes of school newsletters, a self-awareness is developing among
the new schools, a sense of themselves as part of a growing movement.
Much of this increased consciousness is due to the work of the New
Schools Exchange, an information clearinghouse that grew out of a
conference of 200 schools a year ago. During its first year, the exchange set up a directory of new schools, put teachers and kids in
touch with schools, and schools in touch with teachers, kids, materials
—and even, occasionally, money. In that year, too, 800 new names
were added to the exchange list, and the exchange helped many
through the labor pains of birth by offering nuts-and-bolts information about how to incorporate a school, and ways to get through the
bureaucratic maze of building, fire, and health regulations.

But the mortality rate among these new schools is high. Harvey
Haber of the Exchange estimates about eighteen months in the average life span. This includes those that endure for years and those
that barely get off the ground. Money is universally the biggest
hassle and the reason most commonly cited for failure. Even those
schools that endure are seriously hampered by the constant struggle
for fiscal survival that too often must take precedence over education.
Most schools are started by people who are not rich, and charge little
or no tuition, in an effort to act as an alternative for the common man
(the rich have always had alternatives). Teachers work for pennies,
when they are paid at all. "How do I survive?" one teacher laughed
a bit anxiously. "I found a nice landlord who doesn't bug me about
the rent. I dip into my savings, and get my parents and friends to
invite me to dinner—often. Then, there are food stamps, of course.
Mostly we rely on each other for moral support and help over the
really rough places."

This kind of dedication, however, is too much to ask of anyone for any length of time. Working with children in an open classroom with few guidelines makes tremendous demands on teachers, Anita Moses of the Children's Community Workshop points out. Furthermore, teachers must often give their time for planning, for parent conferences, or for Saturday workshops with new teaching techniques and materials. There are intrinsic rewards for this, of course, but extrinsic rewards are also necessary, Mrs. Moses stresses, and those rewards should be in terms of salary.

There are other hurdles besides money—red tape, harassment by various state and city bureaucracies, and hostility from the community at large. In Salt Lake City, for example, a citizens committee tried to close a new Summerhill school on the grounds that the school was immoral and the teachers were Communists.

But perhaps the most fundamental factor for survival is the degree of commitment on the part of the teachers and parents. For brochures, newsletters, and other public pronouncements, it is possible to articulate the concept of freedom and its importance to emotional and intellectual development of the child. But basically the appeal is to a gut-level longing for love, joy, and human community, and often the schools are run on this romantic basis. "If you stop putting pressure on the kids, the tendency is to stop putting pressure on the staff, too," one teacher observed. Schools that fail within a few months of opening tend to be those begun by people merely interested in trying out a new idea. When the idea turns out to be more complex, and its implementation more difficult than anticipated, the original good feeling evaporates and a deeper determination is required.

Parents and teachers who have worked out their ideas together, who have similar goals, who know what they want for their children and why, have a better chance of keeping their school alive. Nonetheless, almost every school follows a similar pattern. If they make it over the physical hurdles of getting money, finding a building, and meeting bureaucratic regulations, they run into the spiritual struggle. Usually, somewhere in the first three to six months, according to Harvey Haber, comes the first great spiritual crisis: "structure" vs. "nonstructure." Having experimented with the idea of freedom, and having discovered its inherent difficulties, many parents and teachers become impatient and anxious. Are the children learning anything, they wonder, and does it matter? Frequently there is a slowdown in the acquisition of traditional academic skills. Children, it turns out, would rather play than learn to spell, and the blossoming forth of innate genius in a warm, benevolent atmosphere fails to occur. Anxious adults begin to argue for more structure to the school day, more direction for the kids, more emphasis on the familiar three Rs. Others insist upon maintaining the freedom, and upon learning to work with children on a new freer basis that really tests its limitations and possibilities.

As Robert Greenway, whose sons were enrolled in the Redwood Association Free School in Sonoma County, California, wrote:

> It seems to me that this anxiety that gets aroused about "what's happening to our kids" is understandable and inevitable. In a public school, we turn our children over to the wardens; there is no illusion about the possibility of influence to torture us. . . . But a truly cooperative venture arouses every possible hope about involvement in the growth of our children—and probably every latent frustration about what we think *didn't* happen to us as well. . . . I suggest that, unless we find a way of dealing with the real anxieties and concerns that this type of enterprise arouses, then we'll fail before we've hardly started (I'm responding to my own growing sense of frustration and anxiety, and to the sign of sudden and/or premature withdrawals from the school, and to the growing hue and cry for "more organization").

The Santa Fe (New Mexico) Community School went through this crisis in the middle of its second year, a bit later than most. Parents were willing to go along with the school as long as the teachers seemed confident about what was happening with the children. But when one teacher began to articulate the fears many parents had tried to suppress, the situation came to a head. There was a period of trying to impose more order on the kids, and the kids rebelled and refused to take it. Some staff members were fired, and parents demanded more teachers with bachelor's and master's degrees, but found they could not get them for a salary of $200 a month. There were endless pedagogical debates, and finally some of the parents simply took their kids back to the public school. "Unfortunately, those who left were the ones with the most money," sighed one teacher. "We're poorer now, but the people here are here because they're dedicated."

After the crisis, the school was reorganized. Previously ordered by age clusters, it is now divided into activity centers, and children of all ages move freely from one center to another. On a bright

Southwestern day a visitor may find a couple of boys sitting in front of the building, slumped against a sunwarmed wall, eating apples and reading comic books. Inside, in the large front room, a group of children may be painting pictures or working with leather or looms. In a quiet, smaller room, someone else is having a guitar lesson. A room toward the back of the building is reserved as the math center; a couple of teachers are math enthusiasts, and many of the older children pick up from them their own excitement for the subject.

In the playground behind the building is an Indian kiva built by students and teachers learning about the culture of local Indian tribes. The Southwest is a multicultural area, and the Community School has tried to draw on all these cultures. There are Indian and Spanish children enrolled, as well as white, and each is encouraged to respect and learn from the cultures of the others.

But despite its efforts to reach into the Indian and Spanish communities, the Santa Fe Community School remains essentially a white middle-class school. The Chicanos and Indians, mainly poor or working-class, tend to shy away from such experiments, partly because their cultures are traditionally conservative with highly structured roles for adults and children, and partly because the poor cannot afford to take a chance on the future of their young. Middle-class whites can always slip back into the mainstream if they choose. But for the poor, neither the acquisition of such intellectual tools as reading and writing nor a place in the economy is guaranteed.

These fundamental differences show up clearly in the community schools operated by and for black people. Black people on the whole bring their children to these schools, not merely because they believe in freedom for self-expression or letting the child develop his own interests, but because their children are not learning in the public schools, are turning sullen and rebellious by the age of eight, and are dropping out of school in droves. The ideology in many of these schools is not pedagogical, but what one school calls "blackology"— the need to educate the children in basic skills and in pride of race. In the black schools there is much more emphasis on basic intellectual training and much more participation on the part of parents. By and large, parents are the founders of these schools; they are the main source of inspiration and energy. They have the final say in selecting both teachers and curriculum, and their chief criterion is: Are the children learning?

As in the white schools, classrooms for the younger children are frequently patterned after the Leicestershire model. But the approach is deliberately eclectic, providing closer guidance and more structured activities for youngsters who need it. The academic progress of the children is carefully observed and quietly but firmly encouraged. "We want teachers who will try a thousand different ways to teach our children," said one mother.

Equally important is a teacher's attitude toward race. Although some schools would like to have all-black faculties—and in a number of cities, parents are in training to become teachers and teacher aides—they must still hire mainly whites. "When I interview a teacher," said Luther Seabrook, principal of the Highland Park Free School in Boston, "I always ask, can you think of a community person as an equal in the classroom?" Many teachers cannot, either because of racial bias, or because of notions about professionalism. Even after a teacher is hired, the going is still rough where feelings run high on the part of blacks and whites, but there is a determination to confront these problems directly through open discussion and group sessions.

The same approach applies to daily work in the classroom. Teachers and aides are encouraged to talk openly about their successes and problems in weekly planning sessions, to admit mistakes, and to try out new ideas. Such sessions are frequently the keystone of the teaching process in these schools. They are the times when teachers can get together and evaluate what has been happening in the classroom, how the children have responded to it, and how the teachers have responded to the children. "It's a tremendous place to grow," one teacher remarked. "You're not tied to a curriculum or structure, and you're not afraid to make mistakes. Everyone here is in the same boat. We get support from each other and develop our own ways of handling things."

There is little doubt that the youngsters prefer the community schools to traditional schools. The humane and personal atmosphere in the small, open classrooms makes a fundamental difference. The children work together writing stories or figuring math problems, working with Cuisenaire rods or an elementary science kit. They are proud of their work and show it eagerly to visitors. There is virtually no truancy, and many youngsters hate to stay home even on weekends according to their mothers.

But perhaps the greatest achievement of these schools is with the parents. They develop a new faith, not only in their children but in themselves. "Now I know," said a New York City mother, "that,

even though I didn't finish high school, it is possible for me to understand what they are teaching my child." In changing their children's
lives, these parents have discovered the power to change their own
lives, as well. Parents who are not already working as aides and
coordinators in the classrooms drop by their schools often to see how
Johnny is doing. At the East Harlem Block Schools in New York,
stuffed chairs and couches and hot coffee put parents at ease, while
teachers talk with them as equals and draw them into the education
of their children.

Nonetheless, black schools share many of the problems with the
community that white schools have. People are suspicious of new
ways of teaching, even though their children obviously are failing
under the old ways. Parents who enroll their children out of desperation still grow anxious when they see the amount of freedom allowed.
In integrated schools, like Santa Fe or the Children's Community
Workshop, there is the added problem of race and class, as middle-
class parents learn that all the children are not necessarily going to
adopt middle-class values and life-styles, that cultural differences are
valid and must be accepted.

Some schools are fed up with "parent education"; it takes too
much time away from the children. A number of schools already are
taking only children whose parents are in sympathy with their aims,
parents who won't panic if the child doesn't learn to read until he is
eight or nine.

But as a school grows more homogeneous, it faces the danger
of becoming an isolated shelter against the reality of the outside
world. Instead of educating kids to be strong and open enough to
deal with a complex world, the schools may become elitist cloisters
that segregate a few people even further from the crowd.

Once again the free schools must ask themselves what they are all
about. If one assumes (as many free schools do) that any healthy,
happy youngster will eventually learn to read and write, then what
is the purpose of school? Is it enough simply to provide one's children with a school environment more humane than the public schools,
and then stay out of nature's way?

At a California high school in the Sausalito hills, teachers and
students think that that in itself is quite a lot. After going through
a typical cycle of kids getting high on freedom and doing nothing for
six months, getting bored, and finally facing the big questions—What
am I doing? Where am I going?—students and teachers think they
have learned a lot about themselves and each other. But as the

youngsters return to studying and start to seek answers to those questions, they find the teachers have little to offer besides a sympathetic ear. Some kids return to the public school feeling better for their experience with freedom. (Feeling, too, perhaps, that it didn't work, that they really do need all the rules and discipline their parents and teachers demanded.) Gradually, those who remain have forced the teachers back to the traditional textbooks as the chief source of knowledge.

The humane atmosphere remains, but missing is a curriculum that truly nurtures the independence of thought and spirit so often talked of and so rarely seen. It takes extraordinary ingenuity to build on students' needs and interests. A few brilliant teachers, such as Herbert Kohl, can turn kids on, meet them where they are, and take them further—can, for example, take a discussion of drugs and dreams and guide it through the realms of mythology, philosophy, and Jungian psychology. But what do you do if you're not a Herb Kohl? According to Anita Moses, you "work damn hard." There are other things, too: You can hire a master teacher familiar with the wide range of curriculum materials available. Little by little you can change the classroom, or the school itself, to make it do the things you want it to do. And little by little, through working with the children and hashing out problems with help from the rest of the staff, you begin to know what it is you want to do and how you can do it.

But even this does not answer the deeper questions—questions that are implicit in every free school, but that few have faced. Is it only a new curriculum or new ways of teaching that we need? Or do we need to change our ideas about children, about childhood itself, about how children learn, what they learn, what they need to learn, from whom or from what kinds of experience? It is clear that our ideas about teaching are inadequate, but is it possible that they are simply false? For example, children can often learn to read and write without any formal instruction. This is not a miracle, it is a response of an intelligent young being to a literate milieu. It is also clear that children learn many cognitive as well as social abilities from their peers or from children but a few years older than themselves. What, then, is the role of the adult in the learning of the child?

In simpler times, children learned from adults continually, through constant contact and interchange, and through their place close to the heart of the community. Today, the society has lost this organic unity. We live in times when children often see their fathers only on weekends. We live in a world that separates work from play, school from the "real" world, childhood from personhood. The young are isolated from participation in the community. They seem to have no integral place in the culture. Too often schools have become artificial environments created by adults for children. How is it possible to forsake these roles?

Young people are trying. Many will no longer accept without question authority based solely on tradition or age. They are seeking alternatives to The Way Things Are. But the venture into unfamiliar territory generates enormous anxieties. The young are painfully aware of their own inexperience; they lack faith in themselves. But who can help them in their conflicts both within themselves and with the outside world? Surely, this is a function of education. But in today's world there are few adults who can do this for themselves, far less for their children. For who can respond with assurance to the anxieties of young people over sex, drugs, and the general peril in which we live? Who knows how to deal with others when the traditional roles are gone?

And yet it should be possible for adults to relate to young people in some constructive way. It must be possible because the young, in their alienation and confusion, and the culture, in its schizoid suffering, demand it. In the words of Peter Marin, former director of the Pacific High School, a free school in California:

> Somebody must step past the children, must move into his own psyche or two steps past his own limits into the absolute landscape of fear and potential these children inhabit. . . . I mean: we cannot *follow* the children any longer, we have to step ahead of them. Somebody has to mark a trail.

Is this what the free schools are all about? Few of them have asked these questions. Few will ever want to. But the questions are implicit in the movement. The free schools offer alternatives— alternatives that may be shaped to meet new needs and aims. At least, they offer a first step. At least, the possibility is there.

Jonathan Kozol

# 35. FREE SCHOOLS: A TIME FOR CANDOR

For the past six years free schools have almost been pets of the media. Too little of this coverage, however, has focused on the deep and often overwhelming problems that confront some of these schools: the terrible anguish about power and the paralyzing inhibition about he functions of the teacher.

The difficulties begin with a number of foolish, inaccurate, and dangerous cliches borrowed without much criticism or restraint from fashionable books by fashionable authors who do not know very much about either life within the cities or responsibilities that confront a free school for poor children in a time of torment and in a situation of great urgency and fear. It is almost axiomatic that the free schools that survive are those that start under the stimulus of a neighborhood in pain and that remain within the power of that neighborhood. Those that fail are, time and again, those that are begun on somebody's intellectual high or someone's infatuation with a couple of phrases from the latest book and then collapse after six months or a year of misery among the cuisenaire rods.

It is time for us to come right out and make some straightforward statements on the misleading and deceptive character of certain slogans that are now unthinkingly received as gospel. It is just not true that the best teacher is the one who most successfully pretends that he knows nothing. Nor is it true that the best answers to the

Involved in the free-school movement since 1966, Kozol is known for his book *Free Schools.* His earlier experiences in the Boston public schools are conveyed in his award-winning *Death At an Early Age.*
Source: Jonathan Kozol, "Free Schools: A Time for Candor." Copyright © 1972 by Saturday Review Co. First appeared in *Saturday Review*, March 4, 1972. Used with permission.

blustering windbag of the old-time public school is the free-school
teacher who attempts to turn himself into a human inductive fan.

Free schools that exist under the siege conditions of New York,
Boston, or one of the other Northern cities should not be ashamed to
offer classroom experience in which the teacher does not hesitate to
take a clear position as a knowledgeable adult. Neither should these
free schools be intimidated in the face of those who come in from
their college courses with old and tattered copies of *How Children
Fail* and *Summerhill*. Many of these people, fans of John Holt or
A. S. Neill though they may be, are surprisingly dogmatic in their
imposition of modish slogans on the real world they enter. Many,
moreover, have only the most vague and shadowy notion of what the
free school represents.

Free schools at the present moment cover the full range of beliefs
from the Third World Institute of all black kids and all black teachers, operated by a group of revolutionary leaders wearing military
jackets, boots, and black berets, to a segregated Summerhill out in
the woods of western Massachusetts offering "freedom" of a rather
different kind and charging something like $2,000 or $3,000 yearly
for it. The free schools that I care most about stand somewhere in
between, though surely closer to the first than to the second. The
trouble, however, is that the intellectual imprecision of the school-
reform movement as a whole, and the very special imprecision of the
free schools in particular, allow *both* kinds of free schools to advertise
themselves with the same slogans and to describe themselves with the
same phrases.

The challenge, then, is to define ourselves with absolutely im-
placable precision—and to do so even in the face of economic danger,
even in the certain knowledge of the loss of possible allies. "This is
what we are like, and this is the kind of place that we are going to
create. This is the kind of thing we mean by freedom, and this is
the sort of thing we have in mind by words like "teach" and "learn."
This is the sort of thing we mean by competence, effectiveness, survival. If you like it, join us. If you don't, go someplace else and
start a good school of your own."

Such precision and directness are often the rarest commodities
within free schools. Too many of us are frightened of the accusation
of being headstrong, tough, authoritarian, and, resultingly, we have
tried too hard to be all things to all potential friends. It is especially
difficult to resist the offered assistance when we are most acutely conscious of the loneliness and isolation of an oppressive social structure.

The issue comes into focus in the choice of teachers and in the substance of curriculum.  In an effort to avoid the standard brand of classroom tyranny that is identified so often with the domineering figure of the professional in the public system, innovative free-school teachers often make the grave mistake of reducing themselves to ethical and pedagogical neuters.  The teacher too often takes the role of one who has *no* power.

The myth of this familiar pretense is that the teacher, by concealing his own views, can avoid making his influence felt in the classroom.  This is not the case.  No teacher, no matter what he does or does not say, can ever manage *not* to advertise his biases to the children.

A teacher "teaches" not only or even primarily by what he *says*.  At least in part, he teaches by what he *is*, by what he *does*, by what he seems to *wish to be*.  André Gide said, "Style is character."  In the free school, life-style is at the heart of education.  The teacher who talks of "redistribution of the wealth" yet dresses in expensive clothes among the poor and spends the Christmas holidays in San Juan gets across a certain message, with or without words, about his stake in some of the nice things privilege can offer.  A black woman with a conspicuous Afro and a certain definite quality of suppressed intensity in her manner and voice gets across a whole world of feelings and biases concerning race and rage and revolution.  A white woman who dresses in old sandals, blue work shirt, Mexican skirt, whose long hair is frequently uncombed, who wears love beads or a molded-steel medallion on her breast, who calls things "neat," "right on," "downers," and "together" presents a living advertisement for a whole body of implied ideas, political tendencies, and ideological directions.

In certain respects, the things a teacher does not even *wish* to say may well provide a deeper and more abiding lesson than the content of the textbooks or the conscious message of the posters on the wall.  When war is raging and when millions of people in our land are going through a private and communal hell, no teacher—no matter what he does or does not do—can fail to influence his pupils.  The secret curriculum is in the teacher's own lived values and convictions, in the lineaments of his face, and in the biography of passion (or self-exile) that is written in his eyes.  The young teacher who appears to children to be vague or indirect in the face of human pain, infant death, or malnutrition may not teach children anything at all about pain, death, or hunger, but he will be teaching a great deal about the capability of an acceptable adult to abdicate the consequences of his own perception and, as it were, to vacate his own soul. By denying his convictions during class discussion, he does not teach objectivity. He gives, at the very least, a precedent for nonconviction.

It is particularly disabling when a strong and serious free school begun by parents of poor children in an urban situation finds itself bombarded by young teachers who adhere without restraint or self-examination to these values. Not only does such behavior advertise gutlessness and weakness to the children, it also represents a good deal of deception and direct bamboozlement. The willingness of the highly skilled white teacher to blur and disguise his own effectiveness and to behave as if he were less competent and effective than he really is provides the basis for a false democracy between himself and the young poor children he works with. The children, in all honesty, *can't do nothing.* The young man from Princeton only *acts* as if he can't. The consequence of this is a spurious level of egalitarian experience from which one party is always able to escape, but from which the other has no realistic exit.

I believe, for these reasons, in the kind of free school in which adults do not try to seem less vigorous or effective than they are. I believe in a school in which real power, leverage, and at least a certain degree of undisguised adult direction are not viewed with automatic condescension or disdain. I believe in a school in which the teacher does not strive to simulate the status or condition of either an accidental "resource-person," wandering mystic, or movable reading lab, but comes right out, in full view of the children, with all of the richness, humor, desperation, rage, self-contradiction, strength, and pathos that he would reveal to other grownups. Nevertheless, some of the free schools that describe and advertise their high-priced, all-white, innovative education in the pages of *New Schools Exchange* seem literally to build the core of their life-style around the simulation of essential impotence, with competence admitted only in those areas of basic handiwork and back-to-nature skills where no serious competition from the outside world exists. "Wow!" I hear some of these free-school people say. "We made an Iroquois canoe out of a log!" Nobody, however, *needs* an Iroquois canoe. Even the Iroquois do not. The Iroquois can buy aluminum canoes if they should really need them. They don't, however. What they need are doctors, lawyers, teachers, organizers, labor leaders. The obvious simulation-character of the contruction of an Iroquois canoe by a group of well-set North American children and adults in 1972 is only one vivid example of the total exercise of false removal from the scene of strug-

gle that now typifies the counterculture. There may be some pedagogic value or therapeutic function in this form of simulation for the
heartsick or disoriented son or grandson of a rich man. It does not,
however, correspond to my idea of struggle and survival in the streets
and cities I know.

In the face of many intelligent and respected statements on the
subject of "spontaneous" and "ecstatic" education, the simple truth
is that you do not learn calculus, biochemistry, physics, Latin grammar, mathematical logic, Constitutional law, brain surgery, or hy-
draulic engineering in the same organic fashion that you learn to
walk and talk and breathe and make love. Months and years of long,
involved, and—let us be quite honest—sometimes nonutopian labor in
the acquisition of a single unit of complex and intricate knowledge
go into the expertise that makes for power in this nation. The poor
and black cannot survive the technological nightmare of the next ten
years if they do not have this expertise.

There is no more terrifying evidence of the gulf of race and class
that now separates oppressor and oppressed within this nation than
that so many of those people who are rich and strong should toil with
all their heart to simulate the hesitation, stammer, and awkward in-
direction of impotence, while blacks in Roxbury, in Harlem, and in
East St. Louis must labor with all their soul to win one-tenth of the
*real effectiveness* that those white people conspire to deny. If there
is a need for some men and women to continue in that manner of
existence and that frame of mind, and if it is a need that cannot be
transcended, then let there be two very different kinds of free schools
and two very different kinds of human transformation and human
struggle. But, at least within the urban free schools that we build and
labor to sustain, let us be willing to say who we are and what we think
and where we stand, and let us also say what things *we do not want*.

Those who fear power in themselves fear it still more in those
whom they select to lead them. Several free schools that I know first-
hand have gone through nightmarish periods in which they all but
pick apart the man or woman they have chosen to be their headmaster
or headmistress. The process is dangerous and debilitating not only
because it does so much direct damage in terms of simple pain and
hurt to many decent and courageous men and women but also because it wastes our time in minor skirmishes and diverts us from the
serious struggle for the well-being and real survival of our children.

More importantly, however, fear of power places a premium on
mediocrity, nonvital leadership, insipid character, and unremarkable

life-style.  An organization, of whatever kind, that identifies real excellence, effectiveness, or compelling life-style with the terrifying risk of despotism and authoritarian manipulation will, little by little, drive away all interesting, brilliant, and exhilarating people and will establish in their stead norms of communal mediocrity.  The label reserved for those who do not learn to respect these norms is "ego-tripper." Without question, there is a need for realistic caution, but not every straightforward, unequivocal statement of position can be construed as an instance of ego-tripping.  The perfect way to avoid an ego trip, of course, is to create a community of utterly alienated, dull, and boring people.  There is no risk of ego-tripping if there is no ego. But there isn't any life or strength or truth or passion either.

Free schools, if they wish to stay alive and vital, must learn to separate the fear of domination from the fear of excellence.  If a free school were ever able to discover or train a leader with the power and vision of a Jesse Jackson or, in a different sense, a George Dennison or a Truman Nelson, I hope it would have brains enough not to attempt to dull his edge or obscure his brilliant provocations with communal indecision.  "Participation" and "the will of the full group," inherently eloquent and important aspects of a democratic and exciting free school, can easily turn into the code words for a stylized paralysis of operation and for a new tyranny of will and function.

It may well be that certain free schools, within a rural, safe, and insulated situation, will find it possible to function and survive without formal structure, leadership, or power apparatus.  It is their choice if they should wish to do it in that way; but those who look for leaders, place them in power, and invest them with the trust and confidence of numbers ought then to stand beside them and help to make them stronger and less frightened in the face of the dangers they confront.  Angry parents who never before had power in their hands and young white people who have forever hated anyone who wielded it, can together paralyze the operations of a free school and can gradually destroy the finest qualities in anyone that they select to lead them.

Statements of this kind run counter to a large part of the jargon that the media tend to associate with the free schools.  Jargon, however, does not often correspond to the realities of struggle and survival.  In every free school that has lasted longer than two years there is—*there always is*—some deep down and abiding power center.

Free schools do not hang photographs of unremarkable individuals. They put up photographs of Malcolm X, of César Chavez, of Martin Luther King, of Tolstoy, of José Martí. What is true in history and on the poster-photographs is also true in our own numbers: Some women and some men *are* more powerful and more interesting than others. Behind every free school that survives are the special dedication, passion, and vocation of one woman, one man, or one small and trusted group of men and women. It is by now almost a rule of thumb that the less the free-school bylaws speak of "power" the more one person or one group turns out to hold it. It may be only by a look, a shrug, or a sense of peace within the quiet center of the pedagogic storm. Is A. S. Neill the "ego-tripper" or the "power center" or the "ethical fire" in the heart of his own school? Ask anyone who has ever been to Summerhill.

Still another dangerous tendency included in the syndrome of pretended impotence and threatening the survival of urban free schools is what Bernice Miller speaks of as an inclination toward The Insufficient—or what I think of sometimes as The Cult of Incompletion. It is the kind of hang-loose state of mind that views with scorn the need for strong, consistent, and uninterrupted processes of work and aspiration and, instead, makes a virtue of the interrupted venture, the unsuccessful campaign. I have in mind an almost classic picture of a group of rural free-school people I know, sitting on the lawn of someone's country farm or "radical estate" in an almost too comfortable mood of "resting on our elbows at a place of satisfying retrospect on our own failure" or at a kind of "interesting plateau of our half-success."

I think that it is time for us to face head on this problem of our own inherent fear of strength and effectiveness. We must be prepared to strive with all our hearts to be strong teachers, efficacious adults, unintimidated leaders, and straightforward and strong-minded provocators in the lives of children. We must work with all our hearts to overcome the verbal style of debilitation and subjunctive supposition—the interposition, for example, of the preposition or conjunction of arm's-length invalidation ("like") before all statements of intense commitment or denunciation. I know some free-school leaders and writers who now begin to justify and defend the will-to-failure by making a virtue of the capability to start and stop things in response to sudden impulse. It is a curious revolution that builds its ideology and its morale upon the cheerful prospect of surrender. Men who walk the city streets with minds uncluttered by their own internal need for self-defeat, aware of the pain around them, could not make barbarous recommendations of this kind.

The free-school press and writers speak more often of Bill Ayers's free school in Ann Arbor, Michigan, which did not work out, than they do of Edward Carpenter's remarkable and long-sustained success at Harlem Prep. I have a good deal of respect and admiration for Bill Ayers. Still, it cannot be ignored that, insofar as the free schools are concerned, Bill Ayers's experience is perhaps the prototype of the eloquent exercise in self-defeat. I believe we ought to honor people like Bill Ayers in the same way many of us revere the name of Che Guevara. There is also Fidel, however, who was not afraid to sit in the victor's chair, and there are also strong and stable people like Ed Carpenter. It would not hurt to have upon the walls or in the stairways of our little schools photographs not only of those who do not fear to die for their beliefs but also of those who do not fear to win. I think that the children of the black and poor ought to be able to know and believe, right from the first, that the struggle for liberation does not need to end with sickness in the mountains or with steel helmets in Chicago or with a T-group in Manhattan. It can also end with personal strength, political passion, psychological leverage, and the deepest kind of moral and pragmatic power.

I do not intend to mock young people, or myself, or my own friends, who really try and honestly do fail; but I am thinking also of the anguish in success and in "too much effectiveness" of those who look upon effectiveness itself as bearing the copyright of evil men. There is no need for us to choose between a contaminated sense of competence and a benign sense of ineptitude. The opposite of the cold and avaricious doctor earning his $250,000 yearly in the kingdom of lighted pools and begonia hedges in Lexington, Massachusetts, does not need to be the spaced-out flautist in the shepherd's jacket on a mountaintop in Colorado or the mystical builder of the Pakistani mud hut in New Hampshire; it can also be the radical, bold, and inexhaustible young doctor working his heart out in the store-front clinics of Chicago. The opposite of the sleek corporation lawyer spooning up the cool lime sherbet from a silver dish in the air-conditioned confines of the Harvard Club in Boston does not need to be the barefoot kid in blue jeans in New Hampshire; it can also be the strong and passionate young woman who nails down her law degree while working nights to tutor kids within the nightmare of the Pruitt-Igoe projects in St. Louis—and then comes back to be their representative before the law.  The preference for the unsuccessful, for the interrupted enterprise, for hesitation and low-key aspiration is not surprising or inexplicable in a hard and driving nation such as our own.

One final point: Free schools often prove to be almost irresistibly attractive to some of the most unhappy and essentially aggressive people on the face of the wide earth.  In many instances, the very same people who have been "evicted" from someone else's free school precisely for the pain and hurt they cause will shop around until they come to us.  There is, as many people in the free schools find, a rather familiar kind of man or woman who does not, in fact, care a great deal about children but who enjoys a power struggle.  There is a kind of "energy of devastation" in such people that can be helpful when it is directed at external obstacles but that can be incredibly destructive when it turns in on our own small numbers.

I have seen one of the kindest black people I know pause, and look gently, almost with sadness, into the eyes of someone of this sort and say quietly: "Well, you don't seem to be somebody that I want to work with.  There has been too much unhappiness among us since you came.  You do not seem to think we are sufficiently enlightened.  You do not seem to think that we have read the right books.  You may be right.  We have not read many books in the past year.  We have been too busy trying to build up our school and trying to keep off people who bring sadness and unhappiness into our ranks.  We think that you are just that kind of person.  We would rather have the courage of our errors than the kind of devastation forced upon us by your intellectual wisdom."

I do not like to end with a passage of this kind.  It shows too much of the bitterness and the deep pain that have been part of the free schools I know.  I am trying, however, to be as realistic and as candid as I can.  There is a time when we must sit down and compose rhapsodic stories to raise money for the free schools; there is another time when we have to be as honest as we can.  In 1972 the free schools have come into their own hour.  It is the time for candor.

1.  How does the revolt today against the public schools differ
    from that of the late 1950's and early 1960's?

2.  Even though no two free schools are alike, what is it
    they all have in common?

3.  How do the free schools act upon Piaget's ideas about play?

4.  Is there a danger that children, once released from the
    constraints of the public schools, will "run wild" in a free
    school atmosphere?

5.  Is it reasonable to expect that any "happy, healthy child
    will eventually learn to read, write, and do basic arithmetic,
    whether or not he is formally taught"?

6.  Does the high mortality rate for the free schools demonstrate
    that they are not worthwhile?

7.  Why do free schools, even though their tuition is usually
    low, attract few children from the Indian and Spanish
    communities?

8.  Are new curricula and new ways of teaching sufficient
    to bring about the type of educational environment needed
    today?   Or is it also necessary to change our ideas about
    children and about childhood itself?

9.  Think about the meaning of "free schools."  Is it a fact
    that children who attend "free schools" are really free?
    Bertrand Russell once stated that he never was imprisoned
    just because the jailer had him behind bars because he
    could think about whatever he pleased.

10.  A great deal of imprecision exists about the free school
     movement.  What is it about the movement that has
     encouraged this lack of precision and directness?

11.  Power can be used to free or enslave.  How should free
     schools use the power at their disposal?

12.  How do you account for the syndrome of pretended
     impotence and ineffectiveness that is found among some
     in the free school movement?

13.  "A teacher 'teaches' not only or even primarily by what he
     *says*.  At least in part, he teaches by what he *is*, by what
     he *does*, by what he seems to *wish to be*."  Draw upon your

own experience for reasons why you would support or reject this statement.

14. Because we have learned to walk and talk and other basic functions without the aid of formal schooling, some believe that we can also learn everything we need to know for living in today's world by such a natural process. Explain your position on this issue.

15. Visit a free school and record the differences observed between their programs, organization, and teacher-pupil relations and those of the local public schools.

# XVIII. Educational Alternatives

*Alternative schools have captured the attention and enthusiasm of many educators, students, and parents even though they have yet to be introduced into most school districts. A significant minority of parents are sufficiently dissatisfied with established public schools that they are willing to see their children participate in alternative schools. Yet few generalizations can be drawn nationwide as to what precisely an alternative school should be. A number of different types of schools have emerged, each with certain distinctive features that may attract one group of parents while repelling another. Since the alternatives are within the public school system, free schools, which usually are private, will not be included in our survey even though, technically, they are an alternative.* Open schools *feature individualized learning activities organized around interest centers.* Schools without walls *utilize the entire community for learning. Learning resources in a large urban area have been concentrated in what have been referred to as* educational parks *or* magnet schools. *And finally,* street academies *and* dropout centers *have organized programs for a specific population. It is also possible that any of these alternative schools could be organized as a unit within a more traditional school.*

*Philip DeTurk and Robert Mackin show the excitement of the young who for the first time have found a joy in learning. They show the range of activities that youngsters are likely to engage in, and why a redefinition of teaching is needed in such schools. Though many questions remain unanswered, alternative schools have made people more sensitive to new educational possibilities.*

*Harry S. Broudy believes that the public schools have not been given sufficient credit for their accomplishments. To base grievances against the public schools on the convictions that all institutions are oppressive and schooling is a fraud perpetrated by the bourgeoisie on the proletariat are untenable, he believes. It is first necessary to raise some fundamental questions about education in general before we can effectively evaluate the need for alternative schools.*

Philip DeTurk
Robert Mackin

# 36. LIONS IN THE PARK:
# AN ALTERNATIVE MEANING AND
# SETTING FOR LEARNING

Much of the energy of the alternative schools movement is devoted
to finding financial backing, convincing school boards, soliciting
community support, gaining sufficient "autonomy" for experimentation, and offering enjoyable and varied experiences for students.
But the question, How much learning is going on? is often lost in
the shuffle. Survival and maintenance concerns sometimes over-
shadow its purpose for being. In fact, that purpose—learning—can
become damnably bothersome. To be sure, the purpose is addressed
rhetorically:

> We want young people to learn more than grammar and
> geometry. We want them to learn in affective as well as
> cognitive areas. We want them to learn responsibility, self-
> direction, and self-esteem. We want them to learn how to
> relate to others and how to enjoy learning. We want them
> to learn how to learn. . . .

Beautiful words are written, but what do they mean and how are they
realized? How do you reassure a skeptical board, a troubled parent,
a frustrated teacher, a bored student, or even yourself that learning
is actually taking place in the alternative school?

Philip DeTurk and Robert Mackin, both Assistant Professors of Education at
the University of Massachusetts at Amherst, have directed alternative schools
and convey some of their observations and experiences in these programs.
Source: Philip DeTurk and Robert Mackin, "Lions in the Park: An Alternative Meaning and Setting for Learning," *Phi Delta Kappan* 54 (March 1973),
pp. 458–460. Reprinted by permission.

One question to ask is whether learning is taking place in the regular school. What makes schooling generally acceptable is the pretense that this is the case. To many parents (and kids and teachers and school board members), homework, teacher certification, and subject matter, bolstered by an evaluation system of testing and grading, give a powerful legitimacy and provide a security that "learning" prevails. The institutionalization of schooling, with its polished and understandable norms, "guarantees" that a service is being provided. Most importantly, from our standpoint, these same standards are also the grounds upon which alternative schools are usually and unfortunately judged.

In light of these accepted learning standards, how do we interpret the following situation? David is a 14-year-old student at the Alternative School in Marion, Massachusetts. Since the age of 8, when he stole a boat from the Marion harbor and sailed out to Buzzard's Bay overnight, he has been in continual hot water with the police and school officials alike. Clearly, his only reason for attending school—even an alternative school—was that he was required to do so. Within the school he stood apart from everyone and everything. The staff took a simple tack: Don't make "school-like" academic expectations of David. Be patient. Concentrate upon making the environment a comfortable and welcome place by treating him honestly and with respect. A breakthrough finally came. After Christmas vacation, David stood up during the morning group meeting and asked, to the amazement of everyone, if there were other people interested in "organizing an English literature group" with him.

In retrospect, we would interject several questions for our fellow educators to consider: Did learning take place for David during those preceding three months? Did David undergo any changes in attitude or behavior? Did his trust in people increase? Did his self-concept and ability to relate to others improve? Obviously, from the data provided, the reader cannot produce meaningful answers. But the answers are not so much the issue here as are the questions. Clearly, we must recognize that there are different priorities for different students at different times. How do we begin to address these varied concerns within alternative schools?

Differences in background, self-concepts, socializing abilities, and the like require different "success contexts." It becomes essential for alternative schools to ask and re-ask themselves the fundamental question, What is learning? in order to create such contexts in as personalized ways as possible. We suggest further that the school must view the way the student values himself and his needs, the way the student relates to other people, and the way the student operates within the institution of schooling. Within each of these dimensions lie variables that will affect what a student learns at a given place or time.

### Setting Individual Learning Priorities

In the Pasadena Alternative School, David and Greg learned their math not because of expert math instructors, but because of special private trips to the park where they alone fought imaginary lions; because of their own post office where they operated a student information center; and because of hours spent at a parent farm and a parent cooking class where they planted, prepared, and ate not-so-imaginary food; and because school for the very first time was the very best place they could think of being. David and Greg, two 9-year-olds, one Jewish and one black, learned their times tables because a Mexican-American mother devoted practically every day as a volunteer to bring them together, to make them happy, and to give them a sense of importance.

Students come into the alternative school, just as they do in any school, with different social, academic, and psychological backgrounds. The alternative school genuinely attempts to accommodate to those differences. Each student must learn what the learning options are, which ones he is interested in, and how deeply he wants to learn within each option he chooses. Comments which some Pasadena students made in the spring of 1972 about their Alternative School experience reveals this range of needs and interests:

> I've been independent, have been able to do what I wanted to do—like reading books, observing nature—that I never paid attention to before.
>
> When I read, I read what I want to read about, like my pigeons, instead of reading out of an old regular school book with boring stories.
>
> I didn't want to take French or typing, and now I feel I really like them.
>
> Never had any intentions to take photography and things like that before. They really turned me on.

As was the case with David and Greg, academic content is some-times secondary to an environment which stresses and builds inter-personal relationships and self-confidence. The learner must learn how to be comfortable in order that he may be receptive to learning of any kind. He must learn how to learn.

To establish a school environment which allows students and staff to set differing learning priorities we need to develop programs with several dimensions:

- accepting each individual as an individual and as a con-tributing group member,
- making school acceptable and comfortable,
- defining new responsibilities for teachers,
- developing new responsibilities for students, and
- recognizing additional sources of learning.

## Accepting Each Person as a Human Being

In Marion, Massachusetts, in 1972, camping trips enhanced the "com-munity" approach to learning. These trips took place during school, after school, on weekends or vacations. On one trip to Vermont, 15 high school students and two staff members confronted each other well into the night, dealing with a wide range of personal problems. "Fantastic" was the word they used to describe the experience, an experience which allowed many of them to learn things about them-selves—through the feedback of others—that they had never known.

At this same school (Bent Twig was the name they chose), daily soccer games with 20 or more on a side included kids with the widest range of ability. Since the ages ranged from four to 16, however, everyone had a place. The superintendent of schools, when he re-alized the kinds of kids who were excited about athletics for the first time, called the "physical education program" at Bent Twig the "best in the state."

## Making School an Acceptable Resource for Learning

One of the more subtle goals of the alternative school is to rebuild for the students a trust in the school as a place to learn and a belief that learning is a respectable and meaningful activity.

In a June survey at Pasadena, parents agreed that fostering a "joy of learning" was the greatest achievement of the Alternative School. Students called it a "freedom to learn." One student cited her greatest achievement as "loosening up to do work, overcoming my own resistance to work, getting interested in things and wanting to learn them."

This freedom to learn results from a redefinition of teaching. In the alternative school, the teacher transcends the traditional intellectual relationship with students. One youngster remarked, "I learned to make friends with teachers, to know them as persons in their own life." Another added, "Since the school is not forcing knowledge on students, they really want to learn."

## The Teacher Has New Responsibilities

An undergraduate intern in Pasadena wrote, "The students received a fresh idea of what a teacher should be and most importantly could be." The teachers in the alternative school do consider a student's academic progress, but they also consider his interests and relationships with specific staff members and other students, home situation, and, of course, needs. The staff tries to provide an appropriate environment conducive to learning for the particular child. Teachers try to localize the problems so that they are not prescribing aspirin for a broken arm or math drill for a broken heart. In the case of Greg and David, the prescription called for lions in the park.

## The Learner Also Has Responsibilities

A student might spend 50% of his time on his own writing a book, or artistically-inclined students might spend a day and a half each week in the art museum completely unsupervised. There were student-initiated learning experiences in the Pasadena Alternative School last year. One Pasadena student said: "I have learned to get along with all ages, and I have learned from little kids as much as I have learned from teachers." Another remarked: "I learned about cutting diameters in wood by teaching Blake, who cut it wrong." A third student commented: "I learned to do for myself, because if I don't do for myself, nothing will get done."

Students, with the help of adults and other students, begin to learn that learning is something which they must control, not something which is done to them. Freedom to learn requires individual responsibility. At a residential alternative school for 14- to 20-year-olds in Jefferson, New Hampshire, one option allowed students to tutor younger children in the town. Tutors were paid for this work, but half of their pay was kept in a school savings account. If students broke their own community rules—in this case taking a car, having sexual relations, or using drugs or alcohol—they lost their savings.

### The Teacher Does Not Do All the Teaching

In our alternative schools, students and adults become part of a learning community. Teaching and learning become a single act by a single person, or by a group! At the Alternative School in Jefferson, no one on the staff could teach foreign languages. Two students, one Puerto Rican and one French-Canadian, took over the task. The format was simple—students wishing to take French or Spanish sat at the French table or the Spanish table for all meals and during that time were not allowed to speak English.

At the same school, each student taking English through using media learned different skills of film making—camera operation, lighting, developing—and was then required to teach "his" skill to the others in the class.

The entire institution of schooling has been built around the role of the teacher as attorney, judge, and jury of learning. The presumption follows, therefore, that learning has a causal relationship to teaching. In the alternative school, however, learning can go on without teaching, and teaching can go on without teachers!

In the alternative schools we have worked with, everyone becomes "teacher"—the teacher's wife who comes in twice a week for jewelry class, the white mother who devotes her mornings to one black high school boy, the black high school boy who devotes his mornings to one white mother, the grandmother who comes in to teach geology, the sheriff who holds a mock trial, the mother who teaches sewing at home, the mother who teaches yoga in school, the intern who helps individual students with their math, the three university students who give science demonstrations, the secretary who teaches typing, the alternative school student who teaches what she has learned in the art museum about ceramics to other alternative school students, and the learning community who teach each other the meaning of respect and privacy and sharing and need.

### *Learning Becomes a Student Rather Than a Teacher Agenda*

Bringing the student as well as the teacher into the evaluating role, and stretching the context of learning beyond the school walls, introduces some dramatic pedagogical questions:

- Why do we identify certain things as "subjects"?
- Why do we have requirements?
- Why are some subjects more important or "major"?
- What is curricular and what is extracurricular?
- How do we define "teacher"?
- What is a school?
- What is learning?

A junior high girl in Pasadena wrote that in public schools almost everything is done for the student:

> There the teacher tells him what to do and he does it regardless of its value to learning. In this school, the kid will be the judge about what books and materials will be useful to his learning, with some exceptions. . . . Self-motivation comes from within and the atmosphere and classes will try to be ones that will bring it out and develop it.

Not all student analyses of their learning are comforting or complimentary to the alternative school. One high school student in the Pasadena Alternative School made the following comment half-way into the first semester: "My achievements? I've met 45 new people and learned a few things about others. Is that going to help me for college?"

But at the same time a friend wrote:

> I've learned more in these two months than in two years of my other school, and that is the sincere truth. I've learned algebra, poetry, politics, and in an interesting way. I've learned about leather, clay, jewelry, photography, witchcraft, Black Panthers, typing, and little kids.
>
> Most of all I've learned about people and myself and a little bit about how our minds work. I've learned that I learn when I'm given freedom—more than when I'm imprisoned in school. I like the Alternative School, and I'm for the way we

are trying to revolutionize the old system of learning, which
I hate.

"College" or "revolution," learning to these students is obviously
in the eye of the beholder. And the breadth and depth of learning
(or lack thereof) are important dimensions which are often unac-
counted for in traditional evaluations of student progress.

In summary, the alternative school itself is learning some things about
learning. There are many questions which are unanswered, and
there are also a host of new questions to ask. The authors suggest
that educators who look at the evaluation of learning in schools keep
the questions as well as the answers (grades or whatever) in mind.
Are we asking these questions?

- Are students learning to learn?
- Are they preparing for future learning competence by
  building self-confidence, gaining an appreciation of
  group structures, using the school and other resources in
  a productive way?
- Is a student learning to overcome his special set of obstacles to effective learning?
- Is a student learning what there is to learn and which of
  those options he wants to take advantage of?

Learning in these terms requires a very broad alternative context,
a context that allows each student to develop his potential. Does
learning take place in the alternative school? The answer depends
on the individual under consideration, what is meant by learning,
and who is making judgment. If the alternative school has done
nothing else, it has at least made us sensitive to the depth and scope
of this essential educational concern.

Harry S. Broudy

# 37. EDUCATIONAL ALTERNATIVES—
# WHY NOT? WHY *NOT*

The dual title of this paper reflects the current ambivalence toward the demand for alternatives in education. "Why not?" says that since we cannot think of good reasons against alternatives, let's have them. Or, more cynically, since nothing we do in education seems to make much difference, what have we to lose by trying something—anything—else?

"Why *not*" implies there may be good reasons for not trying this or that alternative, and that good and bad alternatives can be distinguished. In defending the second interpretation of the title one does not reject alternatives to the current school organization. However, one is not compelled to admit that alternatives are *necessarily* productive of freedom, intelligent choice, the satisfaction of individual differences, creativity, and zestful involvement.

The claims for alternatives can be defended (or attacked) on logical grounds or empirical evidence, or both. On logical grounds it may be argued that a multiplicity of alternatives would be more likely to meet a wider variety of individual needs than a single system. Or one might appeal to the principle that cultural pluralism is a self-evident good and that therefore educational pluralism is also good. Such arguments can be attacked only by challenging the inter-

Harry S. Broudy is professor emeritus of educational philosophy at the University of Illinois. Former editor of the journal *The Educational Forum*, Broudy's books include *Building A Philosophy of Education, Paradox and Promise, Psychology for General Education,* and *Democracy and Excellence in American Secondary Education* (co-editor). His most recent book is *The Real World of the Public Schools.*

Source: Harry S. Broudy, "Educational Alternatives—Why Not? Why *Not*," *Phi Delta Kappan* 54 (March 1973), pp. 438–440. Reprinted by permission.

pretation of the concepts and principles and the conclusions drawn
from them.

However, the claim for alternatives is sometimes defended empirically by pointing to experiments that claim to have achieved the
benefits expected of them. According to Albert Shanker (*New York
Times,* April 23, 1972), such claims are being made for the results
achieved by such alternative schools as the Parkway project in Philadelphia and Harlem Prep in New York. Shanker notes that even if
the claimed results or improvements did accrue, the comparison with
traditional schools is faulty. He cites the small size, the availability
of funds from special grants, and pupil selectivity as characteristics
that could not be duplicated throughout the public schools. Conceivably, however, there could be enough decentralized alternative
schools to enable *all* pupils to attend small, selective, tailor-made
schools. Aside from the extreme unlikelihood that the funds would
be available, what about the principle that each parent is entitled to
choose the type and amount of schooling that he judges his children
need, and that to implement this principle a large number of alternative schools must be available at public cost?

The principle is false if the state supports schools because education is a *public* good and not *merely a private one.* The same distinction is invoked to justify taxing people for roads that they may
or may not use or the fluoridation of the water supply of which they
may or may not approve. Those who argue for alternatives on the
ground that choice of schooling is an individual right are thinking
only of individual benefits, or they are asserting that the public good
can be satisfied by whatever educational alternatives parents choose.
The first argument simply misunderstands the nature of social institutions; the second overlooks the historical evidence to the contrary.

I shall not try to assess the success of alternative schools, because
"success" is about as firm a criterion as a water bed floating on a
pool of mercury, and we all know about the no-fail characteristics of
educational experiments. Nor can I subscribe to the notion that one
can ignore the possibly irreversible adverse effects of educational
experiments, because I do not believe that nothing we do in education
makes any difference. Instead, I propose to analyze the concepts
underlying the claims of the alternatives advocates to produce greater
freedom and creativity, promote more intelligent and responsible
choice, and provide for individual differences in educational decision
making.

## DO ALTERNATIVES
## PROMOTE FREEDOM?

The literature in favor of alternative schools abounds with references to freedom. Sometimes the freedom is from rules governing the personal lives of pupils, e.g., hair styles, class attendance, deportment, etc. Sometimes the freedom wanted is from the control of schools by the Establishment bureaucracies; sometimes it is freedom to do one's own thing whenever and wherever the person is moved to do it Sometimes it is freedom from the established curriculum. Presumably the advocates of free schools are not in agreement as to the sort of freedom that is crucial or that alternative schools are attaining it.[1]

At any rate, alternative schools are supposed to enhance freedom for the pupil from diverse kinds of educational constraints. Are there, however, some educational constraints over which we have no control? Two sorts of constraint cannot be evaded if we are to have *formal* schooling. One kind is the constraint implied in the formal schooling as a process; the other kind is the constraints imposed by the demands of the culture in which one intends to participate fully or, at the least, adequately.

As to the first kind of constraint, what one learns in school does not come naturally. If it did we would not bother with schools. Schools are deliberate interventions in uncultivated modes of human experience, i.e., in what comes "naturally." Uncoerced or painless schooling is to the schoolmaster what the Holy Grail was to Sir Galahad, something to be forever sought and rarely found.

Furthermore, if schooling involves induction of the young into the intellectual resources of the culture, then the logical structure of those resources (the disciplines) as well as their results become constraints. To free the pupil from these constraints, as some counterculture reformers urge, is to free him from knowledge itself. Are alternatives that promise this kind of freedom good alternatives?

As to the second sort of constraint, one must ask what the culture demands as conditions for coping with it. At least three kinds of demand are imposed on all of us: occupational adequacy, civic adequacy, and personal adequacy. The first is needed to earn a living,

[1] A special issue of the *Harvard Educational Review* on alternative schools, August, 1972, catalogs the confusion.

the second to plan one's role in a social order, and the third to live as a fully developed, authentic human individual.

It is unrealistic and mischievous for a school system to ignore these constraints, however much one may wish to reform the way in which they operate. It is mischievous deliberately to maladapt the young to the culture, for those who are so maladapted cannot survive in it, let alone reform it. In this sense alternative schools in which the "standard" English dialect is denigrated in favor of ethnic minority dialects are mischievous, because the important transactions of society are carried on in the standard dialect. That is all that "standard" means, and those who do not master it cannot participate fully in the society. It is one thing to urge multilingualism as a means to learning the "standard" communication medium; it is another to use it as a means of evading the need to master it.

In short, alternatives are good if they increase the freedom of the pupil to achieve the three kinds of adequacy mentioned above; they are not good if they simply free the pupil from the task of achieving them.


## DO THEY PROMOTE BETTER CHOICES?

What about the claim that the more alternatives the greater the opportunity for intelligent and responsible choice? An intelligent choice presupposes that one knows the end and can evaluate a diversity of means purporting to reach that end. The child, especially the young child, qualifies on neither count. Parents and educators may make a stronger claim as far as ends are concerned, and the educator is supposed to be more knowledgeable than parents about means.

As to ends, aside from very specific vocational training, there is neither consensus nor clarity. Educational goals can be formulated in terms as general and abstract as the good life here or in the hereafter or as particular and concrete as learning to do subtraction in arithmetic; and it is difficult to keep controversialists on the same level of objective[2] for more than a minute at a time. About the nearest we get to agreement on objectives is the objective of moving from one step in the educational ladder to the next. This works pretty well if there is agreement about the desirability of making the journey

---

[2] I have tried to map this morass in "The Philosophical Foundations of Educational Objectives," *Educational Theory* (Winter 1970), pp. 3–21.

up the ladder; when alternatives to going up the ladder are proposed, even this agreement vanishes. As to means, aside from well-developed vocational curricula, there is no more consensus than on ends. To make the situation comical, the educators who have claimed authority over the schools on the ground of superior expertise now proclaim that their expertise lies in finding out what their clients would like to have them do. And the parents, at a loss as to how to advise the experts and reluctant to have sullen children around the house, half-heartedly embrace the doctrine that the most reliable guide to educational choice is the interest of the pupil at any given moment.

It is also argued that if choice is free and the alternatives plentiful, decisions will be not only more intelligent but also more responsible. Responsible choice means 1) that relative merits of alternatives are taken into account or 2) that the chooser is worried about making the right choice or 3) that he has the means and will to remedy the consequences of the wrong choice. How difficult it is to make a responsible choice in the first sense has already been pointed out; being anxious to choose correctly is a morally admirable trait, but it is relevant only if there is a way of distinguishing right from wrong alternatives, and finally, making good on the wrong educational choices is virtually impossible.

I am sure that many advocates of alternatives do believe that they can choose among them intelligently and want to do so. They usually can justify their choices by some theory of education that in turn is justified by some fairly coherent view about the good society and the qualities of the good life. The advocates of progressive schools, the Montessori schools, and the open classrooms are not responsible. am far less sure about those advocates of alternatives who base their case on "failure" of the public schools to achieve this or that political or social objective, or who justify their advocacy on the general ground that all institutions are oppressive, or that all formal schooling is a fraud perpetrated by the bourgeoisie on the proletariat.

I believe we have reached this stage of cynicism with respect to public schooling and to some extent higher education as well. In time even the most solid ramparts of common sense and intuition are breached by books, articles, and researches that "prove" that there is no positive relationship between school and economic success, civic competence, and personal adequacy. Propelled by the massive impact of the mass media, these messages come through faster and faster, so that to shake confidence takes less time—especially when funds for schools impose heavy tax burdens.

I shall not assay the validity of this literature. I have tried to do so elsewhere (*The Real World of the Public Schools*, 1972), and the tide may turn more quickly than one might anticipate by virtue of the rapidity with which education doctrines change. Nevertheless, at the moment many of the pressures for alternatives can be construed as a flight from responsibility for and commitment to formal schooling.

## DO THEY PROVIDE FOR DIFFERENCES?

Perhaps the most persuasive argument for alternatives is that individuals vary in interests, needs, and competence so much that only a multiplicity of alternatives will save them from the rigidity of a uniform public school system. However, the amount of uniformity in the American public schools is highly overrated. If anything, the diversity in schools is so great that it is only by extreme courtesy that one can speak of a public school system.

Furthermore, not all individual differences require differentiated schooling. For example, we do not believe, in principle at least, that differences in skin color constitute a basis for school differentiation.

Finally, important individual differences such as in learning readiness, talents and aptitudes, and previous achievement often can be met without necessarily setting up alternative schools. Indeed, one important way of meeting individual differences is to allow the individual to make his unique appropriation of a uniform set of studies. He will do it anyway.

So alternatives as such do not of themselves guarantee the satisfaction of the demands of individuality, and certainly not with respect to general education. The case with vocational training, of course, is quite different. Since there are many vocational tracks and since not all pupils will or can follow the same one, alternatives are the rule. But I take it that alternative tracks in vocational education are not in controversy.

## DO ALTERNATIVES
## PROMOTE CREATIVITY?

Not the least attractive argument for alternatives in schooling is that they provide much-needed novelty and freshness in school life. A single system of formal schooling makes for uniformity and boredom; anything that relieves boredom is welcome.

But as with the other claims for alternatives, one must make distinctions. For example, teachers use a thousand tricks to vary the monotony of drill or to relieve the lassitude of the afternoon school hours. Pupils appreciate sprightly variations in speech and clothing on the part of teachers, and indeed any departures from routine. Such novelties are not in controversy. We are talking about "imaginative breakthroughs" such as life curricula, ecstatic expansions of consciousness, free schools, schools-without-walls, store-front schools, and the like. Are these creative variations or not? Is there a criterion for judging, or are we to rely on the intrinsic values of pluralism as such?

Although no definition of creativity will satisfy everybody, we do recognize that there is a difference between trivial and important novelties. If education had a body of highly organized and widely accepted theory and a considerable range of problems for which there were standard solutions, we would know when an innovation was really important. But education has no such consensus, so that all innovation is equally important; unfortunately, more often than not it is sporadic, episodic, short-lived, and faddish. The operative criterion is likely to be the amount of grant money and publicity a project attracts.

Accordingly, the most frequent defense of alternatives in schooling is that ours is a pluralistic society, and that just as a plurality of cultures is desirable, so is a plurality of school designs. But is the matter so simple? William James argued that this may be a pluralistic universe in which entities are related loosely, as beads on a string, and not as premises and conclusions in a monolithic syllogism. Nevertheless, society is never merely the sum of individual beads on a geographical string. For there to be a plurality of cultures, each culture must have some kind of unity by which it can be distinguished from the others, and there must be some unity among the cultures that makes it possible for us to speak of a pluralistic *society* rather than of a coalition of discrete societies. The rationale for a public school system is that, interesting as the diversity of subcultures is, cultural unity is never zero. This constitutes the limit of pluralism in culture and schooling.

Celebrants of alternatives sagely remark that there are many paths to the same mountain top, but tend to forget that when one opts for pluralism for its own sake, there is no *one* mountain top to which all are climbing and by which we can judge whether the goal is being reached or not.

In the absence of consensus on such a goal, indeed if it is denied that it is even desirable to have one goal, then the search for alternatives can be justified either by asserting complete independence of diverse cultural entities or by the need for relief from sameness. The first justification does not make sense so long as we continue to talk about one nation or about one human race; as to the second, inventing and marketing educational novelties can be a stimulating and profitable pastime. Unfortunately, the need for excitement and novelty is insatiable, and the attempt to provide a supply of alternatives to keep up with the demand is a task too exhausting even to contemplate.

Creative diversity is not random pluralism, but rather imaginative variations on a theme. If we can be clear about the role of the school in a genuine society in which basic features of the good life are shared by all the members, then there can be creative diversity within the public school and outside of it, and these variations will be neither random nor mutually destructive.

# Discussion Questions
## and Activities

1. What significant differences from traditional public schools would you anticipate finding if you were planning to visit an alternative school? How could you prepare so that your observations would be more perceptive and discerning?

2. Are there certain general educational conditions that make learning a joyous rather than a coercive activity, or is it strictly an individual matter—hence the need for many alternatives?

3. What differences in preparation do you think a teacher would need in order to teach effectively in an alternative school as compared to a traditional public school? Any at all?

4. If you believe that students must be able to assume control over their own learning, how can they best be shown how to do so?

5. When learning becomes an agenda for the student rather than the teacher, how, then, do we redefine teaching?

6. Can the success of alternative schools be assessed? What are the difficulties involved?

7. Since alternative schools are usually thought to promote freedom to learn, it is important to be clear as to what is meant by the term "freedom" in this context. How would you define it?

8. Presumably, to live in society everyone must be subject to certain constraints. Do the proponents of alternative schools want to free the child from all constraints? If not, how do we distinguish the healthy from the unhealthy kind?

9. Do we always increase intelligent and responsible choice by increasing alternatives? Are children and parents adequately prepared to make wise choices between alternative schools?

10. Has the amount of uniformity in established public schools been overestimated? If so, then how can a case be made for alternative schools?

11. Why is it that educators have difficulty evaluating the significance of innovations and frequently disagree among themselves as to what innovations are important?